He Sends Me Rainbows
And Speaks To Me Through Songs

A Supernatural Love Story

L.J. Hunt

BLIND FAITH PRODUCTIONS

Published by Blind Faith Productions
Traverse City, Michigan

ISBN: 978-0-9671907-3-0

Vision for the cover by L.J. Hunt
Cover and page design by tothepointsolutions.com
Cover Photo: 24994724 © Dmytro Balkhovitin Dreamstin

He Sends Me Rainbows

And Speaks To Me Through Songs

To my children and grandchildren.
May you always remember
Papa Greg and Grammy's amazing love story.

Contents

Special Gratitudes ix

Introduction xi

Chapter 1   Growing Up Paranormal 1

Chapter 2   Dad 9

Chapter 3   Gregory 20

Chapter 4   Signs Of Things To Come 34

Chapter 5   Dreams And Reality 43

Chapter 6   Going It Alone 52

Chapter 7   My Year Of Firsts 59

Chapter 8   The Calm Before The Storm 70

Chapter 9   Living In Dreamland 77

Chapter 10   Gone But Not Forgotten 85

Chapter 11   Starting To Fall Apart 93

Chapter 12   Starting To Accept 103

Chapter 13   On Shaky Ground 110

Chapter 14   Comforted In My Sadness 118

Chapter 15   Beautiful 125

Chapter 16   Trusting The Process 133

Chapter 17   Lonely But Never Alone 140

Chapter 18   Reflecting. 148

Chapter 19   Unbelievable 157

Chapter 20   Close Encounter 165

Chapter 21   It Just Got Real 172

Chapter 22   Loosening My Grip 179

Chapter 23   One Rainbow At A Time 187

Chapter 24   Rainbows And More Grief 193

Chapter 25   Relief At Last 199

Chapter 26   Laughing Again 208

Chapter 27   Relying On Faith. 215

Chapter 28   One Day At A Time 222

Chapter 29   Thanksgiving 228

Chapter 30   Everywhere And Nowhere 236

Chapter 31   Lonesome Lonely. 246

Chapter 32   Dare To Dream 255

Chapter 33   Rainbows In The Dark 262

Chapter 34   Holy Rainbows! 271

Chapter 35   Reassurance From Heaven. 282

Chapter 36   Hope In The Midst Of Despair 291

Chapter 37   It Isn't Raining Anymore 301

Chapter 38   What If I Never Get Over You?. 311

Chapter 39   Rainbowland 322

Chapter 40   Seeing The Future 332

Chapter 41   Rainbow Paradise. 342

Special Gratitudes

First and foremost, this book would not have happened if it weren't for you, my love, Gregory Roy Hunt, my Rainbow. I attempt to express my heart but there are no words to adequately describe what you have meant to me. I met you when I was twenty-one years old and that was the first time you saved me. You kept me safe while I drank recklessly and partied way too much until eventually—12 years later—I eased your burden of worry when I got sober and began to take better care of myself. Thirty years of marital bliss—a few bumps along the road—and I couldn't have asked for a safer, more loving and exciting man to spend my life with. We had so much fun. *You* were so much fun.

You made me a stronger, more loving person. You gave me children and grandchildren that I never would have had. You showed me love like I've never known. We made each other laugh. We often said we were the male and female version of each other. Our love was easy, playful, unconditional. And then, when the unthinkable happened, you saved me a second time by being there for me the moment you left. You took your last breath and jumped straight into my heart where you have been ever since. I could never have imagined in my wildest dreams how you would continue to show up for me after that.

Your nickname was *Rainbow* and you loved it. Your work buddies said it was because you had such a colorful personality. Rainbows represent hope for a better tomorrow. A promise that things are going to be alright. Rainbows are also seen as a bridge between our earthly grounded self and the higher, spiritual self. You've been sending me your colorful gifts of hope since the moment you left this world. My heart swells with love and joy, and tears fill my eyes when I think about the Rainbows and the songs that soothed my aching heart and helped me want to live another day. The word Rainbow appears in this book over twelve hundred times. That's a lot of Rainbows!

These years I've spent with you in our changed reality, with all it's heartbreaking grief, colorful Rainbows and music every day, were a beautiful place to dwell while I recovered. I've had to grieve the loss of that magical time now that I stand on firmer emotional ground. I am who I am because of you, because of the life and love we shared. I carry you in my heart forever and will feel you there whenever I see a Rainbow. With a warm smile I will remember our time together as I embrace my life, and when it's my time to cross the Rainbow Bridge I will sprint to the other side and into those loving arms once again. Until then, our love stays with me.

I want to thank my family and friends who have loved me, worried about me, and prayed for me while I struggled to be well, both emotionally and physically. Who supported me and encouraged me to honor my journey. I'm grateful for my children and grandchildren who make me laugh and remind me of my husband.

I carry in my heart the essence of all those who have passed on but continue to influence my life. Grandma Sue, Dad, Uncle Steve, grandparents and close friends who all left too soon yet walk with me still. I thank God, for that quiet voice of hope and inner knowing that life is worth living and that hardship and heartbreak bring with them unforeseen blessings.

I wish to thank Mary Jo Zazueta and To The Point Solutions. Thank you for bringing my vision to life. Your patience with me throughout the process of making this book was very much appreciated. I'm grateful for all the time you put into this project. You make a writer's dreams come true!

A big thank you to Nancy Kaetchen for proofreading the manuscript in the early stages.

I wish to thank all the amazing and talented singer/songwriters that I mention in this book. Sadly, I was unable to get permission to use the actual song lyrics and it broke my heart to edit out some pretty powerful entries. Still, I attempted to paraphrase the messages in hopes that the magic was not lost in translation. I hope that readers will take the time to listen to these amazing and beautiful songs with their powerful messages of hope and healing.

Introduction

As I contemplated how on earth I can ever write an introduction to this incredible, amazing, unbelievable, book and do it justice, I thought about why my life keeps ending up in books. In 1992 I wrote a book called *Recovering From Life* that never got published. I was still drinking when I wrote it and I'm still not sure what that was about. I do feel that it somehow led me to the next one.

When I got sober a couple of years later I wrote the real *Recovering From Life*. The book sort of just happened and I realize it came out of my desire to share my experience, strength and hope with others, especially those in recovery. I'm a dream interpreter and I'd been studying dreams for many years by this time. I was amazed at how my dreams guided me through those early years of healing with their profound messages and insights. I thought it would help people in their own lives.

My second book, *My Dreams My Self*, took ten years and was not at all the dream book I thought I would write one day. Instead it was very much like the first book in that it was a compilation of my journal entries and dreams at the time. I was doing over a hundred dream groups a year and was never happier than when I was interpreting dreams. I think this book came out of my desire to share what I'd learned over thirty years about dreams and what they mean. When I finished that book, exactly ten years ago, I had no way of knowing what the next ten years of my life would be like or that it would result in another book. Especially *this* book.

There is no way to adequately describe this story. The power of it will impact me for the rest of my life and pretty early on I felt it was something I wouldn't be able to keep to myself, even though I knew it would be hard for some people. The whole thing seems like a dream. I'm grateful for my faithful journal entries, documenting the whole amazing journey because there's so much that would have been lost as I traveled through my days in a fog of grief.

Except for family and close friends, I quit talking about the Rainbows and the unexplainable things going on at my house, early on after getting looks of doubt, disbelief, even fear from people. I kept the magic to myself because as time went on the whole miraculous series of events was unbelievable even for me and I was living it. Deep grief was intertwined with the healing energy of Rainbows and music and the indescribable experience of being that connected to the spiritual world, carried me—almost dragged me—through my life.

Deep grief puts you in a place where it's easier to hear the voice of spirit. Especially the loss of an intimate partner, the one you shared everything with, love, life, passion. It's an unimaginable void. The outside world loses its importance for a while as deep grief and mourning are a world all their own. If we are lucky enough to trust the process it's a journey not to be missed.

I look back and I am amazed by my own story. I believe life's greatest heartache is to lose a treasured loved one, and there is a process of healing that must take place in order to fall in love with life again. I hope this book fills you with hope and faith in not only this life but in the life after this one, knowing that the two are intertwined. I hope it makes you want to seek that quiet place within yourself that allows you to connect to something pretty extraordinary.

I take no credit for this whole amazing thing other than I wrote everything down. I spent ten years of my life here and the past few years working non-stop, sifting and sorting through thousands of journal entries in order to compile the magic as best I could to tell the story. It's been the hardest work I have ever done in my life. The grief alone was a full time job. I find myself exhausted and exhilarated at the completion of it, but the story itself I take no credit for. It just happened to me.

Chapter 1

Growing Up Paranormal

———

1982—In a bar somewhere in Pocatello, Idaho
I was the captain of a women's pool team and we were playing final tournaments. It was late and all of us had been drinking and partying. Well, except Mama, who for some unknown reason, and totally out of character for her—she didn't drink or go to bars—was there that night. Gregory and I were just starting out and he had stopped into the club when he got off work after the swing shift. On my way to the bar for a drink I was overcome with a powerful vision that stopped me in my tracks.

I saw my life with Greg in a flash over the next 30 years and then I saw him die when we were both still young. I saw myself alone and devastated...

I immediately grabbed Mama and pulled her to the side and sobbed as I told her what I'd just seen. I'd never had anything like that happen in my life but knowing the family I come from I was certain it was a premonition. I was practically hysterical as Mama tried to calm me down and reassure me. We said we just needed to pray. I pulled myself together, determined to pray away this unwelcome message. And I managed to do just that for the next 30 years...

I have memories from when I was very small and from those earliest memories I knew there was something special—unusual, extraordinary—about my Grandma Sue, my father's mother. And about Dad too. He seemed to have the same gift she had. That gift, it was understood, was an intuitive one, a psychic phenomenon. The ability to know things you couldn't possibly know.

The first story prominent in our family was when my 19-year-old Mama was pregnant with me, and my brother, Scotty, was 18 months old. We lived in a tiny one bedroom apartment over the garage in the backyard of Mama's family home. My sister was only 2½ . Scotty was at the window waving down to our dad who was leaving for work. At this exact moment, only a few blocks away, Grandma Sue was overtaken with nausea and a cold sweat that had her in the bathroom splashing her face with cold water and praying. When the phone rang she raced to answer saying, *"What happened?!"* Frantic, my parents would explain that the screen gave way and my brother fell from the second floor window, hitting a car parked below before falling to the cement.

As a broken and bloody baby was rushed to the hospital I know the prayers of my family could be heard around the world. They placed him on the table and everyone, including nurses and the doctor, stood back and watched in horror as this little boy let out blood curdling screams as he jerked and jolted and jerked some more until at last he stopped both movement and screams, seeming to settle down and relax. X-rays showed no broken bones. The astonished doctor said, *"He just put himself back together!"* Covered in scrapes and bruises, one week later there wasn't a mark on him.

The first *ghost story* I remember hearing about happened when my dad was about four years old. They lived on a farm in Oklahoma and the closest neighbors were a mile away. My dad often played outside and Grandma Sue kept an eye on him from the kitchen window. He was playing with a ball and she watched as he threw it. From where she stood she couldn't see where it landed. Expecting my dad to run after it she kept watch. All of a sudden the ball came flying back to my dad who picked it up and threw it again to whomever was playing catch with him. Once again the ball came flying back.

Curious and only a little unnerved about who was there, Grandma hurried to my dad. There was no one else outside. She asked him, *"Who were you playing with?"* He said, *"Them,"* and pointed. *"What do they look like?"* she asked. The story goes that my dad described them and my grandma knew immediately who they were. They were cousins of hers. Deceased cousins. He told his mom he played with them in the barn too.

My father says that growing up there were a lot of psychics around. I wonder who they were? How I wish I'd asked. As a small child my dad says he remembers them watching him and saying, *"That child is surrounded by angels."* My father was born with veils over his eyes—as was Grandma Sue—believed to be the mark of a psychic. Was Grandma's mother gifted as well? Her sisters? Oh, to have asked more questions! At any rate, I don't believe my father's encounter with playful ghosts surprised her and she certainly wouldn't have been concerned about it.

Awhile later though when my dad came in frightened of *the boys in the barn*, she told him that he could tell them to go away. She said, *"If you tell them to go away they will."* My dad would tell the story, *"So I told them to go away and they did."* Then a long pause and he said sadly, *"I wish I wouldn't have said it. They never came back."* But *Spirits* continued to surround my father throughout his life, whether he saw them or not.

As a boy, it was his job to bring in firewood from the barn. The barn was a short walk from the house. In the dark he said he'd get a little freaked out so he'd gather way more wood than he could carry so as to make fewer trips. He said he would inevitably drop a few pieces on the way to the house. In the pitch black he couldn't see where they landed so he would look up, and, by the tree or branch he could make out, he would mentally *mark the spot* where the wood was dropped so he could come back and retrieve it. He'd carry his armload to the fire box and when he returned, the pieces he had dropped were neatly stacked on the back porch.

My dad also recounted a story that happened when he was a teenager. His brother, my Uncle Jack, was eleven years older than my dad. He was a gifted mechanic by all accounts and could make any vehicle run no matter what was wrong with it. He bought an old Junker so he could restore it for my dad. When the car was finished—not a detail overlooked—he couldn't wait to show it to his little brother. My dad was excited too until he saw the car. He said, *"I looked at the car and saw it covered in blood."* He told his brother he couldn't take the car. The story goes that Uncle Jack sold it and later heard that some boys over in the valley were killed in it.

I remember one time in the 70's when we were living in Idaho Dad came home from a trip as a long-haul truck driver and told this story. He said he was driving down the freeway in the middle of the night. He pulled out the last cigarette in his pack, crumbled up the pack and threw it out the window. (Note: my father later became an advocate for *not* littering.) He said he drove down the road in the pitch black for about a half hour before he realized that he had tucked a twenty dollar bill inside the cigarette pack.

My parents struggled to support their young family and I know that twenty dollars was a lot of money to them and probably all they could afford to send with him. He said he continued down the road until he saw a turn around and then headed back in the other direction. He said, *"I drove and drove and drove. Then I found another turn around, headed back in the right direction, and drove a little further. I pulled over, got out of the truck in the pitch black, bent down and picked up the cigarette pack."* He just had the best smile on his face and we all had our mouths hanging open.

But the story that stands out strongest in my mind is when I was 14 years old. Dad came home from one of his trips and told us that he knew his brother, living in Michigan, had died. He said he was driving down the freeway in the middle of the night and he felt someone sitting next to him in the passenger seat. He looked, and there was his brother, looking healthy and smiling. He assured my dad that all was well now. Sadly, my Uncle Jack struggled with alcoholism and died at 47 years old. He wasn't found right away so the call from Michigan didn't come until the next day, but we already knew.

I'm as fascinated by these stories today as I was the first time I heard them. While these encounters are practically commonplace in today's world they certainly were not in the 1930's and 40's when my dad was growing up. At least if they were no one talked about it outside of the family. It wasn't a whole lot different in the 60's and 70's. My family was paranormal before paranormal was cool.

We always knew that Dad could find lost items. He was amazing at it. We all went to him anytime something valuable was lost or misplaced. In a panic sometimes, tears others, we would go to him. He was always very calm in that moment. His faith—from his mother—that *nothing is lost in the Kingdom of God*, assured him that God knew where the treasure was. I believe that my father simply asked God where the item could be found and then he would go right to it and hand it to us. The necklace that had slipped behind the mattress, the ring in the backyard, the money in a pocket. Later, when we were grown, we could simply call him on the phone and he would tell us where it was.

About a year or so before my father died he told me that *someone* had been standing at his door at night but he wasn't sure who. I didn't like hearing that but it didn't seem to scare him. I asked if he thought it was Grandma Sue and he said, *"No, they were too tall."* There has always been a sacredness to all of these things with my dad and Grandma Sue, with their faith and reliance on God for everything big or small. A quiet assurance that in the midst of pain and suffering God is there. That in the end all is well. I'm sure his faith was tested when Grandma Sue died a year after Uncle Jack. Dad was only thirty-seven years old and I'd never seen my father cry so hard. He would cry easily after that.

It was at this time in my life that I started experiencing my own visions, although I didn't really know what they were. I was about fourteen years old the first time it happened and basically it was like watching a movie. I saw myself in the future, standing in front of a huge crowd of people, laughing and motivating and making life better. It would be years in between but they always came when I was in quiet, contemplative places in my life, when I was looking deeper at the meaning of things and searching for answers.

I would see this vibrant, healthy, joyful woman and I knew it was me but it was so far from me that I was terrified. I called them *hauntings* for years. Once I got sober and knew I was on the right spiritual path the visions played more frequently and clearer. My drive and ambition in life has always been working toward this illusive vision without any knowledge of how to actually get there. What I've finally come to realize is that I've been getting there all along. It's never been about the destination, it's always been about the journey.

My sister and I experienced a couple of paranormal incidents ourselves in the 70's. In *Recovering From Life* I wrote about nearly driving off a cliff in our drinking days and being magically rescued before we crashed to our deaths. Another time she and I were driving from 'Blurry' (Burley) to Boise after we'd closed the bars in Blurry. Just weeks prior, friends of ours had been killed in a car accident just a few miles from Boise doing exactly what we were doing. The newspaper said the sun was just coming up and they would have been able to see the lights of the city and a sign saying they were five miles from their destination when somehow they lost control of the vehicle and went off the road, rolling several times. I'm sure they fell asleep at the wheel. All three of them were killed.

It goes without saying that neither my sister nor I should have been driving that night and I'm sure the same was true for our friends who also closed the bars in Burley. They would have been approaching Boise about 5 a.m., just as the sun was coming up. Just as we were doing. Sis and I noticed the city lights at the same time and then looked up to see a sign that said, Boise 5. Just then the energy in the car became very thick with a powerful vibration that seemed to go right through us and lingered there.

We were wide-eyed and more than a little freaked out as I sort of squeaked out, *"Do you feel that?" "Oh, yes,"* she said. Every hair was standing up and we were stone cold sober all the way to Boise, so grateful for our friends—whom we felt sitting in the backseat—for keeping us alert through a dangerous part of our journey. We couldn't wait to get back home and tell Dad about our ghost story. He was enthralled, by the way, and believed every word we said. When we were done with our supernatural tale he excitedly said, *"Did it scare ya?"* Boy, did it! In a freaky-cool sort of way.

Other than the visions I didn't think I had inherited any other psychic gifts. That is until I was in my twenties and I started feeling the physical pain of my loved ones. It's not a very fun psychic ability to have and I often wondered why it is that I would get one that involved pain. I'm not sure when I first realized what was happening but there are many instances throughout the years. A few stand out like when we first moved to Michigan and were living in the cottage.

I woke up one morning and felt like I had been kicked in the back of the head. I even said to Greg, "What'd you do, kick me in the head in the middle of the night?" It was later that day that I found out my sister had been beaten by her boyfriend the night before and he had kicked her in the head. She was living nearly two thousand miles away but was flying to Michigan that day.

Thank God it never happened with my brother because he had a lot of injuries growing up and suffered a tremendous amount of pain. But I picked up on Mama, Dad and my sister. The sore shoulder after Dad got a tetanus shot. The knee I couldn't walk on or the arm that was painful after Sis injured hers, the illness, you name it, I felt it and I could never get relief until they felt better. I learned over the years that pain meds did not touch this psychic pain. I was in pain until whomever I was picking up on got relief. It would be one thing if I was taking the pain from them but instead we both suffered. Last year when I was already so sick and broken down I continued to pick up on both Sis and Mama when they were struggling.

Finally I had suffered enough and said a heartfelt prayer. *"Dear*

God, I know that this is an amazing connection I have with my loved ones and for that reason I've never asked you to take it from me. I'm asking you now. Bless my loved ones and surround them with white light. Put up a protective shield around me so that I no longer carry this burden. Thank you, Amen." And from that point on I no longer feel their pain. We'll, except in my heart.

Then this was pretty amazing. From my journal dated 12-9-09—*"It's a blizzard out and I just got back from walking to the mailbox at the end of our alley. As I went to open the slot my eyes stopped on something on the top of the mailbox. Planted in the snow and facing toward me was the most beautiful and delicate salmon colored lily, my favorite flower. I was startled by it. It was so out of the ordinary in the dead of winter. I just stared at it. I felt an eerie calm all around and through me and I thanked whom-ever sent it. It was only on my way home I remembered Uncle Steve died one year ago today. Chills."*

I had just finished *My Dreams My Self* and within a couple of months I was waiting excitedly and somewhat impatiently for the books to arrive from the printer. My dad's health had taken a turn for the worse and only days before they were delivered we got Hospice for him. It was clear to all of us that he was going downhill and we probably weren't going to have him much longer. The books came and I made myself open the box with none of the enthusiasm I thought I would have. They seemed to have lost all the importance I had placed on them. The cover was much darker than it was supposed to be and the disappointment felt like too much. I set the boxes aside.

Chapter 2

Dad

———

March 1, 2010

I awoke with a bit of a heavy heart. I talked to Mama yesterday. Now she's helping Dad bathe. She said he's not eating and seems confused and disoriented at times. She said he's sleeping a lot. I will enjoy spending time with him this morning.

March 11, 2010

What a gift yesterday was. Everyone came to spend the day with Dad. We couldn't believe how good he looked and how alert he was. He was smiling and ended up staying up the whole day. We took pictures of him with each of us, especially with my niece, Kassie's one week old, Hudson. When my daughter, Megan, got there with her children, Kaylee and Cameron, Cameron clung to my dad. A normally very active 3-year-old, he was at Dad's side all day. He'd lay his head on Grandpa's shoulder, he'd hug him, he'd look lovingly into his eyes. It was so precious. The day was a gift.

March 18, 2010

Megan stopped over with the kids and Cameron went right for Grandpa and hung with him. It's very sweet. He'd look at Dad with such love in his eyes, like he knew what was going on and he wanted to give him comfort. Dad just loved it. It's like he wants to reassure my dad that everything is going to be alright. It's pretty amazing. He's Dad's little buddy.

March 27, 2010 (Saturday)

My dad has been unconscious for a couple of days. I told him I want to be with him when he takes his last breath. The five of us women; Mama, Sis, me, Megan, and Kassie, have been with him around the clock the past three days. No one thought he would still be here. At one point yesterday he seemed like he was coming around and with his eyes still closed he looked excited. Then he said, *"Hallelujah!"* I asked, *"Do you see your mom?"* He said, *"No, I'll have to go look for her."* Then he was back in his coma. Tomorrow is my AA anniversary and my dad might die.

March 29, 2010 (Monday)

We sent the girls home to their families last night so just Sis and I stayed with Mama. She went in to tell Dad goodnight and quickly came back out and said he was passing. Sis and I jumped up and sure enough when we got to his room it was silent. Mama fell apart and Sis went to console her and I rushed over to Dad's side. Just then he went, *"Ahhhh,"* as a tiny last breath left his body. *"Hallelujah!"*

My husband has been mostly on his own the past four days while Dad was dying. When I got home yesterday he said, *"If that ever happens to me, don't you do that, you put me somewhere."* I knew my dad wanted to die at home and I just assumed Greg did too. I was so surprised and I said, *"You wouldn't want to die at home?"* He said, *"No."* Good to know.

April 4, 2010

I had an amazing thing happen last night. I was crying and talking to Dad and feeling a little bit sorry for myself that he died on my sober anniversary. I said, *"Why this day?"* Just then I heard my dad say, *"I wanted to die on a day I knew you would celebrate."* Well, alrighty then. Hard to argue with that one. I can hear my dad!

Cameron

My dad loved that little guy and called him *Grandpa's Boy.* I didn't want to face the first time Cameron went to their house because I knew he was going to ask about Grandpa. He did. He went right to Grandma Bette and said, *"Where's Grandpa?"* She cried, so did Meg and I, as we explained the best we could where Grandpa is.

He went over to the Entertainment Center, where, on the bottom shelf, there is a picture of the five of us; Mama, Dad, Scotty, Kristie, and me. He laid down on the floor on his belly facing it with his hands under his chin and just stared at Grandpa. The next day he did the same thing. He said to Grandma, *"I'm sad that Grandpa died."* Another time he asked her why he died, and she told him about his illness. He went to the door of Grandpa's room and just stood there looking in.

Exactly one week after Dad died we had our first Easter without him. Our first anything without him. I wasn't looking forward to it but it was a good day. We gathered, reluctantly, for the family picture no one really wanted to take. But it would have been unfair to Hudson since it was his first Easter. That evening Megan called to tell me something Cameron just said.

His birthday is April 8th and he'll be four years old. It was decided we'd have his party at Mama's since Sis' work was delivering a bunch of food that day and we would all be together. When Meg called it was to say Cameron just said, *"Grandpa's coming to my birthday party."* Megan and Eric, stunned, said, *"He is?"* Cam said yes, and then said, *"I saw him today."* They asked where and he said, *"In Grandma's room. He said he'll see me on my birthday."* I'm so grateful for all of this! It amazes me but I'm not surprised. Those two were so connected. Thank God Cameron talked about it.

April 7, 2010

Gregory and I haven't been connecting very well lately. I feel like I haven't left enough room for him. I called on the way home and told him I really needed to be with him. I'd been missing him all day but a lot last night at Mama's. I got home and ran a bath and we talked about how little time we've spent together over the past two weeks. He's been allowing me to do what I need to do and we've both been grieving. We promised each other we were not going to let ourselves get that disconnected ever again. I need him. I need to include him in everything this week and keep him close, instead of worrying that he doesn't want to be there.

My dad worked hard, played hard, loved hard, and laughed hard. I hear my father in my own boisterous laugh. I will miss hearing his. When I was in the basement looking for pictures for his memorial I had a strange thing happen. I still don't know how but I moved a box from the shelf and set it on the floor. Just then I realized there was a folded piece of paper in my hand! I could feel something weird was going on as I opened it. I recognized Uncle Steve's handwriting right away. He was Mama's baby brother. It was a copy of his handwritten notes for a song he wrote called, *The Way*.

A tear filled my eye and I remembered that we have a cassette recording of him playing the piano and singing. The words are absolutely perfect and I knew that we would play it at Dad's memorial. Steven died just over a year ago or he would have been here to sing it in person I'm sure. He and Dad had a special bond. I know this was his way of making sure he would be there. It gives me such peace to know that Steven was one of the first people my dad saw when he crossed over and I bet he yelled, *"Stevarino!"* To which Steven would have yelled, *"Dickaroo!"* and they would have raced toward each other for a big embrace!

The Way by Steven Isham

You can see my heart … I'm no stranger believe me
When you look inside what do you see?
What I feel is doubt and fear … Help me make it clear

Were at the door, on our opposite sides
You stand there and so do I
Only my soul can let you inside
Show me the way I want to see the light.
Will you please help me through this?
I can't do it alone.
Help me open the door
Show me the light
Show me the way.
Only you know what I've been through,
The heartaches and trials that opened my soul.
I can feel the light
Small and warm inside of me
Begins to glow... I can feel it grow
Now you've helped me through this
Didn't have to do it alone
Now I have my peace...
I opened the door
I see the light
I see the way

April 9, 2010

Everyone was at Mama's last night for Cam's 4th birthday. We tried to be as upbeat as we could for the kids. When it was time for cake and presents Megan put the cake in the middle of the table and lit the candles. We put his presents around the cake and gathered around the table to sing Happy Birthday. Just then the big light that hangs above the table went off..... then on..... then off.... then on.... A total of four evenly spaced flashes before it stayed on. We all stood in amazement. *Well, Grandpa said he was going to be at Cam's birthday party and he was!*

April 28, 2010

Every morning when I open my *Daily Word*—a double issue for March and April—it falls open to March 28th, the day Dad died, and the word for that day: *Hallelujah.* Earlier this morning when my heart was heavy and I was full of grief and crying, Uncle Steve's song broke through and I heard, *"Help me open the door, show me the light, show me the way."* His song has played often in my mind since we played it at Dad's memorial and I have to say it helps. This morning I could feel the despair he felt when he wrote it and the glimmer of hope in asking for a way to survive the feelings.

April 29, 2010

OMG!! Woohoo! Got a doosey of a sign from Dad last night! I still can't believe it! Yesterday at Mama's we were talking about how sad he was when he realized what was happening. The thing we've been most upset about is how he didn't want to die. Once he knew he was dying all he did was cry. It's the hardest thing. We talked about really wanting to know that he's okay about all of that now. That he's not sad anymore.

I had Kassie's wedding album up in our room on the bed. I've used it as a backing when I write out note cards or pay bills. It's the perfect size. It was laying face down on the bed because the front has raised flowers on it and the back is smooth. We came down to eat dinner and I did a few things downstairs so it was a couple of hours before I went back up.

As soon as I entered the doorway I noticed the album was laying open. I knew that was strange and something was off about the air in the room. Still, as I slowly walked toward it I rationalized that Gregory had been looking at it, even though he had been with me the whole time. When I got to it I was shocked. My dad's smiling face was staring back at me, looking as happy as I've ever seen him. All four pictures—as the album lay open—were of Dad.

Greg was heading up the stairs behind me and I quickly met him in the hall and said, *"Did you see the photo album on our bed?"* He said, *"I saw it there."* I said, *"But were you looking at it?"* He said, *"No."* I started to cry. *"You're sure?"* Yes, he was sure, he never touched it. I told him to come and see what I found. When we got to it and he saw Dad's smiling face staring at us he was visibly startled and said, *"You did that!"* and he was freaked out! *"No, I did not! Dad did!"*

For my dad to open that photo album to those particular pages meant everything to me. He was so happy that day. The pictures are of him walking Kassie down the aisle and that's something he'd never been able to do before. Sis hadn't married and Greg and I got married in their living room. I cried, overwhelmed and happy-sad tears. Then I called Mama. The whole thing blew us all away. The rest of the evening I just smiled when I thought about it. It still makes me smile. *"Thank you, thank you, thank you."* My husband, however, is just plain freaked out about it.

July 5, 2010

This morning I had a vision of Dad on the Other Side with all the people we've lost. An overwhelming sense of peace rushed over me. I went outside to water the flowers and thought of my dad when I filled the birdbath. Greg and I got the folks a beautiful birdbath one year and dad set it up, filled it with water, and then said, *"Now all we need is some dirty birds."* I miss him.

December 30, 2010

Wow, a really cool thing happened yesterday at Mama's. Kassie was here with the baby and he was sitting on Mama's lap. All of a sudden he saw *someone* and began talking gently in the sweetest little voice. He would smile so sweet then turn to those in the room and just smile then turn back and start talking to Grandpa again. It went on for a good 15 minutes and there wasn't a dry eye in the place!

January 3, 2011

Kassie dreamed about Dad. He was sitting there talking to her and said, *"I didn't even know I was dead until the knock on the door,"* and Kassie knew he was talking about the funeral home. I remember at the time their knock sounded loud and uninviting.

Kassie said, *"Where were you?"* He said, *"I was in the back room."* That's the den where he liked to play his game on the computer. He hadn't been able to do that for a while. I can just see him wandering around, able to breathe, able to play his game. We were all there so I bet he didn't think a thing about it.

That makes me feel so good about death. After the struggle he went through for four days, to think that he didn't even know he died tells me he sure didn't suffer. Doesn't even remember that part. It tells me he had an easy exit regardless of how it looked to us. That gives me peace. Oh, and the Cardinals. Dad used to complain that there were never enough Cardinals at the feeders. Usually they'd see two, the male and female. Dad always thought there should be more. Yesterday Mama and Sis looked out and the tree was full of Cardinals! They said they counted 8 bright red males and the same number of females! The tree was *full* of Cardinals. Now that's a sign!

February 7, 2011

My brother's 5-year-old granddaughter had a bad accident and broke her femur. They live in Idaho. Poor little thing had to have surgery and is in a body cast from the neck down for six weeks. When I talked to her on the phone she said, *"I still love Grandpa Dick so much."* I said, *"So do I,"* and she said, *"I'm thinking about him right now."* I said, *"So am I."* She only met Dad one time and she was a baby, but she told my brother, *"Grandpa Dick was watching me at the hospital."* It made me cry.

February 18, 2011

I had a *thing* happen two days ago that I haven't been able to really take in, it's so powerful. I was on my way to Mama's and my eye caught two big dark blobs in the sky way up ahead. I knew they were birds but the grouping was really strange like I'd never seen before. The fact that there were so many in two big dark blobs was odd. Then it got really strange. I was watching these birds and they sort of made a dramatic swoosh and turned all at once and headed in my direction. By this point there was a strange feel in the car as time seemed to slow down.

I watched as they flew toward me, fascinated by the shapes they were creating by the formation of their bodies. In that sort of slow motion state I was able to look at other drivers to see if they were seeing what I was seeing but everyone was oblivious. The birds got closer. Once in my total sight, filling my entire windshield, they came into an amazing formation above me and seemed to hover there for a second. They were in the shape of a heart... I stared in disbelief. Then time seem to switch back to normal and I was going 45 mph down the highway. I heard myself say out loud, *"I got that Dad."* My eyes filled with tears and it seemed unbelievable. I did a rough drawing of what I saw.

When time returned to normal I looked behind me and there were *no* birds. They were gone. *"Oh, Dad, thank you."* OMG!! I smell my dad. Right now, his smell, his breath from his coffee, it's right in my face! I love this smell. I always loved this smell! *"Oh, thank you, Dad!"* Mama dreamed about him! She was looking all over for him but couldn't find him anywhere. The phone rang and it was him. He said, *"Hi Honey."* She said, *"Where are you?"* And he said, *"In your bedroom."* I love that so much. She needed it. I cry at some point every day but I'm no longer devastated by those tears.

April 21, 2011

Yesterday was my birthday and I had a rough morning missing Dad so much. I cried a lot and just felt very sad to have now two birthdays without him. Then my dream!

I was standing in our front yard with my back to the house. All of a sudden I felt arms around me from behind and the familiar smell that I knew was my Dad. I held his arms and then said, "I have to turn around for a full hug," which I did and looked at him to make sure it was him even though I knew it was. I could smell him, see him, and I hugged him tight. Then he pulled back and did 'our face,' and said, "Me Love You!"

From the time I can remember my dad and I had this crazy thing we'd do with our faces. We sunk our mouths in like we didn't have any teeth, squint our eyes and in a sort of hillbilly voice we'd say, *"Me Love You!"* Mirror images of a ridiculous face.

*I started to cry and did the face too and said through tears, "Oh, Me Love **You**!" Then I hugged him tight again. He said, "Now you go back up to bed," and he pulled back. I held his hand and looked right into his youthful face—reminded me of when we lived in Idaho 25 years ago—and I said, "Thank you, Dad, you just made my whole life so much better!" He smiled knowingly and then headed off walking down the road, looking back at me as he walked. I watched him until he faded away.*

Yesterday I knew in my heart Dad was going to acknowledge my birthday in a significant way, but by bedtime there was nothing. I will never forget this. Woohoo! Hallelujah!

May 24, 2011

Woohoo! What a great dream I had last night! Dad and Steven! *We were at Grandma and Grandpa's house. All the family was there and we were looking at old photo albums and marveling at how young we all looked. My dad walked in and I ran to him and hugged him and held on tight. He was young and smiling. Then in walked Steven! Long hair, gorgeous, healthy. I ran to him and hugged him tight. We talked and talked. I told him I was so sorry I didn't do more to help him. I told him everything I was sorry for. He told me he should have listened, but it's okay now. I hugged him so tight and then found Dad again and hugged him some more.* It was an amazing dream!

November 10, 2011

Yesterday at Mama's, as Meg and I were about to leave, hundreds of birds landed in the front yard and blanketed the whole lawn. It was an amazing sight. They rose up in unison a few inches from the ground and then landed back down. We couldn't believe it. Only in Mama's yard.

Chapter 3

Gregory

This part is hard for me to write about but it's important. Greg and I were having our first ever *real* struggle in our marriage. In hindsight, of course, it's easy to see exactly what was going on but at the time we were in two different worlds. Greg had been on disability for two years after being forced to retire early in 2008 because of a back injury. Then Dad died and I know it was harder on him than he let on. He wanted to keep my Dad's wedding ring and wore it on his right hand.

After getting near total relief after back surgery in '09, the other side of his back started bothering him. I know he was going through a lot of pain and was becoming more debilitated again. For an energetic guy like my husband it had to have been devastating. He didn't talk to me about it and I didn't ask. I was busy keeping feelings at bay that said I could be losing my husband.

Especially when he started being real grumpy and it was hard to take. His dad was grumpy and got worse as he got older. I was having a hard time with *Angry Guy*, feeling sorry for myself and taking everything personally. He was being mean to everyone at one point. We had a big blowout. I finally told him I wasn't going to live like that and the next day he called a counselor. He went, then I went, then we went together. The counselor asked him what he thought the problem was and I was so surprised to hear my husband say, *"I think I ride a rollercoaster of depression."*

In an instant I saw that none of this was about me. He was hurting and just didn't know how to deal with it. How to tell me what he was feeling. I always say, *"I don't run into mean people, I run into wounded people,"* and yet, I had forgotten that with the one person I love the most. Everything changed after that and we were back to who we had always been. There for each other, loving and kind, playful. In the fall of that year we took a trip to Idaho and had the best time ever. We felt closer to each other and happier than we'd ever been. My own depression lifted.

He would take two trips without me, one to Florida to see an old friend, and another back to California where he reunited with friends he grew up with and hadn't seen most of them for over 30 years. He seemed to be taking care of business and tying up loose ends. Out of the blue he said he was selling his sliver stock and was finally going to have the front porch rebuilt. It was falling down and had bothered him for years. He said we were siding the house and getting a metal roof. We made the last house payment. And then.....

2012

After he started having back pain again he felt it was probably the same issue they'd fixed on the left side. He didn't want to think about another surgery but it only got worse. Looking back I see that he was much more debilitated than I realized at the time. I would have loved to have handled some things differently. Finally in the summer of 2011 we went to the VA clinic here in town and they started him on physical therapy. That went on for a couple of months and only made things worse. They scheduled an MRI in Ann Arbor for January 24, 2012.

January 25, 2012

Ugh! Ugh! Ugh! We drove down to Ann Arbor the night before Greg's MRI since his appointment was so early. Afterwards we hit the freeway and got home by 3:30 p.m. When we unlocked the door the phone was ringing. Greg answered it while I greeted the kitties and started bringing in stuff from the car. When I came back in Greg was in the dining room, still on the phone, and motioning frantically for me to come here. The phone call ended and he said, *"We have an appointment at 9:00 a.m. at the clinic to discuss the mass on my tailbone...."* He looked so scared and I felt a cool numb from my head to my toes.

So there you have it. His pain explained. Now what? He said she asked him if he was sitting down. She said she's right on it and will fill us in tomorrow. She said we're going to be doing some traveling. Oddly enough I became very accepting of that on the drive home from Ann Arbor. We'd made a bed for him in the back of the Jimmy because he couldn't sit. I felt good that I could do this for Gregory. Whatever he needed from me. Now I'm really grateful for that.

Over the next nearly three months we would make one trip to Saginaw for a biopsy, and then, in early February we had a consultation with the Oncologist in Ann Arbor and packed for an overnight trip. A month later we headed home. The mass on his tailbone was secondary to the lung cancer that could not be treated. Our time in Ann Arbor was spent with him mostly in the hospital where the goal was pain management. He also received daily radiation for two weeks on the mass sitting on his sciatica, in an attempt to manage his pain and get us on a regime that would work at home. It never happened.

February 8, 2012

We're in Ann Arbor but I have to write about what happened on the way down here. I was driving and Greg was asleep in the back. I was thinking about him and wondering what we were facing. I started talking to my dad. I said I was so glad I could feel him here but I missed his hugs. Then I remembered how it felt to hug him and I *'gave him a hug'* in my mind. Just then I felt a sort of tingling sensation and a firm squeeze on my whole entire being!

I could feel my dad hugging me from head to toe, inside out! It was so amazing it can't be described! I said, *"I feel it, Dad,"* and I started crying. I could feel this beautiful pressure all over me. I kept crying and letting Dad know I could feel him embracing me. Then he gave me one final squeeze, tighter than the rest, and back to normal. It was so incredible I will never forget it. I sure needed it too. It felt like pure love and pure reassurance.

Reading over my journals during this time I'm saddened by my own denial. I can also see that it served me well. It kept me in the solution and able to be there for Greg. In hindsight the writing was on the wall but we didn't go there. I tried to stay positive for him but his battle was pain management and the poor guy suffered a tremendous amount for months. He lost tons of weight and barely resembled the man he was before. Still, I believed we would get a miracle. I thought we could beat this thing. A dream I had the day before we left Ann Arbor says it all but I didn't fully grasp the meaning.

February 27, 2012
*I dreamed I was coming in our backdoor with a guest, not sure who. As we headed in one of our 'pets' wanted in but shied away because of the stranger. I was like, "C'mon, come in," and I opened the screen door wide. But the **Ostrich**, who was his normal size(!) kept backing away. The guest was quite surprised that this huge bird was our pet! I thought it was perfectly normal.*
I don't even want to interpret this! Ostriches stick their heads in the sand!

That's all I wrote about it at the time. I didn't even look it up in any of my dream books. But this is what *The Dream Dictionary* says, *"To see an ostrich in your dream suggests that you are not facing reality. You are in denial about something and living in a world of your own. Perhaps there is a situation that you are unwilling to accept.*" You must be kidding me. I'm keeping this denial as a pet. I'm letting it in the back door where nobody can see it. I didn't think there was anything strange about it. Ugh. We were headed home the next day and my journal entry the day we left is sadly full of that same denial.

February 28, 2012

Finally we get out of here. My prayer is Gregory will improve at home. We are willing to do whatever it takes to heal him. It's all going to be about his healing now, whatever that takes.

March 20, 2012

We've struggled. I've had a couple of migraines and that makes it impossible to help Gregory. I'm worn out. I had a bad day yesterday. I'm so afraid he will leave me. Afraid we won't be able to get his pain under control. *Fear.* Afraid of everything. I can't imagine my life without him. It scares me breathless. Today I'm not going to think about that. Instead I choose to envision him whole and healthy, to see our future with him strong and full of life. I'm never giving up. Triumph over cancer! Beat the odds! Get a miracle!

March 21, 2012

Reality hit yesterday when I realized that if something happens to Greg I will have zero income. It's not like I didn't know he was supporting me but I guess I never let myself think about something happening to him before I started making money. I called Social Security and the woman said, *"You can collect your husband's social security... In nine years."*

March 28, 2012

Gregory lost another *10 pounds*. He seems so out of it at times, like he doesn't really know what's going on. He truly looks like he's dying. I'm horrified by what is happening to him. Caring for him is a full time job now. When I was helping in the bathroom he looked so bad and was so frail. A feeling of dread washed over me. I said, *"I feel like you're dying on me,"* to which he replied, *"I feel like I am too."* Knowing what it would mean, I said it anyway, *"Do you think we should have Jeremy (our son in Idaho) come?"* And when he said, *"Maybe that would be a good idea,"* my heart stopped. Jeremy is scheduled to fly in this evening.

April 2, 2012

Gregory seemed clearer headed in the shower this morning. He looks better. His face looks handsome again instead of like a POW on the brink of death. He kisses me more every day, grabs my butt once in a while and just sees me again. That was a lonely place to be when he was so out of it and didn't know where we lived. I asked him the other day and he said, *"Pocatello, Idaho."* I laughed and he thought hard and got it right. He knew our address. I asked him what his name is and he said, *"Now you're being mean."* Lol! His sense of humor hasn't left him!

April 10, 2012

Gregory can't be left alone now. He fell a couple of times in the night getting up to pee and forgetting he has no strength. I sleep holding onto him. We managed to get him out to Megan's for Easter but he was out of it and didn't really know he was there. It broke everyone's hearts, mine included. We took our last family picture with the four of us. Jeremy leaves today. He and Megan have been such a help to me.

April 11, 2012

Something is not right with his mind. He is so out of it. Did he have a stroke? Does he have brain damage from all the meds? I just cried as I struggled to get him on and off the toilet, undressed and in bed. Frail and shaky, he bears no resemblance to my Gregory. I hate what's happening to us. I miss my husband so much.

April 12, 2012

Perhaps today will be the day he comes back to me. If my husband's going to die I want to have a conversation with him.

Later that day Gregory was completely incoherent and unable to walk or respond to me in any way. I called the nurse and she told me to get him to the ER right away, that he might have had a stroke. Megan and our nephew Justin helped get him into the car. It was heartbreaking. A cat scan showed he had a huge mass on his frontal lobe. I asked the question I had been afraid to ask all along. *"How long do we have?"* The doctor said, *"I'd say a week or two."* Megan and I cried and cried.

We got him settled in a room and called Jeremy and told him what was going on. He wanted me to put the phone to his dad's ear so he could talk to him. We heard Jeremy say, *"I love you, Dad,"* and then we were shocked to hear Gregory—in the loudest voice ever—say, *"I love you too, Man!"* The nurse in the room flipped around and she couldn't believe it. She said, *"Do you know how much energy that took for him to do that?"* It made us all cry and I knew that it was so important for Greg to make sure Jer knows that he loves him. There was no doubt! It was so incredible.

Later in the evening I was sitting next to his bed and holding onto him like I always do. He seemed to come around just a little bit and he knew I was there. He said very clearly, yet sadly, *"I'm sorry, Baby."* It made me cry. They were the last words he ever spoke.

April 14, 2012

I'm devastated and honestly don't think I can do this thing. I had a panic attack from hell the first night home. I woke up in a panic yesterday. I couldn't be in our house. I turned on every light. I couldn't breathe. Gregory is everywhere there. I'm going to die with him.

While they were changing him yesterday Megan and I waited down the hall in a nice waiting room. A woman in a hospital gown sort of floated in as we got up to leave. Her voice was soft and sweet and she said, *"Don't leave on my account,"* and then stopped me in the doorway and said, *"Who are you here for, dear?"* I told her and she asked my husband's name then said, *"Can I pray with you?"*

"Of course," I said, and she took my hands in hers and said the most beautiful prayer. Meg stood behind me. I cried and hugged her and said how much it meant and then said, *"And the same for you."* She very softly and matter-of-factly said, *"Oh, I'm going to be just fine."* I said, *"What's your name?"* She said, *"Hope."* I will be looking for *God with skin on*, as my friend Dolly used to say, and throughout my day ask God, as I did last night, to help me be in our home, help me find peace there. *Help me.*

April 15, 2012

My life is beyond a nightmare; it's a heartbreak. I'm holding my husband's hand as he stares out into nothingness. I know he knows I'm here. I don't know how I'm going to be able to do this. Losing my Gregory is more than I can bear. They came to talk to me about what we wanted to do in terms of end of life care since he wouldn't be able to stay in the hospital. They asked if I wanted to take him home and have Hospice come in or did I want to put him in Hospice House, which is private pay. I didn't know what to do and I started to cry. I said to Megan, *"This is when I wish I could talk to him."* Just then I remembered what he said after Dad died, that I should put him somewhere. I quickly said, *"We'll take him to Hospice House,"* and knew I wouldn't worry about how I was going to pay for it.

April 16, 2012

We'll get Greg moved today. I can't believe I'm sitting here with my husband as he prepares to leave this world. *Will my spirituality and my faith get me through or am I going to die of a broken heart?* I don't think I'll be able to stay alone after he's gone but I sure wish I could. I've gotten on my knees the past few nights and asked God to surround me with light and love, with peace and comfort to be able to be in our house and feel safe. To be able to be there for our animals. We have four cats, Lacy, Bailey, Gracie and Riley. They need me. I pray that home doesn't feel like a scary place.

"God help me on this journey. Remind me that I will see him again and that I will be okay." I love this man more than words can say and we are connected on a soul level. That can never be severed. I pray to be with him through this process, to help him and be there loving him when he takes his last breath.

(Evening)

We got Gregory moved today. When the paramedics came for him I held his hand and walked beside his bed as they rolled us toward the back entry where the ambulance was waiting. Hospice House is located right behind the hospital but it might as well have been a hundred miles if I had to get Gregory there on my own. The paramedics seemed so sad for me. They put Greg in the back and one said I had to ride in the front. I headed toward the passenger door in a daze and the other one said, *"Never mind, you can ride back there with him."*

I held his hand and it seemed we were in slow motion. It was so close and yet it seemed we rode in that ambulance for the longest time. Once they wheeled him into this beautiful place I felt such peace surrounding us. He has a beautiful view of the woods out a full wall of windows in his room even if he isn't aware of it.

April 17, 2012

Sitting here with Gregory his eyes are open and seeming lost. I am brokenhearted beyond comprehension. He slept all day and looked so at peace after looking distressed at the Hospital. *When will he leave us? What will I do? How will I survive without my Gregory? Is he going to die on my birthday?*

A friend stopped by to visit and I was standing by Greg holding his hand. I told him who was there and he looked at me with a bit of clarity and reached up to kiss me. I immediately bent down and kissed him and then he puckered up and reached up again and we kissed and then again and again. It was so amazing. He just kept kissing me and kissing me and seemed so happy to be able to express his love. I will never forget it.

In the evening his guitar teacher stopped by to play for him. It was so beautiful and I was fine until I saw Rob crying. He played his peaceful, beautiful music as tears streamed down his face. I held Greg's hand and cried. It was so good to hear guitar music. I knew Greg was loving it even if he couldn't show it. I said, *"It's Rob, Honey, he came to play for you. Isn't it beautiful?"*

Up until the ER Doctor no one ever told us Gregory was going to die. When we left Ann Arbor the end of February his next appointment wasn't until May 15th. I asked the Dr. what we were supposed to do until then? What were we going to do about the primary cancer? He said, *"His lung cancer is located in between two major blood vessels. He wouldn't survive chemo or radiation. But don't worry, nothing's going to kill him before May."*

April 19, 2012

My Gregory died at 1:30 this morning. I was with him. God bless him, it was peaceful like I can't adequately describe and he let go effortlessly. He took care of me in every way he could. By not lingering and by not struggling. And although I wouldn't have minded, he didn't die on my birthday. He died the day before so we can celebrate together. I felt so calm and at peace.

Last evening all the family was there including Justin and his wife, Jeni with 2-month old Jordan. They stayed all evening. Gregory had closed his eyes and I knew he wouldn't open them again. A nurse came in and said, *"Yep, he's floating around here now watching his body."* I thought that strange but then felt myself adapt to the idea that Gregory had already left his pain behind.

A bit later Megan was holding the baby when he began fixating on something just over her shoulder. He began to coo and talk and smile and even let out a little laugh, all in response to his

Great Uncle Greg I know. It was amazing. Jeni got goosebumps. Gregory loved the babies, he always has. There was no doubt he was talking to baby Jordan and I would have given anything to see what he could see! There was a light reflected in his eyes from a source we couldn't see.

Everyone left and I settled in for the night about 10:30 p.m. Greg was breathing heavy and somewhat labored but I knew that I could fall asleep to it and yet would know if it changed. I did. Around midnight he began pausing between breaths. I went over to his side and just held onto him for I don't know how long. Then his breath stopped for a moment and then he breathed quite normally for a couple of breaths then stopped. I waited. I kissed his cheek. I laid my head on his chest. Silence.

The room was filled with more peace than I've ever felt in my life. I couldn't even cry. All I could do is thank Gregory for this beautiful experience. I could feel him in my chest. It's as if he took his last breath and jumped right into my heart. I heard music begin to play in my mind. It was Lionel Ritchie's *Endless Love*. The words sang out in my head and in that moment I knew that my husband was telling me that our hearts beat as one now. I could feel it.

I couldn't believe it. That's what Gregory and I have. I felt our bond even stronger and I knew that I get to spend eternity with this man. I'm not blind to how grief will hit me but I asked Gregory to be strong around me and to hold me up. *"Help me survive your death."* Megan called and is having a really hard time. Oh, my poor children. So many hearts are aching.

April 20, 2012

A friend texted me, *"Birthday."* I thought it fitting. I found out I'm going to be able to hear Gregory. I was in the shower yesterday morning. When I washed my breasts I heard him say, *"Let me do that."* Are you kidding me? Lol! That was so him. *Is* so him. I said, *"So that's the way it's going to be is it?"* In truth it was a relief. I felt my heart settle down knowing that I can hear his voice, I can talk to him, he's right here. Pretty amazing. Jeremy gets back from

Idaho today and we have to go to the funeral home and will see
Gregory for the last time. Just like when he was sick I ask for the
strength I need for this day.

There is a feeling of relief when someone passes after having
been so ill that they can't be left alone. I couldn't even take a
shower until the kids got here to be with him. If I needed to go to
the store I had to wait. And watching him go through all of that
was heart wrenching and I'm relieved it's over. There is sadness in
that freedom.

April 21, 2012

We actually got the best news yesterday. The best birthday
present I could hope for. I came out of the meeting and Megan
was waiting by my car, crying. I thought she was just having a hard
time about her dad but as soon as she saw me she hugged me and
was practically wailing as she said, *"I'm pregnant!"* and then just
sobbed. I was so happy! It is no accident that the day after her dad
died our daughter found out she's pregnant. Perhaps this is what
she needs to get her through. Perhaps a new baby is what will get
us all through.

April 22, 2012

The outpouring of love from our recovery community and our
families is overwhelming. Perhaps that is what's carrying me. My
sister has been staying here since Greg died. I found myself alone
yesterday for about an hour and it could have gotten ugly. I started
to panic and the realization of my loss was almost too much to
bear. Gregory helped me. He's going to have to, and perhaps my
spirituality will be the thing that carries me. And feeling him,
having very cool signs from him. I'm counting on it.

It hits me in waves—the panic—trying to steal the life out of
me. Every time I opened the medicine cabinet his things loomed
at me like some kind of threat. I took everything out, his shaving
cream, shaver, etc. and then my heart sank with it gone! I felt like
I couldn't breathe. I hurried and put it all back but that was too

painful! I took it out and then filled the empty spaces with my stuff and I could breathe. The same with his stuff in the shower, his clothes in the hamper. Ugh.

I call out to him and I hear him say, *"Breathe."* I do and it's okay for a moment. I said to him yesterday, *"You didn't give me a sign on my birthday!"* and he quickly said, *"Hello?! A **baby**!"* Oh yeah, that is a pretty nice birthday surprise even as it's sad that he won't be here for these little ones. I will be and I will tell them about their Papa Greg. I hurt for my children and perhaps my strength is for them as well as myself.

"It's still unreal, Gregory. Everything went so fast my heart is spinning." There is a spiritual force of some sort that seemed to wrap around us from the moment we entered this journey. Perhaps a gift from the Other Side to keep these things from killing us. There was a point toward the end when he was so sick and I knew in my heart he was dying. I was so distraught, so heart-broken I didn't think I could breathe. The thought came, *"I'll just die with him."* Die of a broken heart and go live out eternity with my Gregory. My grief lifted for a moment and I felt pure joy.

When he died I was filled with a calm I will never fully under-stand and a peace that made the whole thing so beautiful. I know the days ahead will feel lonely but I know my Gregory is still with me and making sure I'm taken care of. People have been giving me money and a friend took up a collection and paid all the medical bills the VA didn't cover, including his stay at Hospice House. I don't even know what to say.

April 30, 2012

The funeral was amazing. Standing room only. The funeral director said probably fifty or more people had to leave because there was no room. I told Gregory, *"We didn't book a big enough space for you, Honey!"* It was a beautiful and memorable tribute to my love. The National Guard standing at the front of the room throughout the service was truly amazing. I said a few words and then an old friend of Greg's played a beautiful piece of the blues on Gregory's guitar.

Our granddaughter, Kaylee, was going to read the poem she wrote for Papa Greg but then was crying too hard. Still, she stood up with her dad, who, through his own tears read it and also shared his love for his father-in-law. Megan cried reading what she'd written and then wanted the funeral director to play, *Dance With My Father Again*, by Luther Vandross, but it wouldn't work. We knew it was probably Gregory pulling his pranks and messing with the system. There was a long silence. When Eric had it playing from Meg's phone and held it to the microphone, the mic went loud with noise and we all laughed. Even the military had trouble with the recording of *Taps*! I know it was Gregory!

The rest of the family that wanted to, spoke, and then Kassie introduced *Somewhere Over the Rainbow*. It was the precious Hawaiian version and gave tribute to Gregory's nickname. Then Jeremy spoke and we played the song he chose, *Simple Man*, by Leonard Skynyrd. It was beautiful. The military did their flag ceremony and my dear friend, Linda Woods, was the one who presented me with the flag. It was surreal.

May 3, 2012

I stayed here alone yesterday for the first time. Sis went back home. It feels so peaceful in the house. I can't believe I'm okay but I am. Maybe because I'm not alone. I miss my husband's physical presence and the sound of his voice and the feel of his touch, but he's still here.

Chapter 4

Signs Of Things To Come

It was fifteen days after Gregory died that I got his first obvious Rainbow. Up to that point I was doing remarkably well. His spirit was so strong with me that I was lifted up. He was speaking to me in songs from the moment he left this world and I was happy with the messages. In the car only a couple of days after he died I got REO's, *"Keep On Loving You ..."* The energy in the car changed ever so slightly and it felt like the words were just for me. He told me that no matter what has happened he will continue to love me forever. And as if the whole song thing wasn't enough, just when I'm beginning to write about the grief and loss—the reality of my situation hitting me—the Rainbows showed up.

May 4, 2012

I've been talking to Gregory and crying. I always feel better afterwards. Then a blanket of dread tries to strangle me and I wonder how I will ever go on without him? How will I survive a dark winter alone? I try to stay in the moment but my now moment is the stark reality that my husband has died and my safe little, romance-filled love story has come to a crashing halt. My Gregory is no longer here. Well, in the physical. I feel him everywhere in the house. That's why I'm able to be here. That's why I want to be here. But I need signs from him. I need help to get through this.

I dared him to send me a sign. *"Come on, Gregory, bring it on! I dare ya!"* Nothing was immediate. I went upstairs and there it was. In front of the keyboard, propped on a pen, was a picture of a beautiful Rainbow that I printed off the Internet the other day. It was buried under papers on my desk and I'd forgotten about it. There it was, my sign from Gregory. This is where I challenged him to send me Rainbows every day. That night after my first Rainbow grief hit me like never before.

May 5, 2012

It means so much knowing he's sending me Rainbows. Last evening I cried like I haven't cried since he died. It was the saddest I have ever felt. The tears streamed down my face, *poured* out of me. I felt like I was crying for both of us. Double the tears, it felt, double the heartbreak. It was like Gregory was crying with me. I cried for about an hour then felt so tired and fell quickly to sleep. In the night I found myself moved to my side, like Gregory and I always slept. It was like I was scooted over to make room for him. I've been sleeping on his side like I always do when he's not home but last night I felt moved over. *"Thank you, Baby. Please keep giving me signs."*

May 6, 2012

Some days I'm still stunned that Gregory is gone. I found his journal in the closet. It made me cry. He talks about me often, expressing his love and it felt as though he were speaking from across the veil to tell me how much he loves me and that he thought I was a good wife. He also has entries about Jeremy and Megan and I know they will cherish them. I found his voice in our pictures file. He was teasing me like he always did. Now I have his writing, his words, his heart. What a gift.

May 9, 2012

Greg's sister is coming over to help me move furniture out of the office so I can restore it to a guest room now that I moved the desk into Greg's man room. Then I need to resolve the issue with the stray, pregnant kitty that wandered into our yard the day Gregory died—and hasn't left—then find loving homes for her and the kittens when they're born.

May 13, 2012

I found a couple of notes from Gregory. In a card for my birthday he wrote, *"Keep a smile on your face and laughter in your heart."* Then I found a picture of a Rainbow. Someone gave it to me years ago. Wonderful words of comfort after losing a beloved pet. I thought that was cool/strange. Something in the carpet caught my eye. I picked it up. It looked like a marble but one side was flat. I looked inside and it said, *"Be Happy."* A gentle shiver ran through me.

As much as I miss him I know he doesn't want me to waste energy on anything that can't be changed. No matter what I may be upset about; the VA not being up front with us about how sick he was, or not getting him to a doctor sooner, nothing will fix this thing. Nothing will bring him back. He seems to urge me quickly not to go there. *"Look forward,"* he says. *"Be Happy."*

May 16, 2012

I woke this morning with a little trepidation. Afraid to think too much. But I did feel Gregory in the night, or I dreamed about him, I'm not sure. But he was here with me I know. It gives me hope for more contact. In January I always choose a 'word' that I will focus on in the upcoming year. I'm always so careful when I choose my word because it can be dangerous. This year my word is *Transition*. Ugh. My first thought when all of this began was what? transition from a married woman to a widow? Yep. The only reason I'm doing as well as I am is he's here and I get

Rainbows every day. Bright, beautiful Rainbows on commercials, in movies, on the radio.

May 20, 2012

I was looking at the picture board from Gregory's memorial and crying. I felt not one, not two, but three brushes on top of my head. I knew it was Gregory, kissing me. Whenever I cry he shows up stronger and I feel joy in my heart. He does that for me. He makes me feel so peaceful and so joyful, even as I grieve. I can't explain any of it. All I know is I have a bond with him that, while different, *is* stronger than it was in life. He is always with me. He doesn't want me to be sad but he certainly understands why I am. So he helps me. I love him so much for that.

May 30, 2012

I can't tell you how thankful I am that Gregory had a man room. It was all him. From where he hung pictures and his guitars, to where he put his stereo and his bookcase full of his favorite movies and CD's. All of that is priceless to me. I'm grateful I could move my desk to where his big chair was and leave everything else the same.

May 31, 2012

I had an appointment with the VA. I wasn't sure what I was going for. Someone told me about a benefit available to me that I believed was a one-time benefit. After filling out all of the paper-work the VA worker left to make copies of all the forms she had me sign. When she returned I asked her what this is for? My monthly bills to maintain the house now that it's paid for, total $600.00. That doesn't include food and gas but everything else; car insurance, house insurance and taxes, utilities, everything. She said, *"It's a benefit that, as long as you don't make any money, is about $680.00 a month."* Can you imagine? *"Oh, Gregory, Honey, you're still taking care of me."* I weep.

June 9, 2012

I named pregnant kitty Jasmine and she had her kittens in the basement. Four baby girls. I moved Mama and babies into the closet in the back room and they seem to be resting and nursing. Jasmine is doing great. What have I got myself into?

June 25, 2012

I see Rainbows practically every time I turn on the TV. Sherwin Williams has the most amazingly colorful Rainbow commercial right now and I seem to see it every time I turn on the TV. Then I had an amazing thing happen. I noticed a row of very tall shoots along the east side fence, with a flower atop each one, that I swear wasn't there before. Upon closer examination I realized the flowers were salmon colored lilies, my favorite! Either those were never there or they never bloomed before! At any rate I cried as I realized they were from Gregory. Very few people know what my favorite flower is but Gregory knew! We never had any salmon colored flowers in our yard before. When did he plant them? Also, the roses are in full bloom like never before.

June 26, 2012

Another niece is having her baby this morning. More babies! This is the third boy in the family since February and Megan is due in December. That's four new baby boys born the same year Gregory died. Wow, I hadn't thought about that until now. Today is a good day.

June 27, 2012

I was so sick yesterday and I forgot what a comfort it is having someone there when you don't feel well. But I felt him here with me. When I was taking a hot bath I said through tears, *"As long as you stay with me, I'll be able to do this, but you have to stay with me."* Right away I heard him say, *"I'm not going anywhere, Babe."* Oh, it makes me cry even now like it did then. I love him so much.

June 30, 2012

I'm sitting on a big rock on the beach watching what promises to be an amazing sunrise! It has been so many years since I've done this. I used to do it every morning in the summer after Gregory left for work. The sunrise is taking my breath away.

(At home)

On my walk back I was struck by how beautiful the trees and the gardens are along the way. I stopped at one point, the sight so beautiful, and said to Gregory, *"This,"* and I spread my arms out wide, *"is our backyard,"* which is what he would often say about our city by the bay. Then I said, in my playful way with him, *"This is where you left me."* To which he quickly replied, *"At least I didn't leave you in Pocatello!"* Lol! Don't you love it?! I feel him, I hear him, I know he's here. He sends me Rainbows.

I remember after he died and I felt like he was crying with me. Well it happened again a few minutes ago. I said, *"It's the kids, honey, I'm so sad for the kids."* My tears poured out double and I knew Gregory was crying with me about that loss now. Sad himself that he had to leave the kids this soon when he was such a good dad and had always been there for them. Gregory just sent me a Rainbow through the TV! I got one yesterday too. Always my attention is drawn to wherever the Rainbow is! I love that my signs from him are Rainbows. His nickname was Rainbow and he's sending me a piece of him. May they never stop coming.

July 9, 2012

I'm feeling restless again. I don't like it. Worries me about how well I have done and perhaps I've just been in shock. What if this is the shock wearing off? I do not feel Gregory with me in those restless moments and that stirs up another fear. That I will quit feeling him. Megan called to say Kaylee, in her room for the night, screamed, *"Mom!"* in a tone Meg had never heard before as she flew down the stairs. Her guitar, nowhere near her, strummed. It's the guitar Greg and I gave her and he had been teaching her to play. I love it!

July 14, 2012

I'm at the beach! Sitting on a big rock. It's nice out. A gentle cool breeze promises to warm up as the air and the sky seem clouded and hazy. Before I walked over here my back room was alive with playfulness and it's been a joy to wake up to the beauty of new life. One of the books I'm reading about surviving loss says to surround yourself with living things like a new plant or a stray kitten. Lol! Perhaps that was the plan all along. Pregnant Jasmine was going to need a safe place to have her babies and I was going to need a lot to keep me busy and make me smile while navigating this new territory.

July 18, 2012

I've been up since 5 a.m. My mornings are quite refreshing. Filled with new life as I bask in watching 5½ week old kittens romp and play. It's quite a gift. I have adjusted my life and adapted a section of our home to accommodate and care for these miracles of creation that somehow found their way to our house.

Throughout this whole time I write in my journals about all the things I'm doing on the house. What I came to call the *living room project*—washing walls and painting—was a big job, and one that Greg and I were going to do this past spring. We already had the paint. I felt I had to do it. I also ripped out carpets and replaced them with new when Gracie peed on everything after he died. I had so much to keep me busy. Funny how life shows up to help us in ways often overlooked while in survival mode.

July 21, 2012

Wow, I just got a beautiful Rainbow from Gregory. It made me cry. I'd been having a sad morning missing him so much and wondering how I can do this. Whenever he sends me a Rainbow my attention is always drawn to it just prior. This one was amazing. I miss my love. I miss my life with him. *Endless Love* played in my mind yesterday and it helped.

July 31, 2012

There was an explosive thunder and lightning storm last night. It was my first big storm without the safety of my big strong man. I was really missing his arms around me last night. Wide awake and in awe of the show out my back window, I felt Gregory in a powerful way.

August 3, 2012

I had a tough day yesterday. Sure hope I don't have many of those. *I saw Gregory in my dream. It was vague but there he was standing in the midst of whatever was going on. He looked more like when we first met, mustache, long hair down.* I look forward to more dreams of him. His presence in my dream was reassurance.

August 4, 2012

When I turned on the TV to check the weather I immediately got my Rainbow. This one was so beautiful. Yesterday it happened too. I felt an urge to catch the last five minutes of a program I had hoped to watch in its entirety but had missed. I didn't, however, miss the beautiful Rainbow that appeared as soon as I turned on the TV.

August 14, 2012

Gregory was in my dream! Only a brief appearance but he was there! *I was working on the house and he was helping me. Just like when he was alive, the two of us working on the project of the day.* I think it was his way of letting me know he's right here with me working on the living room project. I had a couple of sad moments yesterday really missing him but it's all good. Grief has not felt scary to me which I'm grateful for. Instead my grieving moments feel cleansing. My heart is broken but my connection to Gregory never will be.

August 22, 2012

I got a Rainbow in my dream! Woke me right up. I was tired after all I accomplished yesterday. The living room looks amazing. I got curtains and a beautiful big area rug. I used our Mackinac Island money to pay for it. It looks so homey. I can't believe it's done. I thought I would never get to this place. I'm so proud of how nice it looks. *"Look at me! Look at me!"* I'd forgotten about that! After we got into recovery and learned how self-centered we addicts can be, Gregory would have that little saying—for himself or whomever it fit in the moment of recognized self-centered-ness—*"Look at me! Look at me!"*

September 3, 2012

I'm missing my husband's touch. I sobbed through the beautiful love scenes in a movie I watched last night. I find it heartbreaking to remember what we had.

September 4, 2012

Gregory and I would be on Mackinac Island right now having the time of our lives I'm sure. Save for three times—Meg's wedding, Kaylee's birth, and a trip to Idaho—we went to Mackinac Island the week of Labor Day every year for over 20 years. I saw him in my dream again but only briefly. *He always looks like he did when we first met. He was 30 years old. Hair long and he wore it down. Mustache, no beard.* I just can't believe it.

Chapter 5

Dreams And Reality

September 12, 2012

I dreamed about making lunch for Gregory, a sandwich, which he sat there and ate, as did I. It was as normal as can be. In these dreams it's never like he has died. Don't I wish? Shows that he's still in my world. I have so much more hope and promise today than I did yesterday. Thank God. Seems I get through a rough patch and get a second wind to carry on.

September 15, 2012

I dreamed about Gregory. *He was sitting on the end of a couch, me on the other. I kept staring at him then finally went over and curled up around him, amazed that he was actually here. I pretty much didn't let go of him after that, convinced that if I did he would disappear. I wanted to make love with him and we went into a bedroom and began but there was an interruption I can't remember now. I started waking up, aware of my dream, and trying to stay asleep. It worked.*

Then, OMG! I was all curled up with him and we were just talking. I was so curious about the Other Side and said, "I bet you know everything now, like when I'm going to be joining you....

Tell me." He was hesitant but I could tell he knew. He acted like he shouldn't tell me so I sort of begged, "I really want to know. C'mon, Honey, tell me." He looked at me like he always used to when I was getting my way and said, "22 years."

In the dream I felt that was good. Gives me time to accomplish my goals and yet I know how fast time goes and before I know it I'll be with Gregory. Now, however, it's hitting me weird, like is it true for one thing, and then wow, what if it is? *22 years.* I would only be 74. That would be less than half the time I thought I had left. Yesterday was stressful. It was adoption day. I was both wanting this day to get here and dreading it. Jasmine and the kittens are gone.

September 16, 2012

I'm still a bit unnerved by the idea that I only have 22 years left. There's that number again. It's been a theme in my life. I'm wondering why I would ask such a question? Let alone get an answer. I guess if one day I'm journaling and it's 2035, I'll know it wasn't true, but until then I guess it's a good motivator for living as fully as I can and making life count. Still, this feels kind of heavy.

September 25, 2012

Last night at bedtime Lacy was in Greg's room crying. She hasn't done that before but last night she was going from one corner to the other crying out, almost calling out. It was heartbreaking. It got me crying. I guess it finally hit her he's not coming back. It hit me too. I have felt so out of sorts and I don't like it. I miss my husband so much. I guess I'm afraid the worst hasn't hit me. That I'm not going to be okay. I feel out of control. Powerless over so many things.

September 29, 2012

I dreamed I was with Gregory in what seemed to be our living room. There were skylights and sliding doors. I looked up to the skylights and could see really cool clouds. One turned into a funnel and potential tornado so I brought it to Gregory's attention. We could see a small one from the sliding doors headed toward us. We were more fascinated than scared as it zoomed toward the door and dissipated in an instant once it hit the glass, doing nothing more than blowing leaves around like a strong wind. Then we were asleep in bed.

I was starting to wake up in real life. For a moment I thought it was real and Gregory was still alive and lying beside me. Then I was awake and saddened to realize he's gone. I felt beside me to the empty space and said out loud, *"I thought you were here."* A tornado in a dream is an extreme emotional upset. That's the truth. But the dream shows that I am safe, *within*, where my Gregory is standing right next to me.

October 1, 2012

I found a guitar in a case in Gregory's closet. He has four guitars displayed in his man room—two hang on the wall—but I had forgotten about this one. I remembered he was going to sell it just before he got so sick. He'd had it less than a year and never did like it. It was an acoustic/electric and he said it sounded tin-y. I remember he was really bummed and felt he'd made a mistake buying it. *"Oh well,"* I remember saying, *"Sell it if you're not happy with it."*

So it's been 'talking' to me from the closet for a few weeks. I felt Gregory urging me to sell it but I just felt weird about it. I could use the money. When I pulled it out of the closet I told him, *"I'm just looking at it. Not sure I can sell it."* Then I heard him say, *"Switch cases."* It was in a brand new case and the empty case in the closet had a few scratches. I switched them and then found myself putting it in the car. I said to Gregory on the way to the guitar shop, *"This doesn't mean I'm selling it. I'm just going to talk to them about it."*

Downtown is always so busy and the chances of getting a parking space without having to walk a ways were slim. I said, *"If there's an empty space right in front of the guitar shop I'll take that as a sign telling me what you've already been telling me, to sell it."* I drove down and there it was, the only empty space for blocks right in front of the guitar shop. The owner didn't know Greg had died and seemed quite shocked and surprised, saddened you could tell. It made me sad. He said he would put $400 on it and I get 75%. Fair enough.

I stood in the small shop, guitars lined and hanging in beautiful rows everywhere you looked and I felt that with all these beautiful choices Gregory's guitar might take a long time to sell. He said they'd take it on consignment. That was fine too, I thought, whatever's meant to be. It felt very odd for me in that shop. Gregory's presence was so strong. This was Friday and Saturday the guitar sold. I couldn't believe it. When I went to pick up the check—again a parking place right in front—I said I never dreamed it would sell so fast. He said, *"We were all praying."* What a great thing. I could feel Gregory again. A guy was playing the Blues and I had the strongest feeling that it was Gregory playing there at that moment. *Playing the Blues for me.* I had goosebumps everywhere.

Again, I cried when I left. So sad that my wild and crazy guy is no longer standing next to me, sleeping beside me, eating meals with me, watching movies, riding bikes, going to the Island.... *everything*. With me. I'm so sad. And yet the whole thing was a blessing and I felt Gregory's presence every step of the way. I've probably missed so many signs from him because when I really slow down and pay attention they're everywhere.

October 2, 2012

I had the best little dream about Gregory. I was in a crowded coffee shop and went out to the sidewalk where a little boy about five or six was playing a guitar and Gregory, knelt down beside him, was just singin' the Blues! He was so good. Both of them were. Gregory had an amazing voice but I had never heard him sing like that. It was incredible. Then I was inside again wondering where he was and looking for him in the crowded room. I saw him sitting at the counter and then he walked outside. I followed him. He was leaning against a newspaper stand and I walked over and put my arms around his waist and just cuddled him. We stood there and I was so happy, holding onto him and looking up at him. He looked so good.

(Later)

OMG!! I remembered something that has jolted me. Something that was so powerful and yet I chose to forget about it; to block it. I had a vision in 1982 about Gregory where I was shown that I was only going to have 30 years with him. That he would die young and I would be exactly where I am right now. I decided to pray it away at the time and basically forgot about it. Never talked about it again. I see now that I didn't want it to be a self-fulfilling prophecy and I began positive affirmations about the long happy relationship we would have. Ugh.

Gregory continues to speak to me through music—through songs—having done so from the moment he died. Always the comfort or reassurance I need in that moment. But either I hadn't been listening or he wasn't doing it as often and I felt maybe it would stop. One particularly sad morning I got in the car after a meeting and the radio was on. I heard the music at the beginning of Marvin Gaye's, *Heard It Through The Grapevine*.

That song always took us back to our wedding and partying afterwards at the Quality Inn Lounge where I worked. The band did a great job on this song and Gregory and I loved it. To this day it's our song in a way (ignoring the actual lyrics). After getting the money for Gregory's guitar it came on again. I haven't heard that song in years. I miss him so much. People keep telling me how good I look. Every time someone says it I think, *"Well, I guess that's good. Must not look like a grieving widow."* Which I didn't expect to be in my prime!

October 3, 2012

"Happy Anniversary Gregory." I didn't remember until I sat down and wrote the date. Ugh! I feel heavy, empty, sad, lost. I

can't believe it. So hard not to go back to last year and the Island. How can I be here without him? It all happened so fast, didn't it? Some days I look in the mirror and can't believe this is my life. A widow at 52. Never dreamed in my worst nightmare that this could have happened to us. I'm in shock.

He was in my dream the past two nights but just sort of on the sidelines. Last night he was in a tent as I crawled in and the night before we were working on a house and he was building a staircase. They weren't good, clear visions of him or any interaction but he was there! I know he's going to help me get through this day, our anniversary, knowing he's with me. *"Happy anniversary Baby. I miss you. I love you."*

October 8, 2012

Last night I dreamed we were going to the Island. Gregory was there in the beginning but not later. Sound familiar? There was a lot about just trying to get where we wanted to go. We were fussing about making sure we had everything we needed. It felt stressful instead of smooth and easy like it had always been.

Well, it doesn't take a dream interpreter to see what that's saying. It tells me that on some level I'm still trying to go there. Pretend that everything is as it should be. Some days, some moments, I feel completely stunned that Gregory is gone. Every day I'm reminded that he hasn't really left me but his absence in the physical world is still shocking at times.

October 9, 2012

I had a restless, scary day feeling the loss of Gregory. I made myself mow the lawn and do laundry but I pushed for everything. In over thirty years Gregory and I have never been apart this long. I miss him. He was in my dream again just like normal. *I had a plate of eggs and hash browns to share with him. He walked over and took a bite.*

October 10, 2012

Gregory was in my dream again, just there like always, like nothing happened. We were in a hallway. I could see into the other rooms but this felt like a safe neutral place to be. He looked so good. He's always with me and that's the reminder the dream gifts me with.

Halls in dreams are.... drum roll please.... *Transition!* My word for the year. Going from one consciousness to another. That was exactly what I bargained for when I chose that word, never dreaming in a million years Gregory would die and my life would change forever. The year I chose Transition my husband died. *"Way to go, L.J."* I had wanted to transform my fear and self-doubt and finally come into my own. That's what I wanted and why I dared to choose Transition. *"Oh, be careful what you ask for."*

October 11, 2012

I'm missing Gregory something fierce today. It's rainy and gloomy out, the kind of day I usually love. Not feeling it today. I feel so sad. I looked through picture files on the computer just to look at him. I played several short videos with him narrating, just to hear his voice and his laugh. I think today it made it worse although hearing his voice is so good. I'm lost. I feel useless. I have so much I could be doing that I'm not. I would have to push and I don't feel like pushing.

October 15, 2012

This past weekend was for reflecting. For healing. I feel so grateful for my life. I feel peace and joy and faith and trust. Today I feel all of that. And I miss Gregory more than I know how to express. I know his soul lives with me always. I'm grateful for the freedom I have to feel and process my life the way I do. I'm grateful for the Rainbows.

October 17, 2012

I dreamed Gregory was in another room so I couldn't see him clearly. He said something that I wish I could remember now but it was one of his comical jibes that made me laugh and I laughed in the dream. That's my sign and my help from him telling me to lighten up. I appreciate that. I miss him so much. At times I am so sad I can't stand it. Mostly I must be feeling acceptance about everything because I feel at peace.

October 20, 2012

I feel such a responsibility to take care of myself. It was irresponsible for Gregory to have smoked all those years, being a dad, a son, a husband. But I know he's the one who lost the most of all. He lost his life. He always thought he would quit smoking at the first sign of trouble, never dreaming that the first sign would be late stage lung cancer, inoperable, metastasized to the bone. Spread to the brain. Fatal. He would die in less than three months.

October 22, 2012

I have to write about what happened last night! I was watching *Long Island Medium* and when Theresa was reading a woman who lost her husband she asked her if she just got a chill? The woman sort of shivered and said she did! Theresa told her that was her husband! I said to Gregory, *"Alright Honey, if he can do that, you can do that. Come on, give me a chill."* Immediately I felt it. Not just a chill! It felt more like my soul was being shaken inside my body! I couldn't believe it!

I've never felt anything like that in my life. Just a little shake me up and I loved it! I felt it in every part of my body. *"Got it, Honey, thank you SO much!"* Maybe it took a lot of energy for him to do that. Maybe it's harder than we think for the Other Side to get through to us. I told him earlier through tears, *"Thank God I know you're right here with me. Thank God I know that."* Then to get a sign that I knew was from him was an amazing feeling.

October 27, 2012

I had an amazing thing happen on my walk home from Greg's Mom's last night. There was a full moon, glowing through cloudy skies and it felt so peaceful and so magical out. I could feel Gregory with me like never before. I could feel his love showering me, pouring over me. In my mind's eye I saw his sweet face, kissing me, telling me how much he loves me. I told him over and over how much I love him, that I feel him with me, I see his face and hear his voice. It was so beautiful. The moon seemed to be shining the brightest yet softest glow I've ever seen. The energy in the air felt supercharged and I could feel it all through me. I felt it all the way home. I felt bathed in my Gregory.

October 28, 2012

Megan's baby shower was yesterday and it was awesome. There were so many little ones running around I couldn't help but smile. We got a picture with the four babies, Megan with our little one still inside, and us holding the other three baby boys. I'm hoping to have a picture with the four boys for my Christmas card this year. Try to fill in Gregory's absence with boy babies.

Chapter 6

Going It Alone

October 31, 2012

I'm thinking about the new baby and wondering how it's going to feel without Gregory. More new life. It was Jasmine and her babies at first. Something I had to focus on, like it or not. It was a lot of work and I'd never want to do it again but it was such a gift. I've had something to deal with ever since he died. Always things on our list, even as I've worked my way through so much. There will be a time when everything on the list from before he died will be done. We're almost there.

I've been thinking about how sad it makes me that Gregory didn't share with me his thoughts and fears about his disability, his pain. Especially the past two years. He was never one to complain. I'm sorry about a lot of things in those two years. I know I would have handled so many things differently had I known they were to be our last. That's the part that feels so unfair.

I just remembered today is Halloween. I'm not into it this year. Gregory always was. I remember his laugh and joy at seeing the little goblins when he went to the door to hand out candy. He would usually shout out something to the adults standing back. Always a teasing of some sort. One year he stuffed his clothes with hay and a hat and slumped over lifeless in a chair on the front porch like a scarecrow and then when the kids went to ring the doorbell he would spring to life! Oh the things you miss about a person. Only everything.

November 6, 2012

I had a near-panic attack yesterday which was scary for a moment. I felt like I couldn't breathe. It was a day I felt really alone in my world, didn't matter how many people I was with. I'm also aware that I'm lucky to be grieving like I am *because* of what we had. I called out to him yesterday and again this morning. For *"Come here,"* we used to say, *"Mere."* I've been saying, *"Mere, honey, mere. It's time for another sign to let me know you're here. It helps so much."* Yesterday felt empty, void of my love. Not a heavy heart an empty one. Still missing him but knowing he is with me always, gives me peace and strength to get through the day. And the Rainbows don't hurt.

November 11, 2012

I dreamed I was laughing. I was at a casual dinner party with friends talking to a couple of women and telling them something funny. I can't remember what but I laughed so hard in the telling of it, as did my friends, that I fell onto the couch and laughed clear to my gut. Just all out, let loose and laugh to your toes. The way Gregory made me laugh.

I haven't laughed like that since he died. Except in my dream last night. It's always a good sign. Laughter *is* the best medicine for whatever ails you. Laughter is all about healing energy in a dream. It relates to lightening up, not taking yourself so seriously. I know it's true.

I had a good cry here this morning thinking about how unsure I am, how unsure I've always been, as a direct result of my own self-doubt but also that of Gregory's at times. It was hard when he couldn't see my vision and felt he had to be the one to give me a reality check. That was the worst. I had to push through my own feelings of unworthiness and self-doubt, sabotaging here, making progress there. Never really feeling I was doing anything other than one step forward two steps back. Always wanting to beat up on myself and pull back whenever Gregory needed me to abandon everything.

Being unable to let go of my vision, my purpose, I would forge ahead, the weight of all the resistance making it feel like trudging, every step labored. I see that all so clearly now. I cried with the pain of the memories. And then relief and joy as Gregory reminded me that it's all different now. Not only is he with me on this journey, helping me with a support I can feel—and this makes me cry in its truth—he showed me that it had to be that way. That it was meant for my good. That I was going to need to be tough going out into the real world. I could never have handled its harsh realities without having weathered a few of my own.

In that instant, as Gregory showed me this, I said out loud, *"They would have eaten me alive."* And it's true. What I thought was my biggest disappointment was, in fact, the most valuable part of the whole thing. It had to be. I get that now and Gregory gets that now. We both had to do what we did in order for me to be who I am. He needed to challenge me and I needed to stand my ground.

Here's something else Gregory showed me. Our love, our connection from the very beginning. He showed me our hugs at the trailer when we first started seeing each other. How overpowering those were for us, how we stood and hugged and held each other forever. That was our soul connection and we didn't want to let go. It was so much fun. He was fun. I will miss that until the day I die.

November 13, 2012

There's a part of me that feels a real peace about my life, where I'm headed, and all the exciting things that are in store for me. I tell myself it's okay to allow my mind to go to happy places. But I can also see that I stop myself. Part of me says you have to be sad. You lost your husband. You are alone now. I haven't allowed myself to feel the excitement of living alone the way I did when I moved out on my own for the first time. It was an exciting time for me. I miss him. I felt safe in his arms, secure when he was next to me. I felt I could do anything with him by my side.

November 17, 2012

I'd love to be able to say that yesterday was a good day but as I sit here and remember how the day played out I'm saddened to realize that the enemy won. The morning, so full of promise, gave way to an afternoon and evening that can be described in one word: *Sloth*. Oh, and let's not forget about *Gluttony*. Great, not only did the enemy win, but he managed to get me to indulge in two of the seven deadly sins!

November 20, 2012

I dreamed about Gregory! I was sitting Indian style in his room, having finished Yoga. I had my eyes closed and was singin' my heart out to the music that played. I was belting out the words, so into it. I opened my eyes and there was Gregory watching me with the biggest, most beautiful smile on his face. He looked so young and absolutely gorgeous. His beard was really dark, like in his earlier years.

He looked amazing and that look and that smile is one I recognize. It's a look of love and amusement, delighted to see me being myself, letting loose because no one was watching. I always loved it when he looked at me like that. His face just lit up. It makes me cry but I'm so grateful. I would love to see more of him in my dreams. It's amazing to see him look so young and healthy. He looked better than I've ever seen him.

November 23, 2012

Yesterday was my first Thanksgiving without Gregory. It turned out to be a really nice day. I was surprised at how peaceful I felt. I could feel him with me all day and with all of us at Megan's for dinner. I feel very tired today. I told Megan I wanted to see the pictures of Gregory with us last Easter, only eleven days before he died. This is our last family photo with the four of us. So many pics we took over the years and then our last one where Gregory looks barely alive.

I know he had to have mustered it together for that photo with us because he looked better in that shot than in any of the others we took. Still, it wasn't good. He looked like death, like he wasn't even there. It made me cry, especially the one of just him and me where I have a big smile of denial on my face and he looks like a POW. He could barely hold his head up. Four days later he would be in the Hospital with only a week to live. After Easter he never got up again.

(Later)

I just watched a great little movie called *The 5-Year Engagement* and the music was so good. The first Van Morrison song I did okay with and was only reminded of how much I love Van Morrison. The second song, however, proved to be too much and I broke down, remembering weekend mornings when he would put on a little Van Morrison, bring me a cup of coffee and wake me with a kiss. He'd go back to the kitchen and finish cooking a hot breakfast of eggs, toast, and bacon, on one plate with one fork. Then he brought it up to bed and fed us both, a bite for you and a bite for me. We had thousands of beautiful moments like that.

November 27, 2012

I got myself a little tree and was able to manage it by myself. I called on my dad to help me put on the lights since he was always so good at it and it was amazing. It's as if his hands took over mine and it went so smoothly. I felt excited. Putting on ornaments was fun! I couldn't believe it. I could feel Gregory there helping me. I hung our stockings on the fireplace and put candles in all the windows. The house emanates peace.

November 29, 2012

The Holiday letter has been weighing on me. I don't know how to sum up this year. Especially knowing some people out west won't have heard that Gregory died.

November 30, 2012

Greg's mom is in the hospital. She was so sick and they admitted her after discovering she was septic. They also said she has late stage Alzheimers and can't live alone anymore. I'm not sure what our options are. I turn it over to God and Gregory. And the Dads.

December 4, 2012

We moved Greg's mom to a nursing home for rehab. She was full of piss and vinegar all the way there and kept thinking she was just returning from a trip and why wasn't I taking her home? It was so hard. Gregory, bugger, missed out on all of this.

December 11, 2012

I had a couple of really sad moments yesterday and I just sobbed and even wailed at one point. I have never heard these cries before. I have never grieved a loss this big. It's so personal. I miss making love with my husband. I miss hugging him and kissing him. His smell, the feel of him.

December 12, 2012

Next to me on the end table is a scattered pile of pictures of just Greg and I. Thirty years' worth. I can see our wedding hug then all through the years up to a recent one. A glance at those pictures is just how fast it all went it seems. I'm so happy by his side in every picture. I am so lucky to have had a love like ours for so many years.

December 17, 2012

OMG! Gregory sent me a Christmas card! It was in a blue envelope—both our favorite color—addressed to LoriJean Hunt, no return. It has a Rainbow across the front and says, *"Follow Your Dreams."* Inside it says, *"No matter what (anyone) says."* No signature. I stared at it. It's what I needed to hear. *Follow your dreams...*

Watching a movie the other night I had a heightened sense of the energy around me that always happens when something with Greg is about to happen. It felt like the movie was in slow motion as the guy tossed something to a woman who caught it in her hand and closed her fist around it. Then a closeup as she opened her hand and it was a tootsie roll! I knew it was from my Gregory! He always carried tootsie rolls with him and loved to toss one to people when they were having a bad day. *"Keep 'em coming Baby!"*

December 18, 2012

We got Greg's mom moved to an Alzheimer's home and it went very smoothly. She was happy to find her own things in her room, which the family prepared before we got there. She was in a good mood and glad to be out on a sunny day. On the way she looked at me and said, *"Greg?"* I looked at her and she said, *"How is he?"* I started to cry. She said sadly, *"He died..."* and she started to cry. Then two minutes later it was all about the beautiful day. *I* still can't process it, how can his mother with Alzheimer's do it? Perhaps in this case she is the lucky one.

Chapter 7

My Year Of Firsts

December 25, 2012

Christmas Morning. Well, here I sit by the lights of the tree and a small lamp with just myself and four cats. For a few minutes it was hard. I moved cautiously through my morning routine. This has not been like any other morning. It's Christmas morning and I am here alone, opening gifts with only my name on them. It looks like any other Christmas morning in my living room only the pile of newly opened gifts is half what it used to be. There used to be Gregory's gifts and gifts to the two of us.

December 26, 2012

No one can tell you how to grieve. People have written books, taught seminars and counseled on grief, but no one can tell you how *you* will do it. Even my own observations of myself as I go through different stages in this process are mine alone. I know one thing, I believe I am grieving and healing and adjusting—adapting—to my new life as it unfolds. Just as the Creator intended me to.

I never know what's going to trigger a pang of grief. I was just folding clothes in the laundry room and saw our laundry bag for traveling hanging there. A sense of dread enveloped me as a flood of memories hit me, not only from our last road trip in February—nightmare—but also of all the fun road trips we took over the years, like to Mackinac Island. That laundry bag has been hanging there since before Gregory died but this morning the bag let itself be known and in a flash I was again reminded of what I've lost.

December 27, 2012

Megan is having the baby today. She's probably headed to the hospital now to be induced. I'll head there shortly. I think she has been in so much fear that she's holding him in there. Either that or Gregory's doing his usual and hoarding the baby! That's probably more like it. I know Gregory will be there and I pray to be in tune with his energy, able to feel him, see signs of him, anything. *"God help me feel this day with wonder. God bless our baby."*

December 28, 2012

It's been an emotional morning already. It was an amazing, sort of surreal day yesterday. Megan was amazing. They broke her water at 12:50 p.m. and she had him at 1:22 p.m. Kadyn Gregory Niezgoda. Watching him being born was amazing. We all cried. It was incredibly quiet and calm in the room. Megan even said, *"It's so quiet."* The room was filled with peace. Kadyn was so alert, huge eyes wide open. I couldn't believe it. He was so mellow. It sort of feels like a dream, the whole day, the whole experience. Powerful. Sad without Gregory's physical presence but we sure could feel him there.

January 3, 2013

The New Year's cards turned out amazing. So beautiful. They are what I hoped for and more. A picture of me with the four baby boys born in 2012 and one of Gregory's beautiful smiling face. I can't explain how these cards make me feel. I felt Gregory's presence within me so strong my heart swelled up, just like it did after he died. I felt good, happy, content. I knew he was right there.

I knew everything was going to be alright. I talked to him and I could hear him talking to me.

January 11, 2013

I feel like I've been through hell and the enemy got so close it frightened me. Yesterday morning was the scariest as far as my grief and missing Gregory. All week really. I haven't felt well. All I could do for two days was lie around and try not to feel sorry for myself. Hot baths were heaven. But missing Gregory was nearly unbearable. Everything seemed to swirl around me and I couldn't stop looking at his picture, couldn't stop crying when I did. Missing him so much I didn't know if all of a sudden I'd hit a wall of grief head on and not get up again. The Christmas card was harder than I wanted to admit. It was the first one without Greg and I arm in arm. The last one with him in it.

January 12, 2013

Yesterday was better. Mainly because I was with people until about 3 p.m. Then the struggle was on. Darkness threatened to overtake me and I could not make myself do one thing around here once I got home. I felt completely spent. And sad. And feeling bad about myself for not getting busy. For not doing even one thing. I talked and cried with Mama. I talked with Megan. I ate cereal for dinner and went to bed early, praying today would be better. Wasn't sure when I woke up. Headache threatens, back is sore, I'm nauseated and my stomach is on fire. WTF?

Just getting back to journaling is helping more than I already knew. Whew! Getting some relief. Gregory seemed to help me a little last night too. I have two pictures of him on my nightstand, one from about 20 years ago and the one I put on the Christmas card. The one taken when he was last healthy. The guy I last made love with, laughed with, lived with. That guy. I can't stop looking at his picture. With grief and despair lately but last night I felt him tell me to do first things first. Get the New Year's cards done and mailed.

As I looked at his picture his smile was just for me and it was reassuring, loving. The picture seemed to come alive. In an instant I felt him warm in my heart and I had the first moments of light I'd felt all week. It is about first things first. Do one thing you don't want to do that needs to be done. *One thing.* He even told me what that thing needed to be. The cards. In order to get into today I have to close out any tasks from yesterday. From last year. I need to pick a word for this year. I will pray on that. It's always so much easier to get back on track than I think it will be.

I'm grateful for a guiding voice that I can hear when I'm at a standstill. Just do it. The enemy says stay stuck. Sometimes stuck can feel like a comfy familiar zone. And perhaps that's what last week was about in terms of escaping into binge-watching Stephen King's, *Haven* on the Sci-Fi channel. It was a place I could live while I healed. Where strange and bizarre things happen to regular people and usually someone dies.

Maybe it's like after Dad died and I found myself watching every single end of the world movie I could get my hands on, including Japanese dubbed. That was a low point. But they had really cool special effects! Lol! That's change for you. That's life and the forward progression of it. Racing toward the finish line. Always with enough time to do what we're here to do. *Always.* But will we do it? Will we work through the obstacles that block us? Do we believe we have enough time? I do. Even if it is twenty-two years for me. Even if I am running out of time.

I feel so much better today. That dark place didn't kill me. Or keep me. I can do my part today. I can feel my husband with me again, strong like he was after he died. I know he was here all week—I felt him and I got Rainbows every day—but my human heart misses his physical presence here on earth, the sound of his voice, the touch of his skin. It was too much for me to bear in my weakened state. And that's okay. I made it and today looks brighter.

January 14, 2013

"Happy Birthday, Baby." My heart is sad. *"I wish you were here. I wish we were going to an early dinner of filet mignon at our favorite restaurant and making love when we got home."* No present to buy this year.

January 16, 2013

I'm sitting here in stunned silence, missing my Gregory so much I don't dare think about it too deeply. His picture beside me where I always seem to need it, smiles at me like he is right there. *Why isn't he?* But then sitting here I looked to my right where I have a stack of white envelopes from the Christmas cards, and there's a perfect pastel Rainbow reflected across the top of them. I smiled and said, *"Hi Honey,"* and with that—right in front of my eyes—it *slowly* faded away. Wow. You had to be there but I am in tears because it was from Gregory and I felt him. Pretty amazing.

February 5, 2013

I dreamed I was having a conversation with Gregory! It was about his illness. I said, "We missed it," then reminded him about Dr. D. finding a spot on his lung on his last physical before we lost our insurance, which is true.

Gregory minimized it at the time as probably just a cyst. I had one of those on my lung years ago too and it just went away so I was perfectly willing to buy that story. I never thought about it again. Not until he was gone. So we had that conversation in my dream last night.

February 11, 2013

I was holding Kadyn Gregory yesterday and that baby just makes me smile. I love him so much. I cried holding him, missing Gregory while Kadyn had his eyes fixated to my right and even cooed and smiled. I knew that Gregory was right there next to us, talking to that baby, and Kadyn could see him. It made me cry even as it gave me peace.

February 13, 2013

I'm having a dark, sad morning and I need to turn it over. I cried out to Gregory, *"Please honey, show up, help me."* I hate when those moments hit. Not very often, thank God, but it feels like my heart is being ripped out. It's the worst feeling in the world. When it's grief like that I don't think I can go on, or breathe, or do my life. I don't even want to live in that moment. I just want Gregory.

In moments like that I don't seem to care what I have, all the gifts, my life, my family. I just need to be with Gregory. It's a bad place to be. Wanting the impossible. There was no reason for it to hit this particular morning. No reason why the house seemed dark even with the night lamps. No reason it should be hard to breathe. I'm afraid to even think about him. But I'm grateful for my recovery, my spirituality, my faith. Just for this moment, this day, I can live without him.

February 14, 2013

Today is Valentine's Day and my sweetheart is here but unable to kiss me, hold me, take me out for dinner. But he's here. I haven't had a Valentine's Day without the love of my life for thirty-two years. All these years gone in a flash. It's so sad to me. I pray for a time when I can replay with joy the years of fun we had. Gregory was a kick. Until he got crippled up and then sick he was always a ball of energy first thing in the morning. I'm a morning person too but not like Gregory. He was full of it first thing. He brightened everyone's day, whether it was the lady at the donut shop or the waitress at the restaurant for breakfast.

I can't help but think back to Valentine's Day last year. He had been in the hospital all month and when I walked in that morning he had written a big *"Happy Valentine's Day!"* on the chalkboard in his room. He drew a big heart and put *"Greg & L.J."* in the middle of it and then across the bottom he wrote, *"Til the wheels fall off!"* which is something we always said to each other. *"It's you and me, Babe, til the wheels fall off!"*

I stare at his picture beside me smiling like he's right here.

Knowing that he's not. My life feels like a dream. I'm in a grief-laden fog. Things have slowed down and for that I'm grateful. Not time so much as the movements through my thoughts and my day. I've found myself thinking about the twenty-two years I have left and my prayer is that after all the time I've wasted, and still can waste, please let me do some good and make a difference before I go.

(Afternoon)

Wow, do I have a thing to report on my Valentine's Day! I cry about it, amazed tears, grateful tears, just like when Dad showed me the photo album. OMG! *"Thank you, Gregory, for an incredible gift."* I went for Reiki and, as always, she gets us each a nice cup of herbal tea and we chat leisurely while we have our tea. Her room is so peaceful, inviting you to relax, breathe deep, free your mind and indulge yourself in all things good. Then she shares her dreams with me and I help her interpret them.

Then I get on the table, on my back to start. She invites me to take deep breaths and I begin my Yoga breathing. My eyes are closed. Beautiful, soothing music plays softly. The smell of sandalwood further relaxes me as she rubs it on her hands. When she finally does touch me I feel her fingertips gently on my head. It feels remarkable. After the deep breaths, she whispered, *"I invited your husband to join us."* Being Valentine's Day she knew he was here for me anyway but she just wanted to formerly invite him to be with us.

I relaxed and breathed and was amazed. When she laid her hands over mine I felt a tingling that was incredible, like I could feel Gregory holding my hands! After a nice long time, with gentle touch from head to toe, including my shoulders, knees, and stomach, she had me turn over. Here's where it gets quite miraculous. After she made her way over all the main areas she ended at my head. I could feel her hand on my head..... but I could also feel her hand on my foot.

In this relaxed, sort of mesmerized state, I'm thinking, *"How is she doing that?"* She would often touch two different places so I was thinking this is what she was doing but then, while I was a bit confused knowing it's physically impossible for her to reach both places, I realized I could feel *both* her hands on my head..... At the same time I could feel *two* hands, one on each foot, holding them gently but firmly. At this point I'm really freaking out inside. I'm like, *"OMG! I have two distinct hands on my head and two distinct hands on my feet! How can this be?"*

My mind tried to make sense of it, explain it somehow. I gently tried to move my feet, just a little, to see if I would realize it was just a weird sensation from the Reiki. But I couldn't move them because someone was holding them! From my head I heard Angela say I was done and I could get up at my leisure. My thought was what's going to happen at my feet when she takes her hands away from my head? She took them away and I could still feel someone holding my feet! Then slowly one hand let go of one foot and then the other let go of my other foot.... and my feet were free. OMG! I could hardly believe it.

I sort of blurted out to Angela that my husband was holding my feet but she was already standing there a bit overwhelmed herself by the experience she had while working on me. She said she started crying when she held my hands because she felt Gregory holding my hands through hers! She also said she had to stop herself from touching my hair which she found herself doing. I just thought it was part of Reiki because the sensation when she touched my hair felt electric. She said the heart monitor went off in the next room when she got to my heart and no one was in there! I'm just amazed by the whole thing and I cried all the way home thanking Gregory.

Before I left I could see *heavy* snow falling through her closed blinds! She opened them and OMG! It was the biggest, heaviest, most beautiful snowfall I have *ever* seen. The drive home was surreal, like being in a snow globe. It snowed and snowed and snowed and will continue through the night. Gregory knew that this is the kind of snowfall I love so much! Driving home I felt like I was in a dream. I'm just blown away. I've been crying and thanking Gregory over and over again. *"This is what I'm talking about, Dude!"* I love him so much. He came to me on Valentine's Day and gave me a gift. The most amazing and miraculous gift I could have hoped for. *"Thank you, Baby."*

When I got home, there was a package by the front door and a shiver ran through me as an eerie calm filled the house. I opened it, forgetting what I'd ordered. Oh yeah, the plaque. I ordered it quite a while ago so no wonder I forgot about it. It's beautiful, all in black and white....

*And if I should go before you
know that part of me still remains....
You will not see me
yet I will be there walking beside you.
You will not touch me
yet I will live in your heart and memory always.
Have faith that we will one day
walk hand in hand in eternity.
Until then live your life for life is good....
And know that I am with you.*

"Happy Valentine's Day To Me! I love you, Gregory."

February 15, 2013

I'm reading a little each night from, *Loving From The Outside In, Mourning From The Inside Out*, by Alan D Wolfelt, PhD. It's very nurturing to the grieving heart. It validates the very real, very traumatic feelings that come with losing a treasured loved one. Some moments, some days, I can't quite wrap my brain around what has happened. It is painful to remember where we were one year ago. And yet my mind goes there. It's not good. It threatens to rip my heart from my chest.

Oh, I almost forgot, one more gift from Gregory. I've chided him for not giving me more signs with the lights since he did, after all, work with electricity every day. Valentine's night, as I undressed for bed, I took off my shirt and the light blinked. *"Funny, Honey."* I took off my pants and the light blinked twice.

*"**Very** funny, Honey."* I love that. I need that. It's interaction with him. Playful like he was. Yay!

February 16, 2013

I continue to be amazed by what happened on Valentine's Day and I cry big, grateful tears at the memory of it. What a gift. I realized I didn't have any expectations about the day. I guess I didn't want to be disappointed if I didn't get a message from him. My heart overflows now, so excited that he outdid himself! I'd ordered that plaque in early January. They said 7–10 days. No reason it would take so long. I'd forgotten all about it and it then it comes on Valentine's Day?

Mostly I'm hanging onto him holding my feet. That was so incredible. It blows my mind. It makes me feel so special. That Gregory loves me that much still. To let me know—on a day meant for lovers—that he is still here with me, touching me, bringing me gifts, and making me laugh. And he also let me know that he *still* appreciates it when I take my clothes off!

He was such a character. So playful and so appreciative of a woman's body. Lucky for me that mine was the one he loved on for 30 years. That's also what makes me sob at love scenes, like earlier on a show I was watching. It's a beautiful thing to love another in that way. And then? When you lose that it's unimaginable. I thought I could *only imagine* what it would be like to lose my husband but there is no way your mind can take you to that place.

No wonder some people crack under the pressure. But my honey held both my feet and my hands and touched my hair on my first Valentine's day without him. How cool is that? Not a story you want to tell everyone but it sure is a treasure for me. *And* a great contribution to my compilation of cool and freaky supernatural things that have happened in our family, especially since Dad and then Gregory died.

Oh, and speaking of that, I forgot to write about the weight. Last week when I was doing Yoga in Gregory's room I bumped into his big old weight on the floor so I moved it over in front of his stereo cabinet and continued doing my workout. A few minutes later I moved into a position sitting on the floor, legs outstretched, and began side bends from left to right, eyes closed. I stretched my arms out as far as I could, touching my left toes then moving slowly to my right toes, then back again.

Only this time my hands were stopped right in the middle by the big weight! Now this thing is heavy. It does not roll on its own let alone three or four rolls which it would have taken to get where it was. I put it back and tried to get it to move but there was no way. When my hand hit that weight and stopped me it was a twilight zone moment for sure. I was like, *"How did that get here? I just put it over there."* I love it! I could experience those unexplainable things all day long.

Chapter 8

The Calm Before The Storm

February 17, 2013

The sun is shining bright on this cold February morning, accenting everything in this beautiful room. I'm taking my day slow and easy. Things have changed for me since Valentine's Day. It goes to show what I've said all along, those signs from Heaven— from Gregory—do everything for me. It is interaction from my baby, the love of my life. The person who knew the most intimate side of me. The whole heart of me.

For him to do that for me on Valentine's Day, at a time that has been difficult with memories of our last one, means so much to me. It fills my heart with so much joy it makes me cry. It has also strengthened my relationship with him. This new way we have to relate to each other. While I miss our physical relationship so much there is so much that is still intact. Our hearts are one our love the same. It's filling me with a lot of peace and joy to help with all the sadness.

March 5, 2013

I haven't felt very well. Yesterday was hard. There was a darkness over my whole day and by evening my sadness felt scary.

I felt that terrible aloneness that thank God I haven't felt very often. I felt nauseated all day and had no appetite. Money worries plagued me. Everything seemed too much. Thank God it hasn't felt that way except for a couple of times, but man, it was one tough day that I couldn't wait to end. *"Please, God, let today be better."*

March 19, 2013

I cried quite a bit yesterday. I heard Nicolette Larson's, *Lotta Love,* on the radio and was reminded of my date with Gregory early on at Pocatello High School. A Nicolette Larsen concert with Night Ranger as backup. We held hands in the dark and I just wanted to be close to him even then. The memory made me cry. We were just starting out then whoosh! thirty years zoomed past. I cried off and on all day and even at bedtime which I don't always do. I feel better today.

March 29, 2013

Yesterday at the meeting Gregory left his calling card. It was my 19th sober anniversary and I looked at the basket for the money and there was a teal colored guitar pick in it. I know it was from him! I could feel him there.

April 1, 2013

March was a sad month for me. Yesterday I felt angry and sad. Right now time does not seem to be helping my grief. I miss him more as time goes by and my grief is intense lately. Perhaps I am experiencing a bit of depression and that's okay. I am sadder and more alone than I've ever been in my life. I haven't felt really mad as part of my grief until lately. I feel quickly irritated. I spouted off in a group meeting and left embarrassed. I made amends the next day but I'm having trouble forgiving myself. I feel out of control.

April 4, 2013

I dreamed that water came pouring in from a leak in the skylight in my kitchen. It wasn't a drip-drip leak, it was like a faucet turned on full blast. I was so surprised because the skylights have never leaked. I called my dad from the next room and he came in to look and said he would call someone to fix it for me. No surprise. Water is the emotions, pouring into the kitchen, the heart of the home. I cried myself to sleep last night. It is a reassurance dream that says *"All is well,"* and my dad is there to help me.

Then I dreamed I was ready to go home. I had my own car but I wanted someone to drive me if they were going my direction. No one was. When I got in my car I was out of gas but figured I could coast home. The road sloped down so I was getting momentum and steered out of the parking lot and coasted on down the road headed for home.

This part is clear enough. Out of gas; out of energy, out of steam, just coasting. It appears I will get where I need to go but not really on my own power. I am exhausted with everything Greg's sister and I are having to do at his mom's to get the house ready to rent now that we've got Mom settled. I'm coasting. The symbolism would have been better had I been coasting into a gas station to refuel but I was just trying to get home. The dream shows I don't even want to drive myself I want someone to take me. But, alas, no one is going my way. This is a journey I must travel alone.

April 12, 2013

I dreamed about Gregory. He was sitting in a coffeeshop having his coffee and reading the paper. He looked good. One year ago today he left our house for the last time. This is the day we found out his cancer had spread to his brain and it was all but over. Everything seems overwhelming to me right now. But the dream is important. I believe it's Gregory's way of telling me, *"Hey, look at me now on April 12th. I'm just chillin' with my coffee and life is good." "Thanks, Babe, I needed that."*

April 13, 2013

Well I allowed myself a day. A day to grieve. A day to feel sorry for myself. A day to say I don't believe in *Karma* anymore. That the *Law of Attraction* is a lie. That the good guy doesn't win. That life is unfair. That things are really f—ked up. I didn't open the curtains and I holed up in my room all afternoon watching movies until bedtime. I allowed myself one day.

April 18, 2013

I dreamt about snow, like we were at a ski lodge of some sort. I was with a bunch of people, family I think. At one point I was walking up a very steep, snow-packed slope. There were big stair-like places carved into the snow—like little caves—that I was climbing up. It was hard to do because these big holes were quite far apart even though they were really big. People were also positioned here and there on the mountain, so I had to climb over and around some of them.

At the top I got a little too close to a very steep edge with nothing to hang onto. I realized how easily I could fall. I quickly stepped back over and had to practically crawl over a kid sitting there. He had a baby too close to the edge but I chose to continue on and not worry about it and to not look back. Then I was up on the snow-packed road and could see the lodge to my left. I knew I could rest. Another part of the dream we were made to wear certain clothes by a man who seemed to be in charge. I was making the best of it but they weren't really clothes I would normally wear or choose for myself.

The dream makes me think of my path right now. Climbing in the rough tracks made my someone but not used by everyone. Crawling up and over to get to the top. To get where I was going. Not easy but I'm doing it. A few scary places along the way where I could have fallen but I didn't. Made to wear clothes (identity, ideas, beliefs)—*the widow*—that I wouldn't choose for myself yet I'm wearing them. The lodge to my left is my time out. That's me taking a break.

And let's not forget about the baby. *Babies* in dreams represent new ideas, hopes, dreams, goals. I see that the baby could be in danger and I choose not to concern myself with it. *"Don't look back,"* I told myself. *"It's not my baby,"* I say, *"I can't be codependent. If he doesn't take care of the baby and something happens I can't worry about it. I have to move on."* It's my children's book. The illustrator still has it, whether or not he's taking care of it. He called a few months ago and then I haven't been able to reach him since then. Dreams show what you're doing or what you need to do. In this case I think the dream is showing me what I'm doing and it's not necessarily a good thing. I can't just walk away from this baby.

April 19, 2013

Gregory was in my dream last night. In a flash of memory there he was. He had his long hair and full beard. His "Grizzly Adams" look. That hairy guy I miss so much. His beard was really dark like in his younger days. I was so glad to see him.

He died one year ago. *One whole year.* How can that be? I think he wanted to let me know that he is alive and well. I cried right off the bat this morning as soon as I sat down and looked at his picture. I held it to my heart just like I did last evening when I cried deep, sad tears and told him how much I miss him. I asked him if he's been happy for a year in Heaven? And there he was in my dream showing me the look that was most *him*.

I've been watching episodes of *Long Island Medium* and I swear Gregory speaks to me through the readings I'm compelled to tune into just as a husband comes through with messages for his wife. He mostly wants me to hear that he has not left me. That he is still here. I know this is true. I feel him I hear him. Last night a woman said she feels her husband and I said, *"I wish I could feel you right now."*

Immediately I felt a wellness, a joy fill up inside me and I couldn't stop it. My face burst out smiling and I felt like I could laugh out loud! In that moment for him to let me feel him within me as joy, as happiness, was such a gift and I would not be doing as well as I am if it weren't for the Rainbows. Still, I cry for what we had. For what we shared over 30 years. I miss everything about the man. I have yet to go a day without crying and I don't know if I want to.

April 20, 2013

So here I am after a good sob, experiencing my second birthday without Gregory.

I dreamed about a huge Owl standing in the dirt in my back-yard. The bird was about 4' tall and felt somewhat threatening. Like warning me not to get too close when I wasn't even thinking about it. Sort of growling at me and looking mean. I knew it was just scared and trying to protect itself even though it didn't need to. Overall the dream felt threatening and uncomfortable.

Okay, so let's not forget that *Owl* is my totem and has followed me throughout my life. Owls are significant in most Native American cultures. When a dream shows graphic or strange imagery it always means there is an important message. Owls represent wisdom. Also the ability to see in the dark with clarity. I know that anytime something in the dream is bigger or smaller than it should be it has to do with how much importance I'm putting on it. If something is too big it usually means that I'm making something bigger than it is.

So this owl, this beautiful creature representing wisdom, clarity in the dark, is way bigger than it should be and is growling; a warning to back off, stay away. I can only believe the dream is showing me that I somehow view this inner wisdom; inner knowing, as too big, too scary, a threat. It makes sense. I'm not feeling very sure of myself these days. I certainly can relate to the growling part and feeling a need to protect myself even if there is no real threat.

April 22, 2013

Yesterday all the family came over. Megan brought balloons in shades of blue so we could write messages to Gregory on them and then let them go in the backyard. They went up and headed right out over the bay, exactly where we wanted them to go. It was very emotional. Kaylee drew a guitar on her balloon for Papa Greg. He had been teaching her to play before he got sick. It was their little connection. It makes me so sad. It makes no sense to me that he had to die so young.

April 24, 2013

I dreamed about Gregory! He was being playful all around me. Sort of sneaking around and popping up in front of me play-fully, all smiles and looking like he did in his 30's. He was like, "Look! Here I am!" It was very cool. Then he pulled up playfully in a little car. He was there for a while just letting me see him and know that he is with me still. It was so great. It felt so good to see him. I've been missing him more than ever and feeling even sadder than normal since the one year passed.

Chapter 9

Living In Dreamland

⌒

April 26, 2013

OMG!! I just saw an orb in front of me! Right where I always feel Gregory. I can't believe it! It was about golf ball size, maybe a little bigger, and it just slowly floated down right across and in front of me. OMG! This is really amazing. I've only seen them on TV. Even with as many episodes of ghost stories as I've seen people don't often see what the camera picks up. Never in a million years did I think I would ever see one. *Woohoo! I just saw an orb float in front of me! How lucky for me!* I know it was Gregory. That lets me know he's trying to show himself to me. He knows that proof is what humans need. The stories to tell.

April 29, 2013

OMG! Are you kidding me? I'm in my bedroom for the night and I just saw a wavy, smoky mist by the closet door! I don't believe this. First an orb and now this? Never in a million years did I ever dream I would see those two things even as I've seen them so often on ghost stories. I'm still in shock frankly. I'm amazed how the mind tries to explain it away. But there is no way I can. I just saw it. The room filled with a cool vibration. God love Gregory, he's letting his presence be known. He's helping me.

May 4, 2013

Gregory was in my dream all night! He was there with me and he never left. He'd be standing there and I'd go over and just throw my arms around him and hug him and just keep ahold of him which is what I did most of the dream. Yay! I can't tell you how much this dream meant! It makes me cry. He knows I need to know he's still with me. I miss him so much. That dream was so special. He looked so good. *"Thank you, Baby, thank you!"*

May 5, 2013

I dreamed I saw a car pull up out front. It was a 'bad' guy. He stared at the house trying to see in. I slid to the floor and hid behind the coffee table and hoped he didn't see me. I knew I would need to always look at my surroundings and always be aware of what or who was near me so I would never be caught off guard by someone with bad intentions. Later I was walking with a young girl I don't know and telling her about being alert and always looking around so as to keep yourself safe.

(2019) Wow, this dream kind of makes me sad six years later. I didn't interpret it at the time. It shows how afraid I felt, how vulnerable and scared I felt in my world. The *bad guy* was right out my front door and I had to hide myself inside where it felt a little safer but not by much. *Scared Girl.* It shows my whole world felt unsafe and I thought I had to be on high alert for danger at all times because someone might catch me off guard and something bad will happen. The unknown girl in the dream is an aspect of me that I'm going to *train* to be on guard as well. She is *Vulnerable Me.*

May 6, 2013

Yay! Wonderful dream about Gregory! He was with me all night again! He looked so good. He never left my side. We got in the car and I wanted to drive. He was in the passenger seat. Then we were walking around an open market. I was always afraid he was going to disappear so I didn't want to leave his side. He kept reassuring me he wasn't going anywhere. At one point he was sitting leisurely at a table reading the paper and I had to go to another room to get something but was afraid if I left him he would be gone when I got back. He reassured me he was there to stay so I went and did whatever and came right back. He was still there.

He didn't have his beard and looked so young and handsome. I was so happy in the dream, so relieved to know he is still with me. I was just soaking up the time with him. It makes me cry but I'm loving these dreams. *"Keep 'em coming Baby! I miss you."*

May 7, 2013

I dreamed I was with Gregory and he was carrying me, my legs wrapped around his waist and we were sort of dancing in a circle, locked in a kiss and embrace, oblivious to the world around us!

May 8, 2013

Wow, I keep dreaming about Gregory! Last night we got a blanket and went into a room with no furniture, laid the blanket out on the floor and made love! It was a long time too but then.... before we were done he got up and went over to the window and smoked a cigarette! I couldn't believe it. I was so mad that he would take a break to smoke while we were making love! The whole mood left me and I was done. He came back to the blanket but I was mad and said, "You're kidding, right? You can't go without smoking while we're making love?" I felt sad.

Ugh! Bummer, right? Woke up with that same bummed out

feeling that cigarettes had interrupted our love. And that's what essentially happened, right? The consequences of his smoking did interrupt our love. Bummer. I woke feeling bad for being mad at him. Still, I love that we made love in the dream and that I've dreamt of him every night!

May 9, 2013

I dreamed about Uncle Steve! He just walked in the room looking so healthy and handsome. His long hair just how I remember. I threw my arms around him for a big hug. It was so nice. No Gregory but at least I had a visitation from the Other Side!

A crazy thing happened when my friend, Christa was here. Someone walked up on the porch. It was loud footsteps and sounded like the mailman with heavy boots on. Christa looked out the window as I headed to the door. I knew the mailman had already been here and I looked at Christa to see if she knew who it was. She had a funny look on her face. I got to the door and no one was there! Christa said, *"That was loud,"* and it was! Very strange. Gave us both goosebumps.

May 17, 2013

I'm having a hard time here. I spent all day yesterday in a darkened room with a migraine, my back and legs were aching too. I cried off and on. So discouraged. I'm so beaten down I can barely pick myself up. I'm so sad right now. Overwhelmed with my own pain and discomfort. So discouraged and afraid I'll never be well again. Tired and beaten down with trying.

May 19, 2013

I dreamed Gregory and I had gone for a swim. He looked young like when I met him, long hair down, mustache, no beard and thinner. We were wrapped in towels and he went off one direction to change and I went in another. I realized I didn't have my clothes and figured I must have left them in the truck. I spent an agonizing amount of time trying to find the truck and my clothes while trying to stay covered with only a towel. Then I was back at the starting point and found Gregory and started yelling at him for leaving me without any clothes.

Clothes are all about beliefs, identity, and they represent who we are. I'm mad and yelling at Gregory for leaving me without my clothes! Lol! Sounds about right! It seems I'm not mad at him for dying, I'm mad at what it's done to me. I've lost my identity and it's his fault!

May 24, 2013

Before I went to bed last night I told Gregory I really wanted to see him in my dreams. Instead I dreamed vividly about Brad Pitt. Seriously? Is that a joke? It's pretty good when you have a dream about Brad Pitt and you'd rather dream about your husband. I don't even know what to say. *We were just standing there talking casually like friends. It was like we had known each other all our lives but the timing was never right for us to hook up. We both knew it was still impossible but I went over to him and gave him a long, passionate kiss. Yes, yes I did.*

June 3, 2013

I dreamed what felt like a long dream about getting ready for a date with my husband. The kids were helping me decide what to wear. They were young. I wanted to wear my hair up in a loose bun. I wanted the children's approval of how I looked for their dad. Then Gregory was there. We got in the car and drove to a nice restaurant for dinner. That's all I remember.

Still spending time with my husband, going to dinner, and acting like nothing has changed. The kids were little showing I'm going back to how it was in the beginning. Probably not the best symbolism. Never good to go back in a dream. Still, it is what it is.

June 4, 2013

I dreamed about Brad Pitt again. Not sure what that's about. Can't remember much, he was just there. There was also a part about a tiny baby in the basement of a house I don't recognize. At one point I went down there and could hear a baby crying but I didn't know whose it was. I went in and picked up the little baby to comfort her. I fed her a bottle. That's all I remember. I'm still not owning the baby as my own but at least I'm taking care of her!

June 8, 2013

I forget to write about the Rainbows because I'm usually feeling grief when I sit down first thing in the morning. But I get them every day and there's a paint commercial that I seem to catch every time I turn on the TV and it's just loaded with colorful Rainbows! It makes me smile. Tonight I'll be walking the Civic Center with Megan and her family for Gregory. It's the *Relay for Life* walk all weekend long. We're also walking for, and with, Meg's mother-in-law, Pam, who is a cancer survivor.

June 9, 2013

The cancer walk was amazing with luminaries lighting our way. 850 bags were lit in honor of survivors and in memory of my Gregory and all the others who lost their battle. It was so emotional for me. There was a big dry erase board where you could write notes for your loved one. I wrote *"Greg and L.J."* in a heart and, *"Till the wheels fall off,"* like he did in Ann Arbor. I cried all the way but just as we began our first lap—I was pushing Kadyn Gregory in his stroller—he looked up at me and started giggling. Almost the entire first lap he giggled at me. He kept making me laugh and then he would giggle some more. I knew Gregory's spirit was there making him laugh and helping him to cheer me up a bit.

June 13, 2013

I went to bed feeling tired and aching all over. The house is a mess and I don't seem to care. The bedroom—formerly *the Love Den*—is not my beautiful sanctuary like it should be. It's a mess. I need a kick in the butt. I'm sad and overwhelmed and missing Gregory something awful. But I saw my dad Tuesday night on the way home from softball! Two cars ahead of me there was a truck and in the side mirror was my dad staring at me with a big smile on his face! He never turned away. It was my dad! I had my hand to my mouth in disbelief and was crying.

It was a big side mirror and his whole head was visible, facing me, smiling at me, *comforting* me and reminding me that he is still with me. When the truck turned off I went by and looked at the driver. He looked nothing like my dad. I cried and thanked my Pop for that. It was surreal. Amazing. Now I need to see Gregory. I miss my dad and my husband.

June 15, 2013

OMG!! I went for Reiki again yesterday and at the end Gregory held my feet again!!! I couldn't believe it! Even though before we started when Angela was out of the room I asked him to be with me. Then I let it go and had such an amazing and very long session. Again she was ending at my head. Last time I had socks on but this time my feet were bare. I felt his hands on the bottoms of my feet, his fingers wrapping around the tops. Even after she was done I felt it. I didn't want to get up. I just stayed lying face down feeling the touch of hands on my feet when there was no earthly explanation for it. I couldn't believe it. I feel so blessed by it. He's with me. He's always with me.

June 16, 2013

I dreamed I was on vacation at a resort or on a ship or something. I was alone in the room and I heard Gregory coming down the hall. I was so happy it was him. He came in and I said I was hoping he was there to see me. He stood in front of me looking just like he did when he was last healthy. *I put my arms around him and hugged him tight. I just looked at him standing close and in front of me. Then I hugged him again, so glad he was there and I could. It was a very nice dream.*

June 19, 2013

I dreamed about Gregory again. I stood face to face with him and just started kissing and hugging him. The kids sort of teased us, like, "Get a room!"

June 26, 2013

I dreamed about dolls. Babies that aren't real. Ugh! *I found two and then one that had come apart in the middle and was two halves. I knew I could sew her back together since she seemed to be a cabbage patch doll with a cloth body.* Yikes! The babies aren't even real! They are pretend babies. Not good.

Chapter 10

Gone But Not Forgotten

June 30, 2013

I dreamed that Gregory and I couldn't be together but we were both in the same house. I said, "Just take me home with you." He said, "I can't," even though I know he wanted to. I wanted to just leave this place and be with him but it was impossible. I guess reality is sinking in. I know there is something separating us but at least he's still here.

July 3, 2013

I worked in the yard all day and it felt so good. I feel Gregory's strong presence when I'm out there. Last night at bedtime I was missing him so much. Missing curling up next to him in bed. I cried as I asked him to show up for me somehow there in our bedroom and he did! In the dark I began to see and feel a waviness in the air. A sort of electrical occurrence that was visible in the darkness. It was so cool. Then I felt a burst of air go across my arm! The air was charged with activity! It was so amazing! Ask and ye shall receive! I was no longer crying and was able to fall asleep. I am so grateful for those moments when I can really feel Gregory showing up for me.

July 5, 2013

I don't often write about the Rainbows Gregory sends me every day but he does. Yesterday I was in the grocery store and noticed the edge of a Rainbow on a bag of chips or snacks. I turned it around to show my friends and said, *"Here's my Rainbow."* That's when I saw the word *Rainbow* in all caps across the front of the bag with a colorful Rainbow behind the words.

July 6, 2013

Wow! Had an awesome dream with Gregory! We were making love! Kissing and hugging and enjoying each other! I didn't recognize where we were but we didn't care! "Oh, thank you Gregory!" Then this next part is powerful. *I was in a huge VIP facility. It was where you want to be to get things done, to make connections, to succeed. You had to have clearance to get beyond the front area. Everyone was friendly in this area but you couldn't go to the upper levels unless you belonged there.*

There was the cutest, friendliest baby that came right to me. I knew she belonged to a very important and influential couple who were somewhere in the VIP section. I knew she was my 'ticket' to the forbidden areas. With her in my arms I was able to walk right past security and go anywhere I wanted. It was amazing to be in this other part. I felt like I belonged there. I felt I was accomplished, sure of myself, and capable of anything. With this baby in my arms I was free to go anywhere. And I did.

Well, if that doesn't tell me how important the baby is I don't know what will. Still, it's not my baby! Dang! I need to own the baby in a dream otherwise it's someone else's. For the past year I've been so unsure of the vision for my life and have wondered whether or not the plan has changed. But the baby is my ticket and I needed that reminder more than I realized. The baby will get me there. No one questioned who I was or why I was there. As long as I had the baby I was in.

July 9, 2013

Yesterday I took my friend to the airport at 5:30 a.m. I was caught off guard by the memory of picking up Gregory following Hurricane Katrina in Gulf Shores. He'd been on storm work for five weeks, the longest we'd ever been apart. In the crowd coming off the plane he saw me and both arms shot straight up. My arms instinctively went straight up as well as we hurried toward each other and hugged and hugged.

I cried leaving the airport and sobbed all the way home. I turned on the radio just as *Broken Wings* was starting. I love that song. It says that even though my wings are broken I'm going to be able to fly again. When it was over the DJ said, *"That was from Mr. Mister,"* and I cried some more, forgetting that's who the song was by and remembering how often I lovingly addressed my Gregory as *"Mr. Mister."* And he called me *"Twisted Sister."* It was probably my most tear-filled day in a while.

July 10, 2013

I had someone after the meeting suggest that I go on Prozac *to stop the tears.* Are you kidding me? I said, *"Why would I want to stop the tears?!"* He said, *"Well if it's interfering with your life."* It's not! It's healing my life! I told him if I was going to do that I might as well drink. They are no different to me. Dry up the tears, don't deal with the tears. Wow. Scary stuff. Just because I've cried every day since Gregory died doesn't mean I cry *all* day. Or that I'm not still doing my life. Sad isn't bad.

July 16, 2013

I dreamed about Gregory again! I couldn't stop hugging and kissing him. We were standing in a public place and didn't seem to notice or care about anything around us. We just kept hugging and kissing. Oh, how I miss that.

July 27, 2013

Had the best dream about Gregory so far even if it makes me so sad now. He was back. I couldn't believe it. He looked so handsome. Full, dark beard, well-trimmed, he looked so healthy and so full of life. He was smiling and laughing as we hugged and kissed. I couldn't get enough of him. I felt his beard against my face and smelled him and felt him and told him this is what I have missed so much.

He was just as happy to see me, to hug me and kiss me. His smile was so bright, he looked incredible. He was laughing and talking and it was so amazing to hear his voice again. I was the happiest I've ever felt in my life. Home in his arms my Gregory was back. We were both so happy. He said, "I said at church last night that I couldn't wait to give you everything," and there was a twinkle in his eye. I said, "You said that at church?!" He just smiled and held me closer.

We couldn't get enough of each other after so long apart. I knew we would make love again and I couldn't wait to melt into his arms. His beard felt so amazing and I was reminded how much I loved the feel of it on my face, snuggling into the smell of him. His eyes were so bright, he was so beautiful. This nightmare separation was over. My grief was lifted.....

And then I woke up..... and sobbed. I cry still. But I'm so grateful to have experienced my Gregory again, been kissed by him, held by him, heard his voice, his laugh, felt his amazing spirit full of life and energy, smelled him, touched him, kissed him. But now, again, I am without him. It was a beautiful gift. A dream I have waited for even if my reality hits hard when I'm awake. Though tears roll down my face, I am so happy to have had that gift. If only for a few moments I did in fact get to see and hold my Gregory again.

July 28, 2013

I dreamed Gregory was back and I hugged and kissed him and said I was going to cherish every moment this time in case he leaves again.

July 30, 2013

I dreamed I was with Gregory in a busy, crowded place where you could go from room to room. I lost him and started searching all the rooms to find him. This went on for quite some time as I searched through the crowd. I was starting to get frustrated when I remembered he's gone. It's like I realized it was a dream and that I remembered, or woke up to realize, I'm not going to find him so stop searching. I felt sad.

Well, it looks as if a bit of reality is sinking in.

August 4, 2013

Woohoo! What a dream! I still can't believe it. *A bunch of us—family—were all getting ready to catch the ferry over to Mackinac Island for my birthday. Someone had bought all the tickets, including mine. I went to the bathroom and then headed over to the dock with everyone. As we were boarding I realized I didn't have my ticket and must have left it in the bathroom. I rushed back and found a crumpled envelope on the bathroom floor. It had my money in it but no ticket. I was very frustrated as I bought another and hurried out. I seemed to be in slow motion as I tried to get to the dock. I was too late. Here I was the guest of honor and they were all headed over to the Island without me.*

I sat down at a table defeated and heartbroken. I looked up and there was Dad and Grandpa Farris sitting next to me! They both looked so healthy and handsome! They just smiled at me reassuringly. I said, "You guys stayed back for me?" They were like, "Yep, we didn't want you to be alone." I asked if there was another boat we could catch and Dad said no, that was the last one. I kept staring at them. Grandpa Farris looked so good. I was surprised by what a handsome man he was and couldn't believe how long it had been since I'd seen him.

He died in 1980 and always looked sort of old and tired my whole life. He used to pat us kids on the head and say, rather amused, "Red on the head," and that was his loving gesture toward us. He did something with his lips in the dream, sort of rolled his lips over each other softly and I was reminded of him from my childhood. That was something he always did with his lips and I had completely forgotten about it! I was reminded how much I loved him. I said, "I love you so much Grandpa," and I leaned over and gave him a big hug and held onto him for several moments. I vowed to never forget him.

Ugh! Thank God Dad and Grandpa were there for reassurance, eh? Otherwise I'm not liking the symbolism! Missed the boat. The only boat. But it was only a day trip so it's not like I missed the trip of a lifetime. Seeing my dad and his dad was so amazing. I cried when I woke up and realized what I'd seen. Dad looked so beautiful. Healthy, glowing skin, no wrinkles, no stress, just beautiful, calming presence. Both of them looked angelic, emanating love and support. It was unforgettable.

August 6, 2013

Well believe it or not I've been working my butt off and the living room is emptied out, cleaned, and ready for new carpet tomorrow. I have to say that picking out the carpet and tile for the entry by myself seemed so wrong. Gregory and I always made these decisions together. He was with me, I could feel him so strongly that it made me tear up a couple of times. And I feel like he helped me pick out what I did. But it felt so strange. No one's tastes to consider but my own. No one to ask if they like this or that. No negotiating, no compromise. There was a part of me that felt empowered making those decisions on my own but it was just a little overshadowed by missing Gregory. It was the first big house decision I've had to make on my own and now that's done.

August 13, 2013

I dreamed I was so thirsty and was filling a broken, dirty, plastic cup from a drinking fountain. The water was clear and delicious but I was worried because the cup was dirty and broken and would only hold about a quarter cup. Still, I drank what I could get and filled it up again and again never feeling like I got as much as I wanted. I remember filling it for Gregory who stood next to me.

Then I dreamed I was in a café having come in from some lost or misguided place. The café felt like a sanctuary; a safe haven to replenish and gather my thoughts. It was also where people— also lost out there—could find each other. I looked down the aisle at people coming in and saw Gregory! I was so relieved. He was tall and gorgeous, his beard long. He smiled when he saw me and started walking toward me.

This dream shows that I'm thirsty, for clarity, for sustenance, for spiritual awareness. Being sick has made everything a challenge. The dream shows that the cup; my spiritual *vessel*, is damaged. The water is healthy and plentiful. I just have to work on the vessel, it's what's broken right now. I thought the part about the café sanctuary was interesting. Shows I do have a safe place to go and replenish. A place where all lost souls go. And Gregory is there!

August 15, 2013

Gregory was in my dream! It was just as natural as everyday living. A guy was there to fix something up in a really cool sunroom like an attic room with big windows. You had to climb a ladder to get up there but I was excited about this room and said I was going to move my office up there even though I wasn't sure how we could get the furniture up. Gregory was standing in the hall with me at the base of the ladder. He had my back.

The upper rooms are spiritual awareness. It's good that I want to be up there but the dream shows the way up is hindered. Not impossible but not easily accessible either. I have to work to get up but at least I wanted to be up there and was excited about what I could do with the place. And Gregory is behind me! Last year this day I was finishing painting the living room and the kittens were wild in the back room. One year later the living room is complete and Jasmine and her babies have forever homes.

August 19, 2013

I dreamed about Megan as a little girl. She was about five or six. She came and sat on my lap to tell me something about her day. I kissed her and hugged her and held her in my arms. She was so sweet. Yes, yes she was. Still is. I guess the dream shows that my mind keeps going back to a time when life was sweet and the kids were still little. I went to see Greg's mom yesterday and it was nice. She acts like I was just there yesterday not last month. I miss her. What a sad ending to a full, vibrant life.

August 23, 2013

I had a busy day yesterday. I get Rainbows every day but I'm not very good about writing about them. I also get messages from him through songs and I always know they are from him. The energy all around me changes and it makes me smile. I ran an errand and when I got in the car and turned on the radio it was an old song that I loved from the 70's, called, *Fool If You Think It's Over*, by Chris Rea. Love it! Save those tears for another day. It's not over for us and knowing that keeps me wanting to live my life to the fullest. Even as I don't yet know what that means for me now.

Chapter 11

Starting To Fall Apart

September 4, 2013

I got a daily meditation book for grief that I read from each morning in my quiet time for a little help for the day. I cried a lot yesterday. We would have been waking up on the Island. It makes me so sad I can barely stand it. *"Oh, Gregory, why am I here without you? Why? Why? Why? Will I ever go to the Island again? Why did this have to happen?"* Ugh.

September 19, 2013

One of the things on my, *Things I'm Avoiding* list, is the basement. It's a storage area basically as much as Gregory tried to make it his workspace. I have done nothing but add to it since he died. Anything that I didn't know what to do with—his work clothes, climbing boots, guitar stuff—I put in the basement. Now you can't really walk down there. I know Gregory would be horrified to see it this way. I got home from my meeting and took a look down there. I wanted to sort of survey the damage and visually look at each item amidst the mound of hundreds. See what my game plan will be when the time comes to tackle that big job.

I've let myself turn a blind eye to the whole mess since he

died. But now as I let myself really look at what's down there my eyes landed on his router table, his bandsaw, his miter saw, big sander, grinder. Then to the smaller things, everything spread out from here to there; the palm sander, electric drill, drill bit set, hammers, bungee cords, sawhorses.... and the list goes on and on.

Everything well-used for many years, some of it passed down from his dad or mine. So much of a life lived through all of this stuff. My heart sank. I could see him using every one of those tools. My heart froze, I caught my breath. Ugh! The loss. Then his albums, his books, our luggage, the TV he watched while tinkering down there. A whole life lived and played out amidst this huge pile of stuff I haven't dealt with. I was overcome.

On top of his albums was a framed 8x10 black and white photo taken his senior year. So handsome. So clean cut! Not my Gregory at all and yet it is. A quick scan across the basement. The young man, the seasoned vet, the builder, the carpenter, and the fisherman. All the things he loved and utilized on his human journey that is of no use to him now. The saying, *"You can't take it with you,"* has never been so clear. It hit me hard. Unexpected. The loss is huge. How can I still be standing?

September 20, 2013

Boy, that episode downstairs caught me so off guard yesterday. Makes me cry even now. No wonder I haven't dealt with the basement! So much of Gregory is down there. I didn't realize. But I'm obviously preparing for the task and I'll be so happy when it's done.

September 21, 2013

A flood of memories hit me this morning. Of this house and what it was like when we first walked in. There are so many memories that Gregory and I alone share. This whole amazing life that only I have memory of now. Whoa, that's pretty overwhelming. And sad to me. In a most grateful kind of way. Sitting here this morning I'm reminded of those early years. When we still had time and Gregory still had his health. Millions of stored memories.

Oh, before I forget, Gregory continues to send me Rainbows every day. I realize I rarely write about it but he does, indeed, send me at least one Rainbow a day and sometimes a few, like yesterday. I see a Rainbow or hear the word, at some point every day and my attention is always drawn to them. It's my wink or little kiss Gregory sends my way to let me know he's still here.

September 22, 2013

In my gratitude journal there's a quote from Buddha. *"Your work is to discover your work and then with all your heart give yourself to it."* This is what I haven't been able to do. To give myself to it with all my heart... Wow, I just had an Aha! moment. I thought this quote referred to my writing and the dream work. *My work.* But as I was writing I heard it differently. *Your work is to discover your work.* For this day, this time in your life. *That* work. Whatever life and the day sends your way. I'm always so quick to beat up on myself for not accomplishing my goals, for not making money, not supporting myself. But being able to mourn and to process this big life change *has* been my work these past seventeen months, along with taking care of myself, the house, and the animals. I'm filled with gratitude for a life that allows me that and I have been giving my whole heart to it.

September 25, 2013

I found our bike helmets in the basement. Ugh. Blow to the chest. Memories of using those helmets on Mackinac Island hit me. When we were our healthiest we'd take some of the rougher trails where a fall could be deadly. But there I stood, holding our bike helmets, knowing we will never do that again. I'm thankful I'd already given the kids most of our camping gear so I don't have to do that walk down memory lane. All those camping trips with the kids growing up. We loved it. Thirty years of memories. I'm grateful whenever something brings one back.

September 29, 2013

I am haunted by my own premonition in 1982 that told me I would be a young widow. Showing me way back at the start of my relationship with the man I was already madly in love with that I would only have him for a time and that neither of us would be old when that happened. If I'm ever going to 'should' on myself it would be that I should have heeded that warning, honored that insight, and prepared better financially. There would have been no way to prepare emotionally. I never shared that moment with Gregory. I never thought of it again. I pushed it out of my mind. Until 30 years later. Now the memory haunts me. Now I remember it clearly. In hindsight I see how that information was a gift that I did not accept and as a result was unprepared.

October 1, 2013

The reading in my grief and loss book said it all for me. It talked about the need to feel our grief and the dangers of getting into the busies to distract from it. She said it's a mistake to hide from it because it will always find you. It will demand to be heard. And then she said something that spoke right to my heart. That inhabiting our grief comes with its own comfort and is where we need to be for a while. Like we belong there, like being in a safe place where we can rest and recover. Then, at our own pace, we will begin to understand the meaning of it all and can begin to move on.

I need to hear that right now. I've hit a wall. I'm missing Gregory and avoiding painting the front porch like there's a plague out there! The end quote on that day makes me realize I'm being hard on myself. It reminds me not to hurry or worry while I dwell in this place of grief. I need those loving reassurances, especially when I'm expecting too much of myself. I've hit the same wall I must have hit last year at this time. The one that decided the porch can wait until Spring.

October 2, 2013

I've been beating up on myself and then scolding myself for it. Reassuring myself that it's okay that I'm not all productive with projects but feeling bad about myself anyway. Then I wrote the date this morning and I realized what's going on. *Tomorrow is our anniversary.* A flood of sobs followed. Geesh, no wonder I've been feeling heavier. Ugh! Anniversaries. They're never quite the same when one of you is gone.

October 4, 2013

Gregory sent me a Rainbow for our anniversary. I'm always drawn to the TV, the ad, the magazine, or a picture on a wall, when he sends me a Rainbow. Something changes slightly in the air and I feel him. Then boom! Rainbow! Always makes me smile and I always say, *"Got it."* It's the same with songs on the radio. I always know when the words are meant for me.

October 6, 2013

Now I know why people say they feel like they've been hit by a truck after someone they love dies. I didn't understand how true that statement is. Literally feel like I've been hit by a truck. Everything hurts. I miss my love on a soul level. My soul aches to be near him. I cried to him earlier about all the things I miss. Holding his hand. Oh, how I miss that. I miss hugging him, kissing him, feeling his beard on my face, his chest on my mine, eating meals together, going out for dinner, riding bikes, going to the Island.

I just sobbed. My heart is in survival mode while it recovers from half of it leaving. The other half is grieving. It's a weak heart, that's why I'm so fragile. And feeling quite useless I might add, as once again I spent precious time resting. Lying around, weak, tired. I did, however, make myself walk to the Farmer's Market which was really nice. I'm doing the best I can.

October 8, 2013

I want my Gregory back. I miss him. I want my life with him back. *"Oh, God, help me."* I sobbed in the kitchen last night while making dinner. Grilled chicken salads. I was reminded of making those salads together. It hit me hard. I never know what memory is going to trigger a flood of tears. I heard it takes years. Not to get over it but to get used to it. Who wants to get used to this? Who said I wanted to settle into life without Gregory? Piss off!

October 10, 2013

"God has created your wings not to be dormant. As long as you are alive you must try more and more to use your wings to show you're alive." –Rumi

Oh, I needed to read Rumi's wisdom on this page. I *have* to use my wings again. I feel so useless. And yet, I am still grieving. My biggest inner battle right now is knowing if I'm doing okay. Is it okay to do just the bare necessities day after day? Self-care being all I manage; time here to write, eating, Yoga, taking care of our four kitties, meetings, lots of sleep at night, and being account-able to people. *Is* that enough when my grief is so intertwined with all of it?

October 11, 2013

Society fights against the grieving human. I'm grieving a different moment in our lives every time I cry. It hit me hard in the shower yesterday. So sad the longer it goes. Seventeen months is a very long time to be without the one you love. Today's *'solution in a pill'* mentality fights against authentic anything. Or the time it takes, whether its grieving or healing the body from illness or injury.

My everyday actions challenge that mindset at every turn. I have to *'positive up'* nearly every first thought that comes. I hear, *"You're lazy. You just want someone to pay the bills while you do nothing. You'll never accomplish your goals. The vision isn't real. It's too late for you. Better figure out how you're gonna get*

through your life. You may need to go to work at the video store.
Suck it up. Just do it. Forget about the dream." It would interfere
with my grieving process if I let it.

October 15, 2013

I feel like a weight has been lifted. Especially after the messages
I got from Gregory yesterday. First I want to write about the cold
spots. It's been happening the past few days. I'd feel a definite
cold spot right next to me on my left, sort of toward the middle.
I'd think, *"Where's that breeze coming from?"* Then I'd check all
the usual stuff; did the heat just come on, cold at first? Did I leave
a window open? Is the fan on? Check. Check. Check. Hmmm.
Nothing on or open. *Strange.*

Then it happened again. I felt the cold area on my left side like
someone was standing right there. First impulse, check windows,
heat, fans. Nothing on. Through my already tear-filled state, I
said, *"This is you, isn't it? You have been trying for days to show*
yourself to me, to somehow—in a bigger way—let me know you
haven't left my side. You're still with me." I cried happy/sad tears,
visualizing Gregory trying so hard, so determined to blow my
mind, and kick me out of this sad, sad place I've been in.

I checked Facebook to see what Meg had posted about the
kids. Pow! There's Gregory's beautiful face! His image hitting me
like I was actually seeing him again, like running into him on the
street. My heart leapt for joy. There he was, up and out of the
screen in front of me, smiling that teasing smile he always had
when he was trying to cheer me up or play with me. I couldn't
believe it. I cried more happy/sad tears. I needed a sign like that.
I feel him near me—he sends me Rainbows every day—but this
past week has been harder. Sadder. I needed him to show up
bigger and he did!

October 17, 2013

It feels like my life without Gregory will never be happy again.
But that ember deep inside glows ever so gently and I know that

the best is yet to come. I see flashes of it, glimpses into a life complete again. I've had glimpses all my life of this illusive vision. Now I'm 53 years old. My father died. My husband died. I don't support myself. Surely a person would give it up by now, right?

October 19, 2013

I was working at Greg's mom's early last evening. Our little great-niece ran in and told me there was a Rainbow outside. I hurried out, so excited to see my first real live Rainbow in the sky since Gregory died. Rainbows every day but never a real one. And OMG! This Rainbow was it. It was so amazingly colorful and bright and from where we stood on Mom's back porch it appeared to be coming straight out of our house! So beautiful, the colors so vivid. And little Neva said, "It's Unca Geg!"

October 20, 2013

Memories of our life come vividly now. Flashes of this tender moment or that warm embrace. Young, healthy, active, and crazy in love. I miss that most of all. Lately I've been questioning if I should still be feeling such loss, such intense grief. And then my reading yesterday reminded me how very individual and complex the healing process is and that there is no way to measure it on any set calendar.

She goes on to consider all the different factors that go into how long one grieves. The author said that four years after she lost her daughter she noticed a shift and her grief was no longer such a preoccupying burden and dominant fact of each day. Another writer says it takes seven years to recover from the death of someone close. That gave me some peace. I can relax in my process and feel better about letting up on myself for still being so sad and functioning at a slower pace. The reading says we just have to feel our way through and trust the process to reveal its own wisdom. The prayer at the end reminds me to live one day at a time. It helps, truly.

October 22, 2013

Gregory speaks to me through music and this morning it was from *Firefall*, a band I love from the 70's. The song is called, *Just Remember I Love You*. I forgot there is a Rainbow in there. It made me cry when it described how I'm feeling. Those blues come calling as soon as I open my eyes. It feels like it just keeps raining and my Rainbow is gone. But then it reminds me at the end that he loves me and everything is going to be alright.

October 23, 2013

Yesterday it was cloudy and rainy so I kept my eye out for a Rainbow. I left Greg's mom's and turned down our street to park in front of our house. As soon as I did there was a huge Rainbow at the end of the street, seeming to come up from the ground and bursting up before me. I felt a rush of goosebumps. It was magnificent and very obvious it was for me from my Gregory. He is sticking close this week as I seem to be missing him more than I think I can bear.

October 24, 2013

I continue to work in the basement and had a few tough moments down there going through things. I found a picture of the two of us and marveled at how absolutely happy I was in his arms. Then I found a card with a single red rose on it. On the front it says, *"It's a simple thing really..."* On the inside... *"I love you."* And then he wrote, *"Happy Anniversary, G."* It was more powerful this time than when he gave it to me. In that moment of staring at our picture and seeing how comfortable we were together, the simple message, *I love you*, was from him in that very moment.

November 4, 2013

Gregory just sent me a Rainbow! You can't imagine how many ways there are to get a Rainbow. They always feel like winks from him. Like, *"Hello I love you."* Every day. Sometimes two or three in a day. For over a year. Isn't that amazing? But I miss the man.

November 8, 2013

I love that my husband sends me Rainbows every day and speaks to me through songs. I love that it happens in moments I need it most. Speaking the exact words to give me peace. And the Rainbows—a wink here, a wave there—just fills my heart with peace in that moment. He is right here, still interacting with me, in tune with where I am and here to do his best to make it better for me.

November 14, 2013

I hadn't cried yesterday morning like usual until I was in the car on the way for coffee. I just started crying, missing my love so much. Right then, *Somewhere Over The Rainbow* came on the radio. I've only heard it twice now since Gregory died and I cried all the way through it. It's such a beautiful version of the song; the Hawaiian version. The one we played at his memorial.

November 20, 2013

Oh, Gregory pulled a doosey again! Sitting here as I do every morning—Gregory's smiling picture beside me—I looked and his picture was upside down! I kid you not! So playful. So Gregory. It made me smile. It was, and is, his spirit.

November 28, 2013

"Happy Thanksgiving, Gregory. Two without you now." How can that be? How can I still be breathing? So far no tears. That still amazes me sometimes. That I can have a real sense of peace, especially first thing in the morning. I'm so grateful. I know it's Gregory's spirit with me. Letting me feel that I'm never alone. But, man, do I miss being held by him.

Chapter 12

Starting To Accept

December 2, 2013

Just got a Rainbow! As soon as I turned on the TV. Beautiful! *"Thank you Gregory."* I got my Christmas tree and it looks nice. The candles are in the windows and the stockings hung on the mantle. Grief hit me hard last night after a really good day. A day where I felt stronger than I have since he died. But last night and again a few minutes ago it hit me that the life I've known for thirty years will soon take its place in memory. The thought of that and the realization that it's already beginning to happen was—is—too much to bear. Ugh.

Although I must report that on a lighter note Gregory made me laugh yesterday. I had challenged him the night before to make a light flicker and nothing happened. As I was leaving in the morning it was still dark out. I got to the end of the alley and just then the lamp post right in front of me began to flash. On off on off. Not a flicker. Not sizzle fade to light as they will do before burning out. Oh no, this was full on dramatic. Slow but steady, on... off... on... off... without stopping for as long as I sat there. I knew it was Gregory. I could feel his playfulness in my heart and everywhere in the car.

In the midst of this grief journey I must say there is a quiet ember deep within me that still believes in love and that gives me peace. And in one of those stronger moments even a bit of excitement at the thought, *"Could I find that kind of love a second time?"* The end of my reading this morning was a prayer asking for help to let go of worry and concern when I'm in the in-betweens. Help me to walk in peace and show me the path I should follow. Help me relax where I am right now so I can gather the energy I'll need for the journey ahead.

December 4, 2013

I have to write about the Rainbows! While I was decorating the tree I kept getting Rainbows! The glass on the front door will reflect Rainbows in the living room but this was different. This was wherever I was in the room. *The Rainbows followed me.* I saw one on the carpet in front of me. As I was hanging our stockings all of sudden right there on the bricks between two stockings was a Rainbow. Sitting on the loveseat untangling ornaments I looked down and there on the full length of my thigh was a Rainbow. I just stared at it in disbelief. The Rainbows seemed to dance around the room following me! It was really very cool.

December 6, 2013

My morning began with tea and tears as I sat down and the song, *How Do I Live (without you)*, by LeAnn Rimes, came on. I felt that song in a way I never could have before Gregory died. How do I get through my days and nights without you? And even if I do what kind of life is that going to be? If you leave I'm not going to be able to breathe and then how will I survive?

Ugh. As the song played I had a strong feeling that the next song was going to be special. I just knew it. Then in classic Gregory style of speaking to me through songs an old Commodores song came on. *Sweet Love.* It answered the question I've had for Gregory since he died and the one I cried out asking again just yesterday afternoon. *"Can you see my vision now? Is it true for me? Am I to follow? Or has it all been a pipe dream and I need to give it up?"* When is it perseverance and when is it stubborn stupidity? Well Praise God and the song *Sweet Love.* I cried all the way through it.

I couldn't believe it when I heard the word Rainbow. The words speak straight to my heart when they say that he knows I've been searching for understanding and peace while I try to find my way. He says I have to keep on searching, try harder. I could feel Gregory in my whole being and tears rolled down my cheeks. I got the answer I needed. I heard; *"I know it's been hard but you've got to keep on..."* I was so amazed by the song and the emotion and the message that I told Gregory, *"If this is to be then I will follow my dream and I will do my best while I'm here and I will love my life knowing that someday I will be with you again."* And you'll never believe what song he gave me next. Supertramp's, *Take The Long Way Home...*

December 13, 2013

Seventeen days left of this year. It went by in a flash. I have turned a corner with accepting the changes taking place. Gregory's songs for me this morning were all about his love for me—*our* love—and how it was all that mattered. All that still matters. Then one amazing message in a song called *Part Of The Plan*, by Dan Fogelberg. It talks about life and how one moment we can feel strong and the next moment weak and afraid. It says that I should cry if I need to, love when I'm able, and at some point we're all going to understand. It's part of the plan. I can live with that.

December 18, 2013

I had on the music channel and was just about to mute it so I could write when I heard, *"No,"* and felt a gentle pull on my hand away from the button on the remote. I sat back to hear what my husband had to say to me. *Because I Love You*, by Stevie B. What a gift. It's a beautiful song. Tears poured down my cheeks as I was reminded that he loves me and will do anything for me. That he's never going to leave my side, that he's going to light up my life and guide me in everything I do. He says he's always going to be around and I can count on him.

December 19, 2013

The Christmas card this year has a Rainbow on it. The first real, in the sky, Rainbow Gregory sent me. The other spots hold pictures of Meg and her family and singles of each of the grand-kids. It's very nice for the first one without Gregory's handsome face on it. Now I'm over that hurdle.

December 21, 2013

Gregory spoke to me in two songs this morning. First was Dierks Bentley's, *I Hold On*. What a great song. The words, *I . . Hold . . On . .* felt very dramatic to me. Powerful. It says that if I ever worry that he's not going to be there it's never going to happen. He holds on. I couldn't help but think, *"Yeah, me too."* Then just now, *I'll Be Around*, by The Spinners. It talks about the fork in the road I find myself at right now. Heading on a path without him in my physical world. But alas, he reminds me that all I have to do is call him and he'll be there. If I need him he'll be there, that no matter what he'll be around.

While deep mourning and grief still hit me I feel more accep-tance. I feel Gregory with me. I know he is here right now. In those moments it feels like enough. Megan called and she and Eric were both crying over something Eric's mom told them. A few nights ago she babysat the kids and she said she overheard Cameron's prayer at bedtime. *"Dear God, please bring my Papa Greg back. He was fun and I miss him."* Big sobs.

December 25, 2013

As I sat by the light of the tree, alone in my living room on Christmas morning, I had a sudden flash over so many Christmas mornings. The reality that I'm alone for only the second time in

53 years hit me hard. It was worse when I remembered all those years when the kids were little. I cried as I thought about it. How much fun it was. How exciting the morning when children are in the house. Then the memories of all those Christmas mornings with just Greg and me. I cried and cried. *"I used to have children running around! I used to have a husband!"*

December 27, 2013

There is a quiet strength building within me. An inner knowing that dares me to believe in love again. Believe that I could find the perfect man for me twice in a lifetime. This morning, talking to Gregory through tears, I said, *"You took me as far as you could."* I cried some more. Then he reminded me once again to *take the long way home.* I love the part where it talks about looking back through the years and seeing what we would or could have been if only there was more time. But that no matter what we're heading to our final destination so we should take the long way home. And so I will. Gregory's life was cut short but mine was not. All roads lead me back to him, to my Home, my family. Now he's playing, *I'll Still Be Loving You...* *"Love you, Gregory."*

January 1, 2014

The song I got first thing this morning from my Gregory was Rod Stewart's, *Forever Young.* The message was that the good Lord is with me no matter where I go, that I can stand proud, do unto others as I would have done to me. That I should have courage, that the guiding light in my life is strong. But most importantly he reminds me that he's forever young now and that makes me so happy. For him and for me when the time comes. It was powerful. I said, *"Happy New Year, Honey,"* before I was even out of bed. The fireworks woke me up at midnight and I went to the bathroom window and watched the whole thing, Gregory by my side. I could feel him.

January 2, 2014

Gregory just did the song thing. I was having a sobbing moment remembering making love with him. Missing that human connection so much I weep. My attention was drawn to the muted TV and I saw *Together Forever*, by Rick Astley. I listened to the words and felt them to my very soul. He reminds me that we're together forever and will never be apart. I'm beginning to see that.

January 6, 2014

I was sitting here overcome with sadness. I cried and cried those borderline scary times where it just hurts too much in the moment to believe it will ever get better. Through my tears I said to Gregory, *"You never liked me to cry. Well, I've been crying for a year and a half!"* In that moment the Christmas tree lights shone brighter casting a soft light in the corner by the stairs and lighting our wedding picture with its warm glow. Suddenly I just knew he was going to speak to me in song.

I unmuted the music channel just as one song ended and Gregory's song began. *Don't Cry*, by Seal. Really? The words remind me that I don't need to cry because I'm always going to be loved. It's such a beautiful song. I told him through my tears, *"Thank you, Baby. It helps so much. It is you, showing me you're here, speaking to me still. Loving me more than ever. Seeing my tears, hearing my pain. If I didn't have that I would die."*

January 7, 2014

Wow, Gregory started off with a song. I went for the mute button but was stopped by that gentle pull on my hand. I sat back and settled in to hear what he had to say to ease my heavy heart. *Two Hearts*, by Phil Collins, reminding me that our hearts beat as one now and that's it's going to be that way until the end of time.

January 14, 2014

"Happy Birthday, Baby," I said to him as soon as I got up. Two birthdays without him. Seems hard to believe. I turned on the TV to check the weather and heard, *"Make a Rainbow,"* as a garden hose watering the flowers cast a beautiful Rainbow across the ground. Right off the bat a Rainbow! *"Thank you, Honey. I know you are so happy where you are that I can't help but be happy for you. It's me we have to deal with."*

January 16, 2014

Gregory just did the song thing. Brought my attention to it with that indescribable change in the air around me and guiding my hand to the remote. *When I'm Gone*, by 3 Doors Down. Beautiful song. Right up there with *Here Without You*. And what am I supposed to do when he's gone? Love him, that's all, just love him. Powerful.

January 22, 2014

I get great comfort from my daily grief and loss reading. She talked about the peace that comes when the grief work is done and the comfort that comes when the process is honored. It began with a favorite scripture from Matthew 5:4, *"Blessed are those who mourn for they shall be comforted."* She says it takes courage to mourn and those who are brave enough to do the work will find an unexpected blessing. That after all the sadness and all the pain it is as if some loving force of nature envelops you and soothes you, and says, *"There, there, I know what you've been through and it's going to be okay now."*

Chapter 13

On Shaky Ground

———

January 27, 2014

Wow, talk about Rainbows! I've had a couple of really sad meltdowns about Gregory. Missing the man; my friend, my life partner. Feeling so sad to be without him. Always in those sad moments my heart pleads for him to show me he's still here. To comfort me in the only way he can now. So I was watching a movie and the scene was in a classroom. On the bulletin board behind the group was a huge homemade Rainbow. The kid in the movie got up and went over to the board and had his back to us. Across his jacket was a big Rainbow! But wait, there's more! The kid turned to look out the window and there in front of him was a big Rainbow decal on the glass! Are you kidding me?

Next scene is in the auditorium, front row, a girl with a big jacket on, like a letterman jacket. Again, I kid you not, around each sleeve at the top where it attaches to the shoulder a Rainbow band that went clear around. Crazy! I just had to smile. Bombarded with Rainbows! *"Go ahead, hit me!"* Oh, and then it's been the word *Dream* in my face at the same time! Turned off the movie and what song plays? *Dream*. Then, I Can Dream About You. Now he makes me laugh. Dr. Hook, *Better Love Next Time*. It says that he can read me, that he sees my misery. But I won't die from this so I just need to pick my heart up and keep going. And that I'll find better love next time. I guess we'll see about that.

January 28, 2014

Gregory just blinked the light. "Good morning Baby." I was sad when I got up. I turned on the music channel to Whitney Huston's *Run To You*. It says that each day I try to pretend that I'm in control but at night when I come home to an empty house the whole thing seems pointless without someone to share my life with. That my tears are because I need him here and if he only knew how badly I want to run to him.

This song really made me think..... Gregory just turned out the light..... Long pause. Back on. *"Thank you Gregory."* I was about to write that the song made me realize I have no one to love me. Not only am I missing my guy to love and shower love upon but he's not here to love me either. I think that's what Gregory objected to when he turned off the light. He will always be here to love me. He loves me more now than he ever could in life. It makes me smile that he turned out the light. My electrical lineman!

This journey of mine is surreal. If it weren't for Gregory being right here with me every moment I could not be doing this. I miss him more now than I did a year ago. You know what I miss most? That daily contact. Kissing, hugging, laughing, sharing a meal. Holding hands, touching..... Ugh! *"Where's my Rainbow?"* Ha! As I was writing that the light flashed. Then I said, *"Feeling a little feisty this morning, are we?"* and the light flickered, flashed, and dimmed. I laughed out loud! This is so amazing! Interaction with my Gregory. It means everything to me.

"Bear patiently the cross of grief..." Those words appeared on the TV in the sidelines on the music channel. Bear. Patiently. The cross of grief. Oh, yes, it is a cross to bear. It will be two years without my Gregory here in the physical world. And my birthday is on Easter. *"Oh, funny Gregory."* I went to turn off the TV and was stopped. A Journey song was starting. *I'll Be Alright Without You.* I guess we're going to have to see about that.

January 30, 2014

Reach Out/I'll Be There, by the Four Tops, was my song first thing this morning. Love that song. The words are powerful. It talks about feeling like I can't go on, that I've lost all hope and that I don't know if I'll ever be happy again. But all I have to do is reach out and he'll be there, with a love that will protect me from the harshness of life and that no matter what, he's going to be here to see me through.

It was very comforting. Music has been such a healing part of my life these days and I would have stopped listening to music, I'm afraid, if it weren't for Gregory. Now I'm listening to music more than I ever have. I got a Rainbow in a song already this morning too. The song is called *Beautiful As You* by Jim Brickman. It talks about all the beautiful things in this world including a breathtaking Rainbow, but that nothing is as beautiful as you.

January 31, 2014

Last night I turned on the TV and there was a commercial for a sitcom. It ended with two guys standing there and one says to the other, *"Do you like Rainbows?"* The guy says, "Yes," and the first guy snaps his fingers and a big Rainbow appeared behind him. When I was watching a movie there was a fight scene with weapons; pieces of wood, whatever they could find to either defend from a hit or to hit someone. Every time their weapons hit each other—like in a sword fight—Rainbows would shoot off like sound waves echoing through the scene. I couldn't believe it. It was like a Rainbow light show! I just can't tell you what this does for my heart. *Rainbows!* It's divine!

I'm also excited about meeting someone new someday. It is such an exciting feeling. But then I'm always reminded of what I had with Gregory and I quickly return to my grief where I know I need to be for now. *Where I just am for now.* It does give me reason to believe I will make it through this and be better for it. I guess those glimpses into a healed life are signs of the healing itself. But I am too tied to Gregory just now and my heart is full of him. My life is full of him.

February 5, 2014

Oh that husband of mine. *"Very funny."* I sat down with my tea and Green Day's, *Trail of Broken Dreams*, came on. I found myself singing to the chorus about walking alone. I could feel deep inside that I never walk alone. Still, I chose—in a childish, stubborn moment—to indulge in the lyrics, thinking, *"I do walk alone. You're not here."* Just then a funky, hip-hoppity song came on. I started to mute it but something stopped me. *"This is you being a smart ass, Gregory, isn't it?"* The song is by Nine Days, and is called, *Absolutely (Story of a Girl)*. It talks about a girl—me—crying enough tears to drown the entire world.

It was such an upbeat song that I couldn't help but almost giggle at the words giving me crap for feeling sorry for myself. I was practically laughing out loud. Then I cried for a moment and smiled again. It was my Gregory's personality. It did everything for me this morning. OMG! Now he played *Wherever You Will Go*, by The Calling. It talks about wondering who's going to be there to take his place. That I'm going to need love in my life and wondering if I'm going to make it on my own. It talks about trying to find a way back to help me through the darkness and that he hopes that there's someone else out there for me. But no matter what, he's going to go with me wherever I go.

I cried all the way through it. Oh, this journey. I miss my man to hold me and to decide everything together. We had fun. We loved each other so much. *Still do.* So this is where life finds me and I must deal with it. Or cry an ocean and drown the entire world!

February 7, 2014

I've been sitting here staring into space for twenty minutes. Not really feeling a thing from Gregory. No music, nothing. I kept switching channels. Nothing. Haven't felt this disconnected since he died. I told him, *"C'mon honey, nothing to say to me this morning?"* And in that moment, Firefall's, *Just Remember I Love You*, came on and reminded me that even though it's still raining and my Rainbow's gone, all I have to do is remember he loves me and everything is going to be alright.

February 12, 2014

As soon as I sat down with my tea and turned on the TV a Maroon 5 song was playing called *She Will Be Loved*, and Adam Levine was saying, *Rainbows*, in the middle of a sentence where I didn't know it hid. It reminds me that life isn't always unicorns and Rainbows but that acceptance and compromise, is what keeps us moving forward. If I didn't have the songs and the Rainbows and Gregory right here with me I'd never be able to do this and he knows it.

February 13, 2014

Wow, that hubby of mine! *All Of Me*, by John Legend, came on just as I was melting into silent weeping. Sad, sad tears. Then this beautiful music began and he sang about us. And not just the part about one of us being crazy and the other out of their mind! Gregory used to say how he loved that I just gave him all of me. And he gave me all of him as well.

February 14, 2014

"Happy Valentine's Day, Gregory. My second now without you. I said it first, so I win." I couldn't help but go back to our last Valentine's together only the year before last. In that Hospital room with his message on the chalkboard to me for this day. He was here. He was clear headed, able to walk, joke with the doctors. I remember many times after I got to the hospital the nurse would come racing in to check his heart monitor which was going crazy. Gregory would just be smiling and wondering what all the fuss was about. After a while they would come in, see me, and say, *"Oh, it's just his wife..."* That feels pretty sweet to me. Two years ago today I had my Gregory. So far this morning he flashed the light and sent me two Rainbows.

February 19, 2014

This morning the song that spoke to me was Seal's, *Love's Divine*. When it talks about me needing love to know who I am I couldn't help but know how true that is. Being with Gregory, being in love like that, made everything in my world just right. It sent me back to a time in my life where love was the most prominent thing. Without that I'm not sure who I am.

Last night I finished watching something on TV and had a strong urge to pick up the remote as I heard, *"Put it on channel 921 to get your Rainbow."* I did, and Phil Collins', True Colors was just starting. My mind was thinking, *"Well, the song is True **Colors**. It's close to a Rainbow, but since the music channel just plays music—not videos—where am I going to get my Rainbow?"* Just then I heard my Rainbow. It just makes me smile. Gregory interacting with me and saying, *"Go here and I'll give you a Rainbow."* And then he does!

February 21, 2014

Wow. My morning started with not wanting to get out of bed which is unusual really. I sat down with my tea and started crying. The songs playing were all about missing you, or can't go on without you, to I walk alone, which I heard as I sat down. I cried to Gregory—as I often do—saying, *"I miss you, Honey."* This morning as I wept I asked him, *"How am I going to ever stop missing you? How?"* Next song? *Let Me Go*, by 3 Doors Down. *"No."*

I felt myself start to go to that scary numb. The words tried to break through my consciousness making me realize it is something I may have to do someday. *"But not today,"* my whole being seemed to scream, *"Not today."* So I'm not ready yet and that's okay. As the song rang out, *"Let me go,"* I stared at his smiling face beside me and just as the words were touching me in that way they do when I know they are from him his picture did a little tilt—like a nod to me—then went back to still. I stared at it. Goosebumps. No denying that just happened.

I listened to the beautiful song and my heart felt stunned at the notion of letting go. Wow. My honey has never told me to let him go before. The idea is too scary for me right now even as I know that it will happen eventually. But I need him with me in whatever way he can be now. I can't hear the words, *Let me go.* At least not yet.

February 23, 2014

Oh will I ever stop breaking down in sad sobs? Ever since the song, *Let Me Go*, I have been aware of what it means for me to hold onto him. He is here with me. I feel him. I hear him. I talk to him. I cry to him. I cannot let go of that. It almost makes me angry that I should have to. Then I heard Gregory say, *"Okay, okay, you don't have to until you are ready,"* and I said, *"You're damn right I don't have to!"* It makes me feel like I can't breathe, like I can't live without that powerful lifeline I feel all around me.

I still need him. I miss him enough as it is. I cry many, many tears missing him. Missing us. The threat of letting go of any more of him is unbearable at this point. Even as I know it's going to be a part of my grieving process. Then I got Fleetwood Mac's, *As long As You Follow*. I love that song. I didn't realize it had a Rainbow in it. Are you kidding me? Yep, it talks about searching for a pot of gold at the end of the Rainbow.

Then I got the Backstreet Boys' beautiful song, *Incomplete*. And that's how I feel without him. I could relate when it talked about feeling like the world is half asleep but I'm still awake. Like I'm out of synch with my surroundings. Like swimming in a big ole ocean all by myself. Society telling me to move on when I don't know how to do that. Praying for my heart not to be broken. For now that's how I feel.

February 25, 2014

This morning was rough. As soon as I sat down with my tea I broke down into sobs. I cried out, *"Help me, Honey. A Rainbow? Anything?"* With that I looked up to the muted TV just as, *Come To Me*, by Goo Goo Dolls, was starting. A direct and immediate response from him. He says to come to him, feel his heart again, and that he'll love me even more so I don't have to be afraid. And then when this whole thing is over we'll go home and start over. I like that idea.

And after that I got, *Send Her My Love*, by Journey. My baby talks to me and tells me exactly what only he could say in that moment to soothe my aching heart and help me breathe into my life again. I would not be listening to music at all right now let alone all the time if it weren't for Gregory. He took his last breath and jumped right into my heart and with a song he reassured me that our love is endless and that we share one heart now.

Chapter 14

Comforted In My Sadness

February 27, 2014

On my way to Mama's yesterday I couldn't help but notice one of those crazy Rainbows in the clouds that I saw a couple of months ago. This time it was bigger and was like a sideways arc. Then I noticed it was like parenthesis on either side of the sun! Just then *Beautiful As You,* came on the radio and he reminded that he thinks I'm even more beautiful than a gorgeous sunset or a breathtaking Rainbow.

This morning as I sat down with my tea, *Better In Time*, by Leona Lewis, was just starting. I cried through the whole thing. It is clearly written by someone who lost their love. It talks about thinking I wouldn't be able to live without him now that there's no longer the two of us, so it's time to let him go so I'll be free. I'm not so sure about that. As soon as the song was over I cried when I saw the next song. *Second Chance* by Shinedown. It says that sometimes saying goodbye gives us a second chance at life.

I sat in stunned silence, the tears that rolled down my cheeks during the first song were gone now. I felt so much love and peace in my heart as I listened to the words. I cried a lot yesterday. Breakdown, sob, miss Gregory unbearably, go on. Have a thought of something else; a flash of memory, and breakdown, sob, miss Gregory unbearably, go on.

The moments in between the meltdowns are changing. I feel stronger in them. Sadder in the sad moments but stronger in the other ones. As if *all* the sadness has drained into those sad crying moments, making them more sad while leaving the in-between times for nothing but hope, faith, trust, and love. Flashes of a future that shines brighter.

Oh, my. As I sat here silently crying I found my right hand going on top of my left hand with a reassuring rub like you would do to comfort a friend. I felt the right hand was not my own. I could feel it tingling into my left hand. I could feel the love pouring out. It was not mine in that moment. I could feel Gregory's hand and I've never experienced anything like it.

March 2, 2014

From where I sit I see Gregory's last healthy picture beside me. I'm also in perfect eyesight of our wedding picture on the wall. I find my eye goes from photo to photo, feeling as though the progression of years between the two went just about as fast as my eye can travel from one to the other. I mourn the loss of those years with all their precious memories. But I'm healing.

When I was ready to go to bed I kept feeling the nudge to turn on the TV. I did and there it was. A Skittles commercial. A kid is showing all the skittles in his mouth when the Jr. High girl of his dreams walks up and says hi. He smiles a Skittles-filled smile. All the colors of the Rainbow. She grabs his face with both hands and lays a big kiss on him and sucks his Rainbow smile into hers. Then it says, *"Kiss the Rainbow!"* I grabbed Gregory's picture and kissed him.

March 3, 2014

I turned on the weather channel just in time to hear, *"It's a Rainbow of fruit flavors,"* describing a colorful mess of weather. Love it! To have the *word* Rainbow have as much of an impact on me as an actual one—whether in the sky or in a magazine—just makes me smile. The child's framed drawing of a Rainbow sitting in my dining room where it speaks to me every time I walk by, was originally a gift from Kaylee to Papa Greg. It is a gift to me now.

March 6, 2014

The reading was powerful this morning and seems to describe perfectly how I've been feeling. How my sad moments seem sadder than ever before while the in-between moments are better. It's like living in the dark with occasional glimpses of light and then suddenly the light seems brighter and happy times are a welcome change. And then it seems we are returned to our sadness with a force that takes our breath away.

How perfect the description of what I'd just recently experienced as my grief shifted. She describes the relief of being able to engage in life again, feeling free at last from the constant sadness, only to remember, and like falling through a trapdoor, the return is much more unsettling than when grief was our constant companion. So once more I am reassured that my train is right on time. That my journey through losing Gregory is an authentic honoring of the love we share.

March 13, 2014

I cried a lot yesterday and told Gregory I can't do this without him. He said, *"You're doing it."* I knew he was going to say that! But I felt useless and worried it would always be this way. Then Firefall's, *Just Remember I Love You*, came on. I cried all the way through it. Life. Feels like too much some days. Lately for sure. Now I got the Eagle's, *Love Will Keep Us Alive*. This is one of my top favorite songs of all time. So I live another day.

March 15, 2014

My reading gives me so much hope today. It says that as we start to feel better and the grief isn't as heavy, those irretrievable memories begin to fill in the empty spaces in our hearts and we will feel like we have found a long lost treasure, even more precious because they were missing for a time. Those precious memories feel almost lost to me. When one would pop in my mind it made me cry, especially early on. But I'm beginning to get glimpses of a precious memory here and there that warms my heart clear to my soul. To hear that the empty spaces will begin to fill in again makes me really excited.

Maybe then I will dream of him. I cried heartfelt tears at bedtime last night and still no dream. He's here, I know that for sure. He sent me three Rainbows just as I was turning off the TV. He knows how much it helps. Otherwise I don't think I could make it. After the Rainbows I got, *Here Without You*, and it helped. It's a beautiful song and reminds me of how powerful the Blues are. Somehow in the heartache singing the Blues seems to help.

March 26, 2014

I was driving home and turned on the radio just as the song that Gregory had for a ringtone on his cellphone came on. It's an Ozzie Osborn song and it is so distinct that when I heard it my heart sank. I immediately began to cry. In an instant I was right back to a time when Gregory was here and his phone was ringing. I sobbed all the way home. It still hits me, just remembering the sound.

March 28, 2014

I'm a little more emotional as we approach the two year mark for Gregory. My grief is deeper, sadder if you can imagine. Missing him like I'd miss half of my soul. I know this is part of my grieving process. I know it is honoring the beautiful thing we had. If I am destined to endure such a loss as this I'm all about getting out of my own way and letting my life unfold as each day comes. No plan, no agenda, just feel my way through one day at a time. It's also what is giving me such hope for a future that is stronger in the broken places. A life filled with so much joy after a period of so much loss.

April 4, 2014

OMG! This is just incredible. Freaky actually. I'm helping a friend with her meds and she called me first thing in the morning to say she was sick so could I put them in the mailbox and a friend would pick them up. I was headed upstairs so I grabbed the two pills to put in the mailbox, my purse, my toast—eating as I went— and started to leave the kitchen. I looked down and saw hungry cats staring at me. I put down my purse and toast on the stove and put the two pills on the counter next to the stove while I fed the cats.

When I finished I grabbed my purse and went upstairs. I propped up in the bedroom with my journal to write when I remembered I had forgotten to put the meds in the mailbox. I hurried down but when I got to the kitchen the pills were gone. *"Okay, ding-dong, what did you do with them?"* So now I'm retracing my steps and trying to remember if I picked them up even though I was sure I hadn't. My last conscious memory of those pills was as I laid them on the counter.

I checked the floor, the garbage—which is right next to that cupboard—and everywhere in between. I searched every corner of every surface in this entire house. I worried that if I'd dropped them the cats might get them. I crawled through my house on hands and knees searching. I searched cupboards and places they couldn't possibly be. I searched all the trash cans. I searched rooms I hadn't been in. I gave it up, grabbed two more pills from her prescription bottle and put them in the mailbox. Still, I wanted to resolve the mystery of the two missing pills. I had to know what happened to them.

I searched every conceivable place and then some. I was baffled. Throughout the day and during the search I did have the fleeting and unlikely thought, *"Watch them show up in some obvious place in plain view,"* but then dismissed the thought altogether. I finally decided the only thing that I could have possibly done was drop them in the sink but even then I felt there would be residual evidence of that. I had to let it go. Chalk it up to an unsolved mystery and be done with it. Still, it haunted me.

About 4 p.m. I was hungry so I headed to the kitchen and made a salad, cutting up the vegetables on the cutting board next to the sink, then returned upstairs. About 5–5:30 p.m. I brought my plate down and stopped dead in my tracks when I entered the kitchen. There on the cutting board were the two missing pills, touching end-to-end, balanced on their sides....

O... M... G... I even said that out loud, as I began to cry. *"Now you're freaking me out, Dude!"* A crazy numb washed over me as tears filled my eyes and I was genuinely freaked out. Chills rushed through my whole body and I stood frozen in my kitchen—more than a little unnerved—yet so amazed at the whole thing. How? Why? Who?

Of course it was Gregory, right? I felt overwhelmed and afraid. Truly. Feeling scared, I squeaked out, *"Is that you, Honey?"* Because if it wasn't, I was going to be beyond freaked out. I had movies to take back so I put on my boots and coat and got in the car. As soon as I turned on the radio, *Lotta Love* was just beginning. It's him. Of course it's him. But I must say this hit me as hard as the photo album with Dad. The pills were missing for about six hours. Then returned to a place I had just made a salad. I love that sh-t! Even if it freaks me out!

April 6, 2014

My tears and grief seem worse lately. Sadder if that's possible. Still, it's not a hole I fall into. It isn't scary grief where I think I can't breathe. It's just sadness beyond comprehension, tears flowing in amounts thought impossible. A feeling of yearning *and* great connection. It's bizarre. The more I grieve the closer he is. Just as I wrote that last sentence I looked up to the muted TV to see my Rainbow. I love that Gregory does that. Truly amazing. Last night at bedtime I got Firefall's, *Just Remember I Love You*, and cried all the way through it. Oh, those lyrics get me every time. It's still raining but my Rainbow's gone.

April 9, 2014

I turned on the TV and got Nickelback's *Far Away* and cried all the way through it. He's been too far away for too long and I miss him. Dreaming that he'll always be with me and never go away. Says that I might stop breathing if I never see him again. That's how I feel sometimes.

April 10, 2014

When I turned on the music channel it was *Wherever You Will Go*, and the part that really struck me was when it talks about hoping that someone out there can bring my Gregory back to me. In other words, perhaps there's another perfect guy for me. Immediately following was Carrie Underwood's, *I Will See You Again*. It reminds me that this is not the end. We will see each other again. Today that helps me.

April 15, 2014

I no longer know what the future holds. With Gregory gone I don't know anything anymore. I was surprised by my reading this morning although I shouldn't have been. It says that suffering breaks us. Like a tree that's been struck by lightning and is forever damaged, left to wonder if we can survive. But then further reassurance when she says there is no need to hurry. That life is going to unfold whether we're prepared or not. And that much of it will be a mystery. The end of the reading talks about that being part of the journey and the excitement because we don't know all that we can become. And so I do my life in spite of feeling as though half of me died with Gregory.

Chapter 15

Beautiful

—

April 19, 2014

I felt sad and heavy when I sat down this morning. Gregory died two years ago today. 730 days without my love. I wanted and needed him to speak to me but when I looked up at the muted TV to see *Beautiful*, by James Blunt, I sort of silently argued that this wasn't the song or the message I was looking for. When the very next song was *Beautiful In My Eyes*, by Joshua Kadison, I was like, *"Okay, honey, I get it. Thank you, Babe."* Then, almost out of my conscious control, I reached for the remote and unmuted it just in time to hear my Rainbow and I couldn't believe it. Yep, he tells me I'm the Rainbow in his skies.

These are personal little miracles to me. When I got in the car I was crying. I turned on the radio and it was *All Of Me*, right at the part that says I'm even beautiful when I'm crying. Are you kidding me right now? Gregory didn't tell me I was beautiful very often when he was alive, so it always meant so much to me when he did. The very next song was *Beautiful As You* and I couldn't believe it! Then the Rainbow chorus! *"Okay, okay, I get it!"* If I continue to have interactions like this with my Gregory I will be okay.

April 20, 2014

I have seen the number *420* flashed at me four or five times already this morning and I just got a Rainbow. It wasn't until I sat down here that I remembered it's my birthday. I feel disconnected from it now. It feels like it's *just* the day after my husband died. This year is Easter and I find myself wanting to let it be just Easter. Let's skip over my birthday thank you very much. Just now I heard, *"Look up,"* and got yet another song titled *Beautiful*, this one by Christina Aguilera. Who knew there were so many songs called *Beautiful*?! This is unbelievable.

April 28, 2014

This morning I feel... quiet, cautious, unsure. *Unmotivated.* In this moment I feel like I don't want to do my life. Songs that take me back to a time long ago—happy times—make me sad. Like now, Pablo Cruise's, *Love Will Find A Way*. 1978. The year I graduated High School. My whole life ahead of me. And then I got *Endless Love*. *"Thank you, Honey, I needed that."* Followed by the beautiful, *You Are Loved (Don't Give Up)*, by Josh Grobin. I know I will be joyously happy again someday. But I miss my life with Gregory.

May 4, 2014

Holy cow! Yesterday I was carrying yard stuff out of the basement and had my arms full, so with one finger I pulled the door hard so it would slam shut behind me. It immediately bounced off something making a "boink" noise and I looked back to see a broom lying on the floor with the handle in the doorway. I continued on and then went back to close up the basement. When I got back the basement door was shut. I thought, *"What the heck?"* I opened it and the broom was leaned up against the cabinet. I could feel it was my father this time. It was very cool. *"Thanks, Pop."*

May 5, 2014

I woke up just before 5 a.m. to the sound of the back door opening. My heart leapt as I acknowledged, *"Gregory's home."* Then I realized it was a dream and it was like years ago when he was out on storm work and was coming home late. I would always get so excited hearing him come in. I laid there for a moment in the feeling. It felt so real. When I came downstairs and turned on the music I was greeted immediately with, *Good Morning Beautiful*, by Luke McMaster and Jim Brickman. It made me smile. It's such a snappy tune you can't help but feel good. I needed it. Both Saturday and Sunday Gregory sent me lots of Rainbows! He showered me with them actually. Every time I turned on the TV there were Rainbows.

May 6, 2014

Woohoo! Yesterday I had an amazing session with Reiki and at the end Gregory held my feet again! That makes three times he's done that! This time she didn't have me turn on my stomach where he would hold the bottoms of my feet so yesterday he held the tops! Held on too after she was done. She said she felt such an amazing connection during the session. With my eyes still closed I told her, *"He's holding my feet right now,"* and then he gently released his grip and let go. So amazing. I always ask him to join me there and Angela said she always does too. Incredible.

I sob when I see myself moving on. It's so bittersweet. I know there's someone out there for me but I can't let go of Gregory just yet. Not even a little. I never have to let him go but I know there will come a time when I can move my Gregory-filled heart over just enough to make room for someone new. Until then my heart and life are still all about him and I will milk this love affair for everything it's got.

May 9, 2014

I felt a change this morning. I danced to a song and my body feels good. I had a true glimpse into my life. Strong, healthy body.

Strong, healthy spirit. Coming into my own. In that lighthearted moment I felt a change in how I sense and feel Gregory. And it is so good. I burst out smiling. I'm reminded of the Scripture, *"Blessed are those who mourn for they shall be comforted."* I know it's true and it has been for two years now. I am surrounded by love. So much love it overpowers my grief.

May 20, 2014

I have not been feeling well and I'm having to push myself to do everything. I mowed the back lawn but by the time I got to the side yard I was struggling big time. As I was mowing the front a stone caught my eye and I picked it up. One of the things Gregory used to do when he was being goofy is stick his tongue out to the side and make a face. I looked at the small stone. It had that face drawn on it. I kid you not! It was from him I knew. I could feel him when I picked it up. It had a little beard drawn on it.

Another thing he used to say is, *"Who loves you baby?"* I didn't feel well when I came inside after mowing the lawn so I laid down and turned on the TV. *Who Loves You*, by Frankie Valli and The Four Seasons was just starting. It made me smile. I have cried more and felt so sad over the past few weeks while I haven't felt well. Feeling sorry for myself I guess because I'm sick and alone. But I do feel a bit better after these signs from him.

May 22, 2014

I got the results of my bloodwork and tests from my doctor appointment the other day and she said everything looks great! My heart sank. I don't want anything to be wrong but clearly something is. It's disheartening when you don't get answers. I made an appointment with my Kinesiologist and it showed that my liver is not working properly and that's why I feel so bad. I walked out of there with answers and supplements in hand. I had a better night.

In an Epsom salts bath last night I was thinking about my liver and remembering when I was only twenty-two years old, bloodwork showed that my liver enzymes were off the charts. When I asked what those crazy numbers were I remember old Nurse Johnnie saying, *"It means your liver is damaging and you need to stop drinking!"* I remember scoffing at the idea. I was so young. I ignored that advice and went on to drink heavily—and feel sick—for another twelve years. It was only after I'd been sober for a couple of years that I remembered all of that. I wonder if all my years of drinking ruined my liver?!

Then I started thinking about Gregory and it made me sad. I wondered when my grief will lessen so I can remember more happy times with him. Just then I had a memory of him sitting out on the front porch teasing one of the kids next door and making all of us laugh. The kid was locked out of the house and was banging on the door. Greg said, *"Wait 'til you're 18, they'll lock you out for good."* As if in direct response to what I was thinking he gave me a happy memory. I thanked him.

When I got out of the tub I turned on the music channel just in time to hear my Rainbow in *Beautiful As You*. I could feel Gregory's presence so strong. Those are precious moments for me. That's when everything is okay. Gregory is right here with me, loving me and telling me he thinks I'm beautiful. Perhaps as time goes on and I feel him ever closer I will feel complete again. My heart stronger for having been broken.

May 23, 2014

I dreamed I was in a car and the grandkids were in the back-seat. Cameron leaned forward and wiggled his fingers to give me 'the weasel,' which is something Greg and I always did with each other. I got so excited as I connected my fingers to Cam's and said, "Papa always did that!" I woke up smiling. I think it was his way of letting me know that he lives on through the kids.

May 24, 2014

I just finished a sobbing meltdown, crying to Gregory about how he's a hard one to get over. *Just The Two Of Us*, by Bill Withers and Grover Washington Jr., started. I know the song but I couldn't believe it when I heard the Rainbow. In these moments I can feel Gregory so close I can all but see him. At bedtime I reached for the remote to turn off the TV but instead felt that strong urge to put on the music channel. Just starting was, *True Colors*. I smiled all the way through it. Lots of Rainbows in that song! *Love you, Honey*. The song was followed by, *Good Morning Beautiful*, which I enjoyed before I turned off everything and went to sleep.

May 29, 2014

Last night I was watching a movie and had an amazing showering of Rainbows. It was a pretend board meeting where basically it was showing how bizarre it would be to try to pitch the idea of Noah's Ark for a movie. He's pitching the idea and gets to the part after the storm and the ark doors open up and there's a big Rainbow. Then it got hilarious. The board members took off on the Rainbow idea and it went nuts. One idea after the other.

We could have a giant Rainbow, children everywhere will paint a Rainbow on their wall. Everyone will want to know, where does the Rainbow come from? And on it went for several minutes. I was laughing out loud, honestly. Rainbow this, Rainbow that. It was so funny. I could feel Gregory's presence so strong in the room I was in awe as I laughed like I haven't laughed since he died.

June 1, 2014

I love hearing the sound of my chimes on the front porch on a quiet, yet breezy early morning. When I finished writing yesterday I was crying. They were bittersweet tears. Sadness for a life left to memory now combined with knowing Gregory is right here with me as I cautiously and somewhat reluctantly move forward with hope in this wounded heart. I went to the window to open the curtains and let the morning light flood this beautiful living room.

Just now I thought about our road trips with the book when *Recovering From Life* first came out. Those were fun and exciting times. Spending so much time alone with Gregory in the car, in the restaurants, in the motel rooms. Everything. So many conversations. So much love and excitement. It is a time I buried after things did not go as planned and the book was not the financial success I'd hoped it would be. In fact, it cost us way more than Gregory would have ever agreed to—or supported—so it was a struggle at times to justify continuing my work over the next several years.

In the end he surrendered to the fact I was going to do what I was going to do and we continued on having come to an unwritten truce. But I never want to forget how supportive he was with both books and how no one wanted success for me more than he did. That is the truth of it. He was tough on me when I needed it, even as I stubbornly stood my ground. I miss him.

When I have grown accustomed to being here without him in the physical I will rejoice in where he gets to be while still being here with me and sending me..... I just heard in my mind, *"Incoming!"* and looked up to see *Beautiful As You*, playing on the music channel. He's here with me and sending me Rainbows! Last night it was in a movie when I turned on the TV. A beautiful Rainbow in the sky as a couple walked along beside it. A big ole' Rainbow. Just for me. From my love. Blessed in my grief.

Earlier I was watching Oprah with Maya Angelo. Oprah was sharing that when she was going through a particularly desperate moment, Maya said, *"Oh, God has a Rainbow in your clouds!"* Not only did I get my Rainbow I was gifted with the message to thank God for your difficulty, your tears, your despair, because there's a blessing in there. A great lesson or benefit. A Rainbow in those clouds.

June 7, 2014

Today is Greg's mom's birthday and I took her some flowers out of Gregory's garden. It felt really good to see her and hug her and wish her Happy Birthday. Even though I had to tell her it was her birthday five or six times. Always with the same response, *"Whose birthday? My birthday?"* God love her. At any rate I felt better having visited her on her 85th birthday.

I've actually been laughing to tears lately for the first time since Gregory died. He always made me laugh to tears. Yesterday after the soccer game the kids told me they were going to watch Goonies that night and I said, *"That was Papa Greg's favorite movie of all time!"* They were excited. Just now Megan texted me that it was awesome but a little inappropriate in some parts! She said, *"I love the part with the naked statue and they glue on the penis upside down and the guy says if God made us all like that we'd be pissing in our face!"* I laughed and laughed as the tears rolled down my cheeks.

June 11, 2014

As I sat here writing, feeling good about my morning, I looked at Gregory's smiling face beside me and *knew* I was going to get a song and that there would be no doubt it was from him. I looked up to the muted TV and *Heard It Through The Grapevine* was just starting. Woohoo! Big smile! That's it! The song that always takes me right back to our wedding reception and I burst out smiling. Out on the dance floor in my wedding dress, dancing so happy and in love with the man I just married, looking ever so handsome in his mauve tuxedo. What a fun day. *"Thank you, Baby, for taking me back there."*

And then I felt the grief hit me. I cried as I told him I wanted him to be here. He said, *"I am here."* "I know," I cried, *"But I wanted to pay you back. For all the years you supported me. For everything."* I waited. Nothing. *"I can't hear you, honey."* I began to sob. *"Talk to me."* Then I heard him. He said, *"Do it for the kids and the grandkids. It will be from both of us and that will be your gift to me."* I am empowered by this journey through grief. Something is changing in me. I'm feeling excited about my life and the possibilities that lie ahead.

Chapter 16

Trusting The Process

June 17, 2014

Whew, I had a moment of terrifying grief and was freaked out for a minute. It was Gloria Estevan's song, *I See Your Smile.* It kills me when it talks about seeing his smile when I close my eyes and how it shines a light in my darkest moments. I really miss that smile. Scary grief. I can't take it. I cried out to him, *"I need a sign, Gregory. Right now."* I turned up the volume on the music channel just as Firefall was beginning. *Just Remember I Love You.* The part that stood out, besides *just remember I love you*, is at the end where it repeats that everything is going to be alright. I know it's true but it helps to hear it. I still cry at some point every day but haven't felt panicked but a handful of times since he died.

June 18, 2014

Last night I was ready for lights out, Gregory and the day still heavy on my mind and heart. His songs help so much and I always get my Rainbows. I held his picture to my heart. The 5x7 lands between my breasts. I heard Gregory say, *"Over..."* Are you kidding me? It was so him and exactly what I needed in that moment. It made me laugh. The TV was on, turned low, until it almost shouted, *"There's a Rainbow in you!"* and I looked up to see splashes of brilliant colors on a paint commercial.

In case I don't write every day that he sends me Rainbows doesn't mean he didn't. I get Rainbows every single day. I just glanced at the muted TV and *Just The Two Of Us* is playing. I heard a gentle, *"Turn on the sound,"* and when I did I heard my Rainbow. *"Thanks Babe! Oh, funny, Gregory."* Next song? Daughtry's *Life After You*. The words that rang out were about just wanting life to be full of laughter. Gregory always made me laugh and he still does.

June 20, 2014

Wow! I sat down to write and turned on the TV just as David Cook's, *Time Of My Life*, was starting. I was about to mute it when I heard, *"Leave it."* As a gentle shiver ran through me, I settled in for what I would hear and couldn't have been happier when I heard *Rainbow*. But then it talked about looking for that Rainbow that I couldn't see until I let go and holding onto things that are no longer here. Dang.

I was sitting here trying not to feel sorry for myself because I don't feel well. Not wanting to cry but crying. Telling Gregory I haven't had a day since he died that I've felt well, no pain, nothing hurting. That's when I got my Rainbow. Isn't that amazing? What a thing to be my sign and gift from him. Just even what the Rainbow means. A promise that things are going to be alright. But right now I'm feeling pitiful. Just got *True Colors!* Phil Collins. I listened to the words. Tears rolled down my face as the song addressed me as the one with those sad eyes.

July 1, 2014

Gregory spoke to me right off the bat this morning when *Lotta Love* came on first song. Then *Endless Love*. Followed by *Two Hearts* by Phil Collins and another reminder that our two hearts are beating as one now.

July 2, 2014

I had a strange thing happen that I can't explain. I came down last evening to get Gracie in for the night. She wanted no part of it. Several attempts later I left her out and walked over to Greg's mom's to check the self-clean oven I'd turned on hours earlier and to close all the windows. When I came back Gracie was nowhere to be seen. When I got inside she was sitting on the stairs looking at me. *"How did you get in?"* I said with a quiver in my voice. *"Did Dad let you in?"* The house was locked. I live here alone. No explanation.

July 3, 2014

This is a powerful morning. It started with turning on the music channel just in time to hear the word Rainbow in a song. But more than that is how I feel my grief changing. My tears are mixed with joy and gratitude and awe. They have lost some of their sadness. As the vision of my life continues to play with more detail I cried to Gregory saying I didn't want him to just be the guy that brought me to this point. I wanted him to be *with* me, by my side.

In that moment his energy went from out in front of me—where I normally feel him—to, in a flash, right by my side, pulling me tight as I heard him say, *"I am here, by your side,"* and with that I melted into sobs. Joyful, amazed sobs mixed with grief and so much hope for the future. Feeling alive again. Feeling Gregory's playful, energetic spirit within me.

July 4, 2014

This morning, as I heated my tea, I wept deep, heartfelt, silent sobs. It felt like this beautiful mixture of sadness, acceptance, and immense gratitude for my life with Gregory, before, and since, he died. A new level or stage of my grief. The change—*the shift*—is palatable. I feel Gregory even closer, his spirit so bright and full of life and love for me. My memories flood back over 30 years and all the fun we had.

July 11, 2014

I just got my Rainbows! The kind that take your breath away! I wanted to hear *that* song this morning and sang the chorus to the TV just a few minutes ago. And then it came on! I cried all the way through it.

July 12, 2014

Gregory has sent me two Rainbows since I started writing here. Earlier I was watching a show and a woman was wearing a pajama top that had Rainbows wrapped around each sleeve! Are you kidding me? I just got another Rainbow, then another before I could write about the first one! Good thing because I'm so tearful here this morning, so sad without him. And I cry for me. I cry for the loss of my best friend, my lover, my companion and life partner. I feel sorry for the young, 54-year-old woman who had it all and is alone now. Gregory being here always made whatever I was going through okay. And just now I heard him say, *"I'm still here."*

July 18, 2014

I've been crying already this morning. Missing Gregory so much my heart aches. Then I turned on the music channel just as *Second Chance* was starting and I cried new tears, bittersweet tears at the idea that sometimes you have to say goodbye to the past in order to get a second chance. I know it's true. I have beautiful pink roses next to me from my Gregory's garden. They remind me of when he was alive. He would often cut roses and I'd be in the kitchen and he'd come in with his hands behind his back. Or I'd just find them in a vase on the kitchen counter. He always loved to give me flowers and I always loved getting them.

July 19, 2014

I watched a movie last night where a woman was getting her life back on track after losing everything—including her daughter—due to her alcoholism. The movie ended with her showing her daughter her bedroom at Mommy's new house. When she opened the door to a beautiful room my eyes were drawn to the big Rainbow above her bed and I sort of gasped in excitement. *"There's my Rainbow!"* Then the little girl said, *"It's a Rainbow! I have a Rainbow room at Daddy's!"* To which the mom said, *"Well now you have a Rainbow room here too."* The little girl saw the fishbowl on the desk and she yelled, *"Goldfish!"* and ran over to it. She said, *"I'm going to name you Rainbow,"* and the movie ended.

July 29, 2014

The cable was out last night and after about 45 minutes on the phone with the cable company they couldn't find the problem and said they could send someone out the next day. I really wanted to watch TV and then I heard Gregory say, *"You hit the plug in the basement when you moved the dehumidifier."* *"I did?"* I had, in fact, moved the dehumidifier earlier so I ran downstairs to check. Sure enough it was unplugged! *"Thank you, Baby!"* Cancel service call.

July 30, 2014

Wow.... I just had an amazing thing happen. I still haven't felt well and I have to drag myself out of bed. I sat down and turned on the music. *Crazy* was just starting. There are a handful of songs that make me get up and dance no matter how I'm feeling and *Crazy* is one of those. I got up and started moving this tired old body. I felt a cool chill all through me and the hairs on my arms stood straight up. I felt like my whole aura was cool and a bit electric. I have never been so engulfed in a feeling so physical yet so spiritual, so surreal.

I danced and moved from a place where I can see our wedding picture. That's the one that draws me in and connects me to the healthy young man that I know he is again. But it made me cry. I got sad and my dance changed. I lost my connection and the feeling all around me and through me was gone. In my mind I cried out to him to come back and felt myself re-connecting to the soulful movements. There it was once again, enveloping me and permeating my entire being with a cool vibration. I felt like Gregory had his whole being wrapped around me, hugging me. Reassuring me, is what he was doing.

Then, *My Immortal*, by Evanescence, came on. Hauntingly beautiful song about living without the one who was always there. About trying to accept the fact that he's gone but feeling like sometimes the pain is too real. And that even though he's still here I'm alone. Such powerful words that had me mesmerized.

Last night I was getting ready to watch a movie. I came downstairs and on my way to the kitchen I thought, *"Hey, I haven't got my Rainbow today,"* to which I heard Gregory playfully say, *"Well maybe you're going to get it in the movie you're about to watch."* I knew in that moment I would. The movie goes along and there's a scene in the common area of the children's wing in a hospital. BIG Rainbow all across one wall. And there it is! Then I noticed down on the right side another smaller Rainbow. Take that.

August 6, 2014

Whoa... Last night at 5:47 p.m. the phone rang. I was watching TV and caller ID shows on the screen. It said, *Gregory R. Hunt*, and our home phone number. Um..... I looked to the telephone ringing next to me. It says, *Hunt, Gregory R.*, and our number. How is that even possible? I was freaked out as I picked it up and hesitantly said, *"Hello?"* No one there. Well, not that I could hear. Tears rolled down my face. I had goosebumps. My baby just called me on the telephone! I keep looking at the caller ID even now. I can't believe it. Later I tried calling myself from this number and you can't do it, you just get the busy signal! *Freaky*. In a good way. OMG....

August 12, 2014

I turned on the music on my way to the kitchen this morning and, *Who Says You Can't Go Home*, was just starting. It's a song by Jon Bon Jovi and Jennifer Nettles that I hadn't heard before and I had to laugh when I heard the part about kidnapping a Rainbow and then smashing into a pot of gold.

August 14, 2014

I sat down and turned on the music just as *Crazy* was beginning and I felt Gregory pull me up to dance with him! It's indescribable how I can feel him inside and out. A cool/heat vibration and chills all through my body! The air around me electrically charged. Hair standing straight up, goosebumps everywhere. I love it! *"Thank you, Baby!"*

Chapter 17

Lonely But Never Alone

―

September 1, 2014

Today I'm trying not to be sad knowing we would be waking up in either Mackinaw City or St. Ignace. Eat breakfast and catch the first ferry to the Island for a fun-filled, romance-filled week. Boohoohoo! Remembering lots of years and memories there.

September 14, 2014

Rough weekend. Have not felt well at all. Liver not working properly and making me feel like I have a hangover. Felt scary sad this morning and have cried sad, sad tears missing Gregory. He sent me Rainbows all weekend. One time I was just staring at the colorful commercial and could feel his strong presence. I knew my Rainbow was coming. Smile on my face and boom! Rainbow across the screen! I laughed out loud.

September 29, 2014

I just got my Rainbow! I was sitting here thinking about Gregory and when I looked up there it was. And then? *Endless Love!* And now?! *True Colors!* OMG! *"Thanks, Babe! Bombard me with Rainbows, why don't you?"* Yesterday I was standing at the counter making lunch. Gregory's picture, notes and cards to me, are on the side of the fridge behind me. I had the music on and heard, *"There's a Rainbow over your shoulder..."* I looked over my shoulder and there's my Rainbow! Gregory's smiling face!

October 3, 2014

I woke up at 4:30 a.m. and said, *"Happy Anniversary, Baby."* When I sat down and turned on the music channel Journey's, *Send Her My Love*, was just starting. After that was, *Heard It Through The Grapevine*! *"Happy Anniversary!"* I got up and danced! No other song could Gregory have played on our anniversary than the one that takes me right back to our wedding day.

"Thanks, Babe! I miss you."

October 5, 2014

I dreamed about Gregory and my dad! *I was walking hand in hand with Gregory and I just kept staring at him. He looked so handsome, full dark beard, beautiful. Then we walked into Mama's. I saw my dad across the room and he looked so handsome! I hurried toward him and wrapped my arms around him.* Then I woke up! Woohoo! Finally! It feels like I haven't remembered a dream in a year.

October 9, 2014

My song from Gregory this morning took be aback for a second. Only because I wasn't expecting it. *Dare You To Move*, by Switchfoot. Hmm. The message—the feel of it—was clear. My husband is challenging me to move. Physically. On with my life. On with my work. Toward the vision. Pull yourself up and get moving!

October 13, 2014

I sobbed again yesterday. Deep, hard, sad crying for what I've lost. But, I had the mattress pad folded on the couch after washing it and was headed to the basement when I noticed a bright

Rainbow across it. Not just a Rainbow but two! And they were wavy…. no kidding. Alive with colors in movement. I searched for the source and couldn't find it! I have never seen anything like it. I watched it dance for quite a while. It was amazing!

October 17, 2014

I've had my tears this morning. As soon as I turned on the music I got *I Miss You*, by Klymaxx. Beautiful song. It talks about thinking I heard his voice and turning to say I love you only to realize that my mind was just playing tricks on me.

October 22, 2014

First thing this morning when I turned on the music I got *Beautiful In My Eyes* right at the Rainbow. As soon as it was over I got Keith Urban's, *Memories Of Us*, and I don't think I've ever truly listened to the words to that song either. Certainly didn't remember the Rainbow.

October 25, 2014

Wow. My husband is turning it up and it's a good thing because I've been really sad this morning. I heard the music to *True Colors* as soon as I turned on the TV. Next was, *Beautiful As You*. After that? My favorite Firefall song of all time, even if the lyrics make me cry. *Just Remember I Love You*. Three Rainbow songs in a row! But there's more! Driving home last night an old Bread song from the 70's came on called, *Make It With You*. I couldn't believe my ears when I heard yet another Rainbow.

October 31, 2014

I cried to Gregory last night before bed and told him I never thought I could do this but I am doing it. Just then I heard him joke, *"Look at me! Look at me!"* His funny little ways I love and miss so much.

November 1, 2014

Grief hits me out of nowhere, like a few minutes ago. Remembering a conversation on the phone with my daughter-in-law in Idaho when she called asking what was going on after Jeremy made a quick trip here. I said sadly, *"He's dying."* Then we both cried. I always cry when I remember that conversation. I had never really said the words until then. It was a devastating moment.

November 24, 2014

The dark moments no longer have to overshadow what Greg and I had. The regrets can be let go. They are unimportant. He bombarded me with Rainbows on Saturday. I texted a friend asking, *"Have you ever seen snowflakes made out of Rainbows?"* Then added, *"I have."* I saw them on a commercial when I turned on the TV. I just knew he was going to send me another one and he did! A car commercial. The car was zooming along with tracers of light—Rainbows—trailing the car's movements.

Then a father dancing with his two small children and the little girl has a Rainbow across her dress! Then—and I knew he was showing off!—Paul Williams on Oprah. The first mention of his many, many songs was, *The Rainbow Connection*, and they sang it! I love when it asked the very question I've wondered myself lately about why there are so many songs about Rainbows.

November 25, 2014

Powerful session with Reiki and Angela! Woohoo! My honey was there and we both felt him. OMG. It was incredible. I talked to him on the way there and said I'd love for him to show up big. Still, I had no expectations because I did the same thing last time and he didn't show. At least not that I could feel. Three times he held my feet and then nothing. But he did it again and blew both of our minds! She said his energy was so heavy she was having trouble balancing. It was so incredible.

November 27, 2014

This morning I turned on the weather channel. It was 4:40 a.m. *Strangest Weather On Earth* was on. This particular show was on *Secrets of the Earth*. C'mon, try to guess what segment was just beginning? *Rainbows*. I couldn't believe it. My ear is so trained to hear the word that I giggled after about the fifth or sixth time it was spoken. Not only were they talking about Rainbows and telling how they're made, I was seeing them.

Beautiful Rainbows. I was crying at this point, giving Gregory *the weasel* and thanking him for the miracles. This was unreal. So many different types of Rainbows. There's a *Red Rainbow* or a *Scarlet Red Rainbow*, pure red and absolutely breathtaking. A *Glory*, which is a Rainbow reflection circling an image. A *Round Rainbow*. There's the *Double Rainbow*. There are *Moonbows*, which are all white and truly beautiful. But with the right kind of intense camera you can see that it's really a regular, colored Rainbow!

For a full ten minutes I was bombarded with Rainbows as happy tears poured down my face. Then a commercial. More Rainbows! The Rainbow snowflakes then another car commercial and the road was a Rainbow! Are you kidding me? Then the final segment about the green space that can be seen just as the last of a sunset disappears. A flash of green almost never seen. The whole thing was more Rainbows! The *cause* of the green space and other flashes of color and light is the same. I continued to be bombarded by Rainbows for another 10 minutes!

OMG! I just realized it's Thanksgiving Day! We used to see who would remember the holiday or anniversary, and say, *"Happy Whatever,"* first, before the other one. *"Well, Honey, you win this one! You showered me with blessings right out of the gate! I love you so much!"* To start my day—Thanksgiving Day—showered with Rainbows first thing is a priceless gift.

December 12, 2014

I push myself to write that Lacy has the same aggressive cancer on her mouth that Cali had. She's almost 17 years old. She is frail, and got more so, after Gregory died. I'm afraid I'm not going to have her for very much longer. When Gregory first died I couldn't relate to those younger pictures of him, but now I just put up one from about 25 years ago.

December 14, 2014

Gregory just pulled one on me. I have to say I was feeling a little sorry for myself before I sat down to write. I was feeling like I'm not getting as many Rainbows as I was getting. Maybe only one a day for the past couple of days. I told Gregory that I noticed and sort of teased him that he was falling down on the job. A few minutes later I heard a vehicle pull up out front. It's Sunday morning, what the heck? I looked out and it was the mail truck. On Sunday? *Oh, yeah, Christmas.*

Thinking it was one or more of the gifts I have ordered, I excitedly opened it. First thing I see is a big Rainbow and the words, *Over The Rainbow*. It's the calendar I'd forgotten I ordered for myself for Christmas. There you have it. Then I heard Gregory say, *"Here, take seventeen Rainbows and quit yer bitchin!"* It makes me laugh. Then I thought, *"Seventeen? What's he talking about?"* I counted them. Sure enough there was a double Rainbow *Bonus Image* and then three of the months are double Rainbows. Seventeen Rainbows. *"Lol, Gregory!"* Take that!

December 16, 2014

Lacy having cancer affects me. She wanted to be held all day yesterday and I find I choose to sit and just hold her instead of doing all the things that need to be done. As soon as I wrote that I found myself understanding that holding my little Lacy, who not only has cancer, but liver disease, is exactly what needs to be done right now. When she's gone I doubt I'm going to regret the chores that didn't get done while I loved and held her all I could. While I could.

December 17, 2014

I'm re-reading *My Dreams My Self*. I am nearing the end and read about an experience I had forgotten about. It reminded me of who I am, where I come from, and what I'm capable of. An amazing, powerful experience that I feel compelled to also include in my Rainbow book.

There was a woman at the women's AA meeting that I'd never seen before. She had red hair, and was probably in her late 50's. She came in late and pulled up a chair in the doorway. She shared that she had had 15 years of sobriety but had relapsed. She said her daughter, Jackie, was going into the treatment center the next day, and she named the one where I do my dream groups.

After the meeting, I went right over to the woman, and gave her a hug. I told her that I did dream groups at the treatment center, and I would be meeting her Jackie, and would take her under my wing. She hugged me and said thank you. I could tell it meant a lot to her. When I got to the treatment center the next day, I took roll, and Jackie was last on the list. I noted that she had arrived the day her mother said she would. I said to Jackie, "I talked to your mom, and she told me you were coming in. I told her I'd keep an eye on you." Jackie looked at me strangely and didn't say anything. I said, "Did she tell you about me?"

The color seemed to drain from her face and she said, "My mother Is dead." I was like, "You're kidding, right? Red hair? Had 15 years of sobriety and then relapsed?" She seemed stunned, and I said that now I was really confused. Then she said, "Funny thing is, my mom had 15 years of sobriety when she relapsed." Now I'm really freaked out and said, "She didn't have red hair though, right?" To which she replied, "Actually, she did."

I'm still not sure what to make of it. I've tried to come up with every possible explanation, but there isn't one. She's the only Jackie at the treatment center. She got there the same day her mother said she would. I described her mother perfectly. Since my grandmother was psychic, and my father saw dead people, when I told my family about it, my sister said, "Welcome to Dad's world! How's it feel to see dead people?" Very funny, Sis.

I feel very blessed by this experience. I pay closer attention to people since then because we never know when we are entertaining angels unaware!

December 30, 2014

One of my Christmas gifts to myself this year was a powerful book about Native American healing herbs and remedies. It moved me to tears when I read that injury and illness are a result of an imbalance and disharmony in the spirit, mind, and body. Then I really cried when I read that first the spirit must be healed before balance is restored and the mind and body can begin to recover. In those two beautiful sentences I am reminded where the healing needs to take place. I am relieved and enlightened to realize why I've been so unwell since Gregory died. Grief has caused an imbalance and disharmony of the mind and spirit which manifested in the body. That is the balance I feel being restored. My mind and spirit healing just a little bit.

Chapter 18

Reflecting

—

January 2, 2015

    Life feels good. Even as I cried and grieved earlier, holding Lacy under my chin. She clings to me now and she's never been like that. I had to put her food on a plate instead of a bowl. She couldn't seem to get a mouthful with that big walnut bulging out. We have a moment of peace. Even as I'm losing Lacy, my life feels manageable. The key is staying in the present moment. Just for today I can manage everything on my plate.

January 7, 2015

    Yesterday was a tough day with Lacy. She just wants to be curled up on me. I cry a lot now when I'm holding her. Grieving the loss that is imminent. I know her time is near. I cried off and on all afternoon and evening and Gregory—not to go unnoticed—sent me Rainbow after Rainbow. On the TV mostly but also in the written word. Never have I felt such love and support from him at a time when we would have been sharing this heartbreak.

January 8, 2015

Gregory sent me a Rainbow right off the bat. I've had my tears of disbelief this morning too and came pretty darn close to being mad at him. *"You owed it to me—to us—to quit smoking."* But the anger quickly turns to the real emotion and I cried my eyes out missing the love of my life and everything we shared. Knowing he paid the highest price of all.

January 9, 2015

Gregory started right out with a Rainbow. Between Lacy and missing him I was having an emotional morning. I asked him to help me. *Endless Love* came on and my heart melted. After that was, *Wherever You Will Go,* and that has become the theme song for my life right now. A reminder that he will always go with me. It's also a gentle push to move forward with the beautiful hope that there's someone else out there that's perfect for me. Then I got another Rainbow and then flashes of Rainbows reflected across the TV for no apparent reason. Well, to anyone but me.

January 14, 2015

Today is Gregory's birthday. I have cried sad tears here this morning. No gift to buy. No filet mignon at our favorite restaurant. No making love. Lacy's cancer continues to grow and is big on her lower jaw and mouth. It breaks my heart. The first sign of labored breathing or other distress and we're done. I told her to 'give me the look' when it's time. I turned on the TV and got the most beautiful Rainbow in Northern Lights on a wilderness show. Spectacular!

January 28, 2015

Last evening I was thinking about Gregory and my life with him. My heart seemed to hollow out and felt empty. The grief in that moment was the worst. Flashes of the life I've lost and I cried out a new cry. A different cry than I have ever heard from myself. A soulful mourning that was so incredibly sad and heartbreaking.

A gentler, quieter version of that guttural heart-shattering initial grief. Feeling the loss on so many levels. Shocked that I find myself here. And yet, reminded that I knew. 30 years before, I knew.

I just got *Broken Wings*, by Mr. Mister. My message from Gregory. It's time to mend these broken wings so I can fly again. When the song ended I said, *"Thanks Mr. Mister,"* to which he replied—like he did when he was alive—*"No problem, Twisted Sister."* I smiled through my tears and said, *"I know you know how much it helps, so I thank you."* I got three Rainbows yesterday. I also got a new book called, *I Wasn't Ready To Say Goodbye*. I'm reading a little every night.

January 30, 2015

I sat down crying. Big, sad, tears. A flash of an entire amazing life with Gregory and the memory of my premonition at the start of our journey. Now a beacon of what was to come, as clear and a part of the story as any other memory. I see his smiling face beside me. That glimmer in his eye. The light of life inside of him that shows the love he had for me. When he looked at me that way I melted into him. I got three Rainbows last evening as I watched TV.

February 1, 2015

I turned on the music channel and *Let Me Go* was starting. *"No!"* I said to his picture, *"No! Not only that, I demand a Rainbow!"* And right on cue I got a Rainbow of reflected light across a still photo of Celine Dion, as *Let Me Go* ended, and her song began. I don't know that I'll ever be ready to let him go. His reassurance Rainbow tells me I don't have to. *"Oh, funny Gregory."* I looked up to see Mariah Carey's, *Can't Let Go*. Story of my life.

February 5, 2015

I had a flash of our years together and how much fun we had. Then I wept deep, mournful sobs. I looked at his picture, kissed it, then kissed the air, reaching out for him. *"I wish I knew where you are!"* I searched the air with my arms, longing to find him. *"Where are you?"* In that moment, I heard him say, *"I'm everywhere. I'm in here,"* and with that my arms folded into myself and my heart was *full.* My whole chest was filled with the spirit and the presence of my Gregory.

In that moment of deep mourning, feeling my loss at great depth, feeling left behind, his presence exploded into our room. My chest felt the pressure of two hearts and the music seemed to be coming from the heavens above. These are moments that cannot be adequately described. You had to be there. Yesterday he sent me no less than four Rainbows. It's absolutely incredible. Lacy sleeps next to my heart. Last night I noticed a change in her contented purr. Just a hint of a rattle. I'm going to love her until she goes to be with Gregory. I just got another Rainbow.

February 14, 2015

I've been so sick with the full-blown flu and so upset that I couldn't be at the hospital this morning with Megan and Eric while Kadyn Gregory gets tubes put in his ears. I felt better after she sent me a picture of a smiling Kadyn at 11:46 a.m., mere moments before they came and got him. The text at noon made me cry. She said, *"He went back holding two ladies' hands. Before they took him they brought him stickers. One was an Army tank and the other was a Rainbow!"* Just then I got my own Rainbow on the TV and then another. I cried and cried. So did Megan. Everything went smoothly with the baby.

I got two Rainbows right off the bat this morning before I realized it was Valentine's Day! Dang! He won. At bedtime last night I thought, *"I'm going to win this time. I'm going to wish him Happy Valentine's Day the minute I open my eyes!"* But I'd been up for 20 minutes before I turned on the Weather Channel and heard, *"Rainbow,"* followed by talk of Rainbow Circles, and demonstrations thereof. Then on a totally different program I got several of these Rainbow circles in quick succession and I smiled. Then teared up. *"What a gift, Gregory. You send me Rainbows, Honey. How beautiful is that?"*

February 17, 2015

I got a beautiful Rainbow right off the bat this morning. Yesterday afternoon I was going through stuff in the office and I came across a card that I was sure was from me to him. It's a gold card and says, *"Love Is Magic,"* on the front. But it wasn't from me, it was from him. I cried all the way through. *"The talks we've had, the laughs, the fun, the special things we've said and done. That smile of yours that warms my heart. The way I feel when we're apart. The happiness you've brought to me and all our plans for days to be—these things I think of when I say, I love you even more each day!"* It says Happy Birthday, and in his writing, *"Forever and Always, G."* It made my day!

February 21, 2015

Yesterday I got no less than four Rainbows. For probably the first couple of years I got my daily Rainbows by hearing or seeing the word. I also got a lot of animated-type Rainbows. Sherwin Williams paint commercials, graphic printing company ads, cereal, or other children's commercials. Prisms of light across the TV screen—which still happens all the time—or in the room. Then I started getting real Rainbows on nature shows or the Weather Channel like I still do. I wasn't very good about writing about them.

February 24, 2015

Rainbows yesterday made me smile. I came down to the living room and a Rainbow was shining across Kadyn's forehead in the 8x10 on the mantle. I stopped to stare. It began to wave, got brighter, then slowly faded away. Unreal. *"Did that really just happen?"* I said to myself. *"Yes, yes it did!"*

March 1, 2015

I've had two beautiful Rainbows plus I saw the word and heard the word. All before 7 a.m. I need them now more than ever. I picked up Lacy's prescription and the doctor asked me if it was time. She's been so much better since the pain medicine. She still wants to play. She looks like hell, but she's basically got the same quality of life she's always had. For now. He said, *"Sounds like you're doing good hospice care."* It hit me as odd and I thought about it on the way home. My mind went back to the last time I was doing hospice care. We were on our way home from Ann Arbor the last day of February 2012, and on this day three years ago, I was so excited to get us home so Gregory could heal. He would die fifty days later.

March 2, 2015

Sitting here in a sad mood this morning, I turned on the TV and got *Just Remember I Love You*. There's truth in that song. I could feel his love all around me and my heart was full of his, as his reassuring words penetrated my entire being. It means everything to me. The next song was *Beautiful*, by Mercy Me. It says that there will be days when I feel worthless and don't have the strength to carry on. Praying for the willingness to keep fighting and the faith that there is more to life than what I'm grieving. That my spirit is made for so much more than what I see in front of me.

March 4, 2015

I have to take Lacy in today. She gave me the look last night. It was in her eyes. *"Too much, Mom, too much."* I've cried all morning. I knew this day would come.

March 5, 2015

Well it's over. Lacy is with Gregory. A friend drove me and I held her fragile little body in my arms and cried all the way to the vet. Once there they gave her a shot and she died in my arms. When it was over I felt a wave of peace come over me that I knew was from Gregory. I couldn't believe it. That peace is still with me and it's mixed with relief.

Last night I dreamed everything was black and white. Then all of a sudden it was Rainbows, Rainbows, Rainbows! Floating and coming from every angle! Colors like I've never seen in this world! It was awesome! It woke me right up and I was like, *"Yes! Woohoo!"* I think it was Gregory's way of letting me know Lacy made it home.

March 6, 2015

I dreamed about the most gorgeous double Rainbow and then woke right up. Then later the same thing. Big double Rainbow and it woke me up. I went back to sleep and saw an upside-down Rainbow that was a smiley face! I woke right up again and I was smiling ear to ear! I haven't remembered a dream in a long time so this was amazing. The Band Perry's song, *If I Die Young*, just came on and I heard, *"Turn it up,"* so I did. I couldn't believe my ears.

The words say that if I should die young send me home with a love song. See me as a Rainbow and I'll send blessings to my mama and when she stands under those colors she'll know I'm safe with you in heaven. This blew my mind. It makes me cry. Looks like little Lacy is also sending me reassurance and Rainbows. I still can't believe how many songs have Rainbows in them. I never could have imagined. It's pretty amazing.

March 12, 2015

I picked up Lacy's ashes yesterday and was way more emotional than I expected to be. In the folder was a *"Certificate of Passing"* and said, *"Lacy peacefully left this earthly existence to wait for us by the Rainbow Bridge."* Are you kidding me? Then another page with a beautiful poem called *Rainbow Bridge*. More confirmation that Gregory's got her.

March 26, 2015

I dreamed about Gregory! Just a little snippet but there he was looking like he did the last time I saw him healthy. More please.

April 3, 2015

As soon as I sat down to write I felt the nudge to turn on the muted TV to the soft rock station and I would get my Rainbow. As soon as I did I saw the word *Rainbow*. A trivia on the sidelines of a Faith Hill song reporting that she sang *Somewhere Over The Rainbow* at an event. I looked to Gregory's picture propped up beside me and it had fallen forward. I stood it back up with a smile and said, *"You **should** take a bow."*

April 5, 2015

Today is Easter and I can't help but remember our last Easter with Gregory. I cried and sobbed through Yoga. Missing him and feeling a little bit pissed off at him. I cried, *"You piss me off, you f—king jerk,"* which was one of those tongue-in-cheek sayings we robbed from a movie and would use on each other in a moment of irritation and it always lightened the mood. Then I really sobbed. *"I didn't expect to be doing this without you."* I heard him say, *"You aren't."* *"Well, without you by my side!"* I argued. *"I am by your side,"* he said. *"You know what I mean, Gregory!"* I cried. I'm doing my workout all through this exchange. Then I sobbed and said, *"I miss you. I miss us. I miss you holding me, touching me, kissing me."* I noticed the silence. *"You don't have anything to say to <u>that</u> do you?"*

April 6, 2015

I know I'm sad about this time of year. I miss Gregory so much. I guess a part of me doesn't ever want to stop missing him. And yet it's so sad. What happens when I let go of that sadness? What happens to Greg and L.J. if I let go of any of it? I still have on our wedding rings. I got his sized after he died and wear it with mine. I still feel married to him.

April 10, 2015

I cried last night at bedtime and it's the worst feeling. I'm so grateful it doesn't happen very often. My mind was full of Gregory as I sat down here with my tea. Random thoughts and memories made me cry. Made me feel as alone as I am now. Even as I smile at some memories and my heart is warmed by the precious moments we spent together. I think I feel sadder because I can feel life pushing me along, moving me forward, making me heal. Threatening to put my life with Gregory in a place somewhere behind me. *In the past.* I can feel my own resistance to the idea.

April 11, 2015

I watched little Kadyn Gregory yesterday and he 'nuggled' on my lap while I read one book after the other. He wanted to pick out each book and would search them carefully before he chose the one we would read next. When we were done he would put it back, get another one, and crawl back onto my lap and snuggle in. A very energetic little boy, he was all too content to just cuddle with Grammy and I savored every moment. The first book he picked out was *Peter Pan*. We opened it and there it was, a yellow Rainbow.

The story begins with a faraway place where the sun is always shining and the sky is always blue. No one ever grew old. Into the book further, when the gang first spots Never Land from a cloud, the Rainbow shoots out from the village center. Of course this would be the book he would choose first.

Chapter 19

Unbelievable

‑‑‑‑‑‑

April 15, 2015

Wow what a morning already. Very powerful. I've talked to my husband and had my sad tears missing him. I've danced my socks off to Adele's, *We Could Have Had It All*, and one slower, sultry song where Gregory danced with me. It's indescribable. I feel him all over and around me, *through* me. I get a rush of chill bumps from my head to my toes and everywhere in between. Like he is the blood flowing through my veins. For a few moments I am in his arms again.

April 22, 2015

OMG! OMG! OMG! I have spent the past half hour in tears, in awe, in praise. My heart swells to overflowing. I am humbled mostly. The impossible has been made possible. A sign especially for me. *My* sign. The numbers '420' that have specific meaning to me. My birthday, but also my sign that I'm on the right path. I see it everywhere. I'm doing *The Artist's Way*, by Julia Cameron, again. It's been ten years. The book is beginning to do its magic.

Last evening I was working on my *Artist Date*, which encourages some sort of fun activity or play every week. I found a couple of magazines and began cutting out all the images that spoke to me so I could make a collage. I had a whole pile of little pictures. I found a whole page filled with pictures of old, well-worn, hotel key tags. Numbers faded so much that a few were nearly worn off.

I searched the nearly 100 tags expecting to find a 4 and a 20. I found a worn 42 and the only usable zero was on a 90 tag. I knew I could overlap them and I'd have my *420* for the collage. I cut out a bunch of images that spoke to me and then I gathered the big pile and put them in a sheet of paper folded in half. I put them on the dresser and placed our address book on top so they wouldn't get knocked over. I went to bed.

I woke up at 4:20 a.m. and did my morning routine. I went back upstairs to check the weather and when I came down I stopped when there was something orange lying at my feet. It was right in

the path I had walked a couple of times already this morning. I bent down to see what it was and couldn't believe my eyes. There were the two key tags, overlapped to show *'420.'* This is what I saw:

I was stunned like I've never felt and as soon as I picked up the numbers I started crying uncontrollably. Those clips (actual size) were mixed in the

middle of the pile in that folder. I would have walked over them on the way to the kitchen and then again on the way back. There are so many impossibilities here. I can almost hear the theme song to *The Twilight Zone*. Perhaps I'm being shown my '420' to remind me about my birthday. That day I just skipped over. I didn't even journal.

April 24, 2015

Things are already starting to change in my world. In small, gentle ways. And of course, not so gentle ways! I looked at Gregory's smiling face beside me just now and before I can say, *"Hi, Baby,"* I am in sobs. I was talking to him and missing him and telling him we knew this would happen with me. I love with my whole being. I know that's what hit him when the last thing he ever said to me was, *"I'm sorry, Baby."* He probably thought, *"Oh, f—k, she's gonna die or drink or something...."*

I also remember a strength not my own that showed itself when I told him it was okay for him to go, that I'd be alright. I'm sure I heard him say, *"Liar!"* as we often—playfully—said. But at the same time, in that moment, our souls knew it was the truth. He could let go of the physical knowing the bond between us would only grow stronger. That was the image I got in those last days with him. When letting go of him was unimaginable yet inevitable. Spirit impressed upon me the clear knowing that what Gregory and I shared in life—the love, the bond—was only going to strengthen once he died. I knew it to be true and it helped me to relax and trust what was about to happen to us. To me.

April 27, 2015

I had a thing happen Saturday. Propped up on my bed where I admit I'm too comfy (safe), I was working on stuff for *The Artist's Way*. I had Gregory's picture propped up next to me against a throw pillow. I like to keep it close. I went to the kitchen and when I came back up it was gone. Gone. I didn't automatically think woo-woo things are disappearing before my eyes. No, I'm thinking it fell over, stuck to the pillow, maybe I tossed it, or it somehow fell into the recycling bag.... that's out in the hallway. There had to be an explanation.

Over a 24-hour period I searched for the darn thing. I said to him a couple of times yesterday, *"C'mon, where is it? Give it back."* Last evening I was watching a show on the computer. I paused it and went to the kitchen. I looked at his picture in the living room and said, *"It's not going to scare me when it shows back up..."* then added, *"Freak me out maybe, but you won't scare me."* When I got back upstairs there was Gregory's smiling face next to the keyboard.... I just stared at it. *"Finally you turn up."*

May 10, 2015

I caught the end of Maya Angelo on Oprah. She asked who's the Rainbow in your cloud? Then added that maybe we're meant to be the Rainbow in someone else's cloud. I've been getting the word Rainbow a lot lately and I love it. I cried earlier and just now, but my day—laying low because I still don't feel well—has been filled with golden nuggets. Mostly about being true to yourself. On Oprah's *Life Class*, Jane Fonda said that our goal is not to be perfect, it's to be whole. Amen!

May 11, 2015

Very telling dream. *I heard Gregory at the front door. I saw him through the glass. I was so excited. The door was locked when he tried to come in. I thought of racing down to let him in but now I was in bed and very sleepy. I wanted to get up, but I just couldn't wake up.*

Okay, there you have it. There's the reason I haven't dreamed about him. I've locked him out! He's trying to come in. Now I have to figure out how I'm doing that. Is it my grief that keeps him out? I've got my Rainbows and a couple of them have been amazing.

May 12, 2015

OMG! Last night I was just about asleep when I felt a kitty on the bed. Light little footsteps behind me. Before I went to bed I checked on the three girls and found them sleeping in their spots. I laid still to be absolutely sure I was feeling what I was feeling. She walked all around behind me, right up next to my back and down. I felt her walk up onto my hips and down to my feet. This is a sensation so familiar to me. This is what Lacy always did. I had to look. No one was there.... OMG. It was Lacy.

May 14, 2015

I keep thinking about my dream where Gregory was locked out. Wow, just now on the muted TV I saw Maroon 5's, *She Will Be Loved*. I turned up the volume and instead of hearing the Rainbow part like I normally do, I heard the part that says you're invited in anytime, that my door is always open. I love that!

May 16, 2015

First thing this morning when I turned on the TV it showed a child's hand coloring a Rainbow. The ad said, *"Create your own cloud and Rainbow!"* Then the Rainbow on a little girl's t-shirt danced with her around the room. Love it! I've had my tears. My life is exactly how I saw it in my premonition thirty years before Greg died.

May 19, 2015

On the way to Megan's yesterday I heard *Here Without You* and felt Gregory with me. Kadyn and I watched Rainbows on TV and he says the word so cute. At one point he was standing in the living room. I was on the couch looking out the sliders to the beautiful deck and yard. I was thinking of Gregory and imagined him standing there. I felt he was standing there, I just couldn't see him. Just then Kadyn turns and says, *"Papa Greg."*

May 25, 2015

Just now I thought of Gregory and simultaneously saw a Rainbow on the TV. In the exact moment. Very cool. Woohoo! Another Rainbow when I just looked up! Thank God he's still here. I sense him, I feel him, and my love for him has never felt stronger. Thank God for his Rainbows.

May 26, 2015

I'm at the beach! I'm not sure if I missed the sunrise and it's just behind clouds but the sky is soft pink and the clouds are amazing. I feel Gregory here. Strong in that peaceful presence. I thanked him for bringing us here. For being willing to take an adventure with me and the children across the country to start a new and better life. *"And we sure did that didn't we, Mr. Mister?"* The golden orange of the sky glows deeper. A gentle breeze makes the trees sway ever so slightly like a morning waltz. I am alive here.

May 30, 2015

As I was coming back from the bay yesterday and walked under the bridge, the bike path veers off to the left and I go to the right toward home. All at once I saw Gregory and I on our bikes gliding past me and following the path to the left where I remember we would go off into the parking lot and then home, avoiding the stairs at the mouth of the river. It hit me hard. Tears rolled down my face all the way home. Still, I'm grateful for those memories playing before me.

The Artist's Way this week is *Recovering a Sense of Strength*. Reading the chapter last night it talked about grieving all the failed artistic endeavors as if they were miscarriages. That hit me hard and I realized that I probably have some grief work to do with all those lost pursuits. All the so-called failures. That is what I have called them. She says no. She says it is gain disguised as loss. Then—powerfully—she suggests we ask questions such as how can this loss serve me or in what direction does it point me? She says that when hit by loss you have to ask what's next not why me? She talks about doing an inventory of our artistic injuries and that no inventory would be complete without acknowledging those wounds that are self-inflicted. *Ouch.*

June 2, 2015

The pictures of Greg and I seem to swirl around me this morning. My heart feels strong in one moment, as I begin stepping more firmly into this life of mine. And then in the next moment I feel that numbing fear, as harsh reality moves in around me. A new shift in my grief. Simultaneously I feel both feelings. It's very powerful. Stunned by the life I had before as it slowly takes its place behind me. Excited, in a fearful sort of way, about all the possibilities that lie ahead. Including love again.

June 5, 2015

The *Daily Word* for today is *Harmony*, and the first word of the reading was Rainbows. *"Rainbows provide a wonderful example of harmony. Each color is clearly defined, yet they all come together perfectly for a beautiful work of natural art."* This morning I turned on the TV and there was an infomercial about the music and times of the 60's and 70's and there were all kinds of Rainbows flashing at me! Love it!

June 8, 2015

I didn't cry for three days! One day at a time for over three years my heart and my life have felt broken. My tears have flowed enough to fill a river, soothing my wounded heart and life and making them whole. I did not give up. I did not.

June 9, 2015

I cried on the way home from Megan's. Our early years together were stirred from the pictures she has around her house of Gregory holding her when she was a baby. This morning I felt a sadness and regret about some things I would change if I could. My whole being felt dark and heavy. I returned to the end of a movie I started watching last night. It's called *True Heart*, about an Elder Native American and a huge bear he was protecting from poachers.

I hear the sounds, the language, the drums and chanting, and it feels like home to me. The Elder had helped two children after a plane crash and had retrieved the girl's locket from the crash site. It had a picture of the children with their parents. The young girl was so happy to have found her locket but then she handed it back to him and told him to keep it to remember them by. He said that remembering is good, but sometimes it's also good to forget and move on.

Last night I turned to the Weather Channel and it was a segment on these strange ball clouds. I can't remember what they're called but it was just about over and I grabbed the remote to shut it off when I heard, *"Coming up..."* and I saw a Rainbow upside down. A smiley face like I saw in my dream! A *Floating Smiling Rainbow*, they called it. Strangely they aren't actually Rainbows because they aren't reflected off the sun. They are seen straight up above your head so most people never notice them. They showed several of them and it just made me laugh. Smiley face Rainbows just before I shut my eyes to sleep.

Before I could shut off the TV there was an ad that shows a Lineman up on a pole, something I've been seeing more of lately, and I always think of Gregory. That was followed by another Rainbow! God love him. The feel of the room always changes ever so slightly and I can't help but be aware of something pretty incredible taking place. And just now, as if right on cue, I felt it, and looked up to the muted TV. A song called, *Since You Been Gone*, by Rainbow! Are you kidding me?

June 16, 2015

My day started with Rainbows. I realize I don't always write about the Rainbows I get every day, but I should. I'm trying to be better about it. Stop what I'm doing and write about it when I get one. Not a day goes by that I don't get my Rainbows. Not one single day in over three years. That's a lot of Rainbows. That's a lotta love.

June 19, 2015

Three years, two months, three hours, and about fifteen minutes since my Gregory died. I turned on the TV first thing this morning and got Mercy Me's, *Finally Home*. Such a beautiful song. Starts out talking about the first thing I'm going to do is run to my daddy and wrap my arms around him and tell him how much I've missed him. That will be after I pull myself away from Gregory.

Chapter 20

Close Encounter

June 27, 2015

The sky was ablaze with red when I walked over to the beach at 5:30 a.m. What a gorgeous scene. A lone fisherman anchors out a short distance from where I sit. When he came out from the mouth of the river his silhouette reminded me of Gregory. Then he took off his hat and glasses to put on a hooded sweatshirt and I've seen Gregory do that a hundred times. He raised his coffee mug for a sip and it was my Gregory for a moment, in my mind and in front of me. I talked to him all the way over here. Thanked him for everything.

June 28, 2015

My day started with Rainbows when I was watching a movie at 5 a.m. like I love to do on Sunday mornings. It was the true story of artist *William Turner*, set in 1832. In an early scene a woman is excited to show Mr. Turner and his father a crystal. She was all excited and, holding it to the light she said, *"It can make a Rainbow!"* Then they closed all the curtains except for a tiny opening and she held it up. They put an easel with a white canvas in the middle of the room and a beautiful Rainbow was reflected perfectly onto the canvas as if it had been painted there. It was such a great little scene.

The movie ended and the TV came back on. It was on Animal Channel and the Vet was holding a big snake and said, *"This is Rainbow."* I couldn't believe it. Twice more I saw beautiful Rainbows on a wilderness show. Then I was watching an Alaskan show OnDemand and there was the most beautiful Rainbow over the water. They commented on it, saying, *"We're going to drive right through a Rainbow!"* Gregory has been very close today.

July 1, 2015

I'm here at the beach on a dark, cloudy morning. No color to be seen anywhere. Maybe that's because I was bombarded with Rainbows on the Weather Channel at 4:30 a.m. Rainbows! Rainbows! Rainbows! Made me laugh. *"Thank you, Baby."*

July 7, 2015

I no longer keep track if I cried this day or not. I know I still cry *and* I believe there are days that I don't. It's taken three years but it's happening. Just got my Rainbow! It's like Gregory is giving me his approval. Just got another Rainbow!

July 17, 2015

Well, we almost lost Mama. She's in ICU at the hospital and nearly died. She's stabilized now but it was scary for a minute. Then something pretty crazy happened about 3 p.m. I'd left the hospital to meet Greg's sister and the neighbor for lunch. He's interested in buying Greg's Mom's house. I came back and joined Megan and my sister in the cafeteria. I was telling them about the meeting and just then Kassie called Meg to see what the neighbor had to say. What I didn't notice as I was telling them what went on was that my sister was watching a guy through the windows between the cafeteria and the hallway, staring at who she believed was Gregory walking by. She was sitting there with her mouth hanging open.

All of a sudden she hit me on the leg and said, *"That guy looks just like Greg!"* I said, *"Where?!"* and jumped up to follow in his direction. He was in blue scrubs and had a tie-dye surgical cap on with a ponytail out the back and a white, neatly trimmed beard. I no sooner headed into the café and he was already headed to the counter. I rushed back to the table knowing he would walk right by us.

My sister was in disbelief. She'd watched in shock as he passed the windows and was unable to speak. She said he stopped at a phone outside the cafeteria entrance and then walked past us. I had my back to the entrance and saw none of this. Neither did Megan. As he headed our way I looked right at him and our eyes met. I had a big smile on my face and could not look away even though we were all staring at him! He had a big smile too and he looked exactly like Gregory.

At this point I'm feeling like I'm in the Twilight Zone! There was a strange feel in the air. I felt like I was in a dream. Everything seemed to be in slow motion. Our eyes continued to be fixed on each other as he walked right to me! Now let me just say that earlier in Mama's room we were talking about when I meet someone new and I said how much I loved that Greg and I were both in recovery and it would be so nice if the new guy was too.

He bent over, took my hand, and softly said, *"Are you a friend of Bill W.?"* This is something that those of us in 12-step recovery sometimes say to each other in order to maintain public anonymity. Bill W. is one of the founders of Alcoholics Anonymous. I said, *"I am."* He squeezed my hand and said, *"That's where I know you from."* Shocked, I said, *"Nice to see you again."* He walked away and I was stunned, unable to move.

Megan sort of freaked out and said, *"He looks just like my dad!"* and she started to cry. My sister was all excited and said, *"See! It's not just me!"* Then, at the same time, they both turned to me and said, *"What did he say to you?!"* I told them, still not believing the whole thing had happened. It was surreal. I felt like I haven't felt since sparks flew with Gregory nearly 35 years ago. I couldn't stop thinking about it the rest of the day. Neither could Megan and Kristie.

I was home by 6:30 p.m. and was nearly giddy as my mind replayed the whole thing over and over again. Sis called as soon as she got home and said, *"Did that really happen?"* Just then Megan texted me asking if I had told Greg's sister about the *look alike* and said she cried when she told her husband about it. I was so excited, giddy, until after 9 p.m. and wondered how I was going to be able to sleep with all this excitement. Then I cried and cried, a mixture of so many feelings. Happy sobs as I felt Gregory nearer to me than I ever have and knowing that somehow he made the whole thing happen. It was him.

I turned on the music and Lenny Kravitz's, *Again* was just starting. The energy in the room was already filled with electricity and the song seemed to echo in and through me. Wondering if I'll ever see him again. The whole thing feels surreal. All I know is I haven't felt that alive since Gregory died. Megan said she wanted to find the guy and give him a big hug. Sis said we'll go to the cafeteria a lot!

Maybe it was Gregory's way of letting me know that I can feel this way again. With someone else. He looked like the healthiest version of my husband. Like what he would look like at this age if he'd never smoked. If he'd taken better care of himself. The magic of that interaction—that three of us experienced—is etched in my mind forever.

July 18, 2015

I barely had the TV on this evening, winding down from a stressful day at the hospital, when I got a Rainbow. And then another and another and another. Lol! Four Rainbows! Gregory has shown up even stronger since my encounter with *Mystery Man*.

July 26, 2015

My feeling now is that *Mystery Man* doesn't really exist, and my sister feels the same way. *It was Gregory.* His spirit anyway. It opened my heart to new possibilities. To hope of finding love again. More importantly, to show me that I'm ready for that to happen. Or at least I'm getting ready. Until then I am here with my Gregory. Missing everything about our life together, even as he's right here.

In the midst of my grieving moments last night I got Rainbows like you wouldn't believe. The most beautiful Rainbows. Probably six or more in the span of two hours. The way I feel when he sends me Rainbows is so amazing. It is more than just seeing a Rainbow. It is his spirit touching mine in a profound way. It is a feeling that can't be described. It can only be felt. Experienced. And it has been a joyful blessing in my life since my husband died.

July 29, 2015

On the way home from the hospital last night I turned on the radio then flipped it to the rock station which sometimes plays Uncle Steve's, *Turn Up The Radio* (Autograph). Instead I got *Rainbow In The Dark*, by Dio. It talks about feeling like I've been left on my own with no sign of the morning light. A Rainbow in the dark. Yep.

August 4, 2015

Last night Meg and I were texting back and forth and I said that I'd texted Jeremy the day before and told him I think of him all the time and I miss him and love him. Before I could send it I got a text from Jeremy and he sent me a Rainbow! I couldn't believe it. I added what just happened to the text to Meg and sent it. She texted that this was weird because she was just texting me asking if I'd heard from Jeremy. I said, *"Were all connected!"* I could feel it. I said, *"It's your dad!"* I could feel Gregory so strong and they could too. It's a gift from Spirit no doubt about it. I'd also gotten two Rainbows just before that.

August 9, 2015

Gregory bombarded me with Rainbows before I went to bed last night. Not only did I turn on the Weather Channel just in time for a segment about Rainbows, but even the commercials had Rainbows! I was laughing and felt so connected to him. I love it when he does that! *Then he bombarded me with Rainbows in my dreams! Twice. Rainbows everywhere. Floating through the sky every which way. All sizes. Lots of little spectacularly colored Rainbows. Woke me right up. Went back to sleep and dreamed about more Rainbows! Woke up! I love it!*

August 10, 2015

Last evening I turned on the TV just in time to hear, *"Rainbow..."* and the people were talking about Rainbows! How can that be explained other than it's from Gregory? I can't tell you how many times it happens. Turn on the TV, Rainbow. Turn on the radio, Rainbow. It's pretty darn cool. And then, as if right on cue, I just got two Rainbows on the TV when I looked up!

August 14, 2015

I haven't been doing well physically. In the middle of the night, as I lie awake in pain, I started having memories of Gregory and missing him so much I started to cry. I remembered when I asked him for a sign one other time in the scary dark and the air came alive with electricity! Wavy sparks of light. So I said, *"Show me something, Gregory."* My eyes stared out into the darkness. Then a little spark of light, purple. Then another. Random bursts of wavy, electrified color, starting small then growing before fading out. Then big balls of pastel white filled the room yet lit up nothing! It was as if the light was coming from within a vast vortex. It was unbelievable.

Amazing flashes into a world of possibility. Then pale peach flashes of light, big, as they swayed across the room! Several more flashes of smaller wavy lights and I wondered if I was really seeing this. It was like fireworks! It was unreal. Then the room faded to pitch black and that heightened sense of energy faded. Incredible. *"Thank you, Baby."* That was something alright! When it ended I felt exactly like when a fireworks show is over. You know it's over and yet you are elated to have seen it. I fell asleep.

August 27, 2015

I've already had three Rainbows this morning and it's not even 6 a.m. I've been thinking a lot about my life with Gregory and what it was like being with him. It was amazing. The memories seem to be coming more easily since I came out of that dark spell. Not that I don't still have moments of heavy grief, but it has gotten so much better. I feel like I can take a deep breath.

August 28, 2015

I feel a swirling of powerful emotions that somehow make up who I am now. A strength deep within that was never there before. A sense of knowing that seems to come with surviving deep loss. With getting to know who you really are because this journey with grief is one that must be traveled alone. Family and supports all around, yes, but surviving that kind of loss on a soul level takes going it alone.

Chapter 21

It Just Got Real

September 1, 2015

I've been emotionally eating and out of sorts again and I finally figured out why. It's this time of year. *It's the Mackinac Island trip.* I feel it in the air, I smell it in the air, I get excited with all it stirs in me.... and then I remember and my heart sinks heavy in my chest and the energy seems to drain out of me. It helps to be aware of this. Now the tears are flowing about the Island.

September 2, 2015

Yesterday I was standing in the health food store waiting for my latte. I felt a gentle push toward the cold case where they have premade sandwiches and stuff. I was surprised by it. Then I heard, *"Go over and read the labels."* I'm like, *"Whatever... no."* I heard it again. I felt pushed over there, and on the way I took out my glasses and started reading labels, scanning the rows, still wondering what the heck I'm doing this for. And then I saw it. My eyes stopped on the word... *Rainbow salad.* I stared at it. *"Hello Baby. I love you, thank you, Honey."*

I turned on the Weather Channel first thing this morning and it was a commercial with a beautiful, uplifting message of hope and reminders of all that's good and beautiful in this world. A crisp, beautiful red apple, a river stream, and then, I just knew what was coming next. I knew I was about to get a Rainbow. Wait for it... boom! There is was. A most beautiful Rainbow. Just for me. From my Gregory. Because he knows this is hard for me.

Even though I'm in my fourth year without him, and have lots of hard grief work behind me, I needed that Rainbow I knew was coming. I needed to be reminded that all is well. That hope is for real. That life is good and full of endless possibilities. That's what Gregory shows me every day with his Rainbows. I love him so much for that. He knows me. He knows how much I loved him, depended on him, was safe with him. He knows I am lost without him. So the crazy guy sends me Rainbows. Every day.

September 8, 2015

I woke up in the middle of the night remembering a dream of being with Gregory. We were walking around in a city. It was night-time. I had my arms wrapped around his waist. I'd get behind him and wrap myself around him and then we'd go further, talking all the way. I cried as I held onto him and told him flat out how hard this has been. I even said, "Think about it, Honey, what if it were switched? What if you were here without me?" I held onto him tight, squeezing him and never letting go.

I cry even now at the memory of it and I thank him over and over. It's exactly what I needed right now. I needed to feel him, wrap myself around him again. In a deep grieving moment yesterday, where I didn't think I could breathe, I pleaded with him to help me. *"Please, Honey, help me."* So he came to me in a dream and we just got to be together. I was able to cry and tell him what I've been through and he just listened and held me. It was amazing. I got what my heart was crying out for most. Just the chance to hold onto him again. Have him be my anchor.

September 25, 2015

The neighbors next door planted sunflowers along both sides of their fence. They are all facing me when I look out because they face east. A bunch are in bloom on the far side of their yard. On my side, one lonely sunflower sticks its head above the fence as if to greet me. I walked outside and there it was, tilting its head from side to side as if it were waving or giving me a playful nod. *There was no wind.* The flowers on the other side stood still. This was amazing. I just stared at it and almost started laughing. I knew it was Gregory. I could feel him.

September 28, 2015

I dreamed about Rainbows last night! Random Rainbows here, there, and everywhere! Vivid colors we don't have here on earth! Woke me right up in the middle of the night and I was just smiling. I love that!

October 3, 2015

"Happy Anniversary, Baby." It feels surreal to me. October 3rd has always been such a great day. Those feelings are forever ingrained in me and I'm grateful for that. And yet it's hard not to remember how this day would be if Gregory were still here. What we would be planning for our special day. It's Saturday so we'd go to the Farmer's Market I'm sure. We'd ride our bikes or walk along the river. We'd just be together.

October 7, 2015

My morning began with not wanting to get out of bed. *"I'll get up when I'm well,"* I said to no one in particular. *"When my body doesn't hurt."* And then I got up anyway. The loss of Gregory felt too heavy and I just felt so alone. This feels like a really sad leg of the journey. It's where I'm going to have to put my life with Gregory in my past. Right now that feels like a terrifying prospect. I'm holding onto him tighter, clutching our memories like precious lifelines. So afraid they might begin to fade. Then I got *Crazy*, and as always I got up to dance with my Gregory. It's him asking me to dance. Pulling me up from where I sit—stunned—and getting me to move.

October 13, 2015

The early pictures of Greg and I are affecting me in a profound way. Remembering how much fun it was. I cried some heart-breaking tears a few moments ago. It's about letting go now and accepting that I'm no longer Gregory's wife. No longer anyone's wife even if I still wear wedding rings. I didn't realize how it was going to feel when I started feeling unmarried.

October 14, 2015

I've been crying out loud. My grief feels like saying goodbye. It makes the saddest tears you've ever known flow out of me like a gentle river. It's sad to me in a way it never was before. Is it denial falling away? Reality checking in? I know I've kept Gregory alive from the moment he took his last breath and jumped into my heart. I have held onto all we had, to all I had with him, to my life as his wife, to everything. I have held on.

October 16, 2015

After I fed the cats a funny thing happened. I was in the back entry to put on shoes to go outside. It's raining and I thought about the coming snow and how it'd be nice to have a plow guy. This led me to think about the show *Northern Exposure,* that Greg and I loved. There was a sort of high society gal who'd come from the big city to see her friend in Alaska and she ends up in the most unlikely romance with *Plow Guy*. He was hunky, outdoorsy, rugged.... *"Yum,"* I thought, and then said out loud with a big smile on my face, ***"Plow guy!"***

Just then I lifted my right foot to put on my other shoe and Gregory shoved me over! I fell into the door only a foot behind me. I laughed out loud! And I couldn't stop laughing! I felt that playful push many times when he was alive. It's what he would do anytime I think he felt a little jealous, which was never serious, but he would sort of shove me over. Like if he saw me looking at a cute guy. It was always cute and funny, and I felt that same playful interaction this morning.

October 20, 2015

This morning feels dark and a bit scary. I hesitated to get out of bed. Feeling like going on without Gregory is too much. I miss him terribly. I turned on the TV and got *Wherever You Will Go*. *"Got it, Honey."* It has to be enough. Then I got Faith Hill's, *There You'll Be*, and it was powerful. It talks about looking back over the years and feeling so blessed to have had him in my life. That he was always there for me. Even now.

October 22, 2015

I dreamed about Rainbows! Four different times I saw a beautiful scene with a magical, colorful Rainbow, and then I'd wake up. I'd think, "Ahhh, a beautiful Rainbow! Thank you, Honey!" I'd go right back to sleep and dream about another Rainbow and wake up! It was so amazing! Four times this happened! Incredible.

October 24, 2015

I woke up in the middle of the night and was thinking about when we took Gregory out of here for the last time. It made me cry. Alone in our bed in the dark of night, missing him so much. *"I don't want to cry in the middle of the night, Gregory. It's too scary."* Big tears flowed out of me and that's all I remember until I woke up from a dream. *It was an amazing, sexual encounter with him. I mean, amazing.* That's all I'm going to say.

November 1, 2015

Life on my own is starting to feel familiar. I hadn't thought about it but I've been treading unfamiliar territory since Gregory died. The fact that my new life is beginning to feel familiar makes me want to cry. That means my life with Gregory is beginning to feel unfamiliar. That's a sobering thought. This year of reflection has been a hard one. It's starting to feel less like he just died and more like he's been gone for a while. Ugh. And yet I feel a glimpse of joy and excitement about my life after my hard grief work is done. When I can say that I made it. I survived Gregory dying.

Something else has been happening. Ever since I married him I've had a vision of what I thought was our second wedding celebration. Our planned vow renewal at twenty-five years. I see the dress, the party, the happy bride, everything. Well, not everything. I realize I've never been able to see Gregory. Since he died that vision has still been playing and it blew my mind the first time it happened. Same exact vision I've always had. *Apparently, I've been seeing my second wedding.* I get excited when I think about that happy bride. I know she is a healed woman that God blessed twice.

November 5, 2015

I dreamed about Gregory and three Rainbows! I dreamed the Rainbows first; a big one and two smaller ones. Beautiful. Indescribable. Then Gregory was sitting in the driver's seat of a vehicle. I was in the passenger seat. He looked like he did when we first fell in love. Long hair, mustache, no beard. He just sat there looking at me. It didn't seem out of the ordinary. I had no emotion like, OMG! he's here! It was just the two of us sitting in a vehicle.

My heart tells me what this dream means. The big Rainbow and two smaller ones represent me and the kids. *Rainbows.* All is well. My heart sank when I wrote the part about him sitting in the driver's seat. He is what's in my driver's seat. You should always be in the driver's seat in a dream. It shows that you're taking responsibility for where your life is going. Gregory sits in that spot, content, yet not. He almost seemed bored sitting there. I get it. That's why this year has been so hard. That's why the pictures draw me in like a trance. Pulling me back to a place I want to be while life pulls me in the opposite direction.

I cry a few times every day but I do not cry all day. I am content. I am at peace. While the rug of life flipped me on my butt I am slowly staggering to my feet. In the car yesterday I turned on the radio just as *Here Without You* was starting. I yelled a big thank you! to the Universe. It made my day! It is my reality. It is beautifully painful. It is powerful. It says that time has made me older since the last time I saw him.

November 9, 2015

I turned on the Weather Channel just as a program was ending. I looked at Gregory's picture and felt a deep pang of sadness and loss. I looked up and there was a double Rainbow! Just at the very moment I needed to feel him with me.

November 12, 2015

This morning I came down early and turned on the soft rock station. First up, Eric Carmen's, *All By Myself*. "Very funny, Dr. Jones." I sang out the words dramatically and sarcastically. Next up, Cher's, *We All Sleep Alone*. Seriously? It talks about needing to be strong when you're by yourself because sooner or later it's going to happen. At some point we all sleep alone.

"Cute, Gregory." Since he seems to be on a roll I waited in anticipation for the next song. David Cook's, *The Time Of My Life*. I leaned back and listened to the words. It talks about waiting for my dreams to turn into reality and watching for some sort of magic Rainbow that I can't see unless I let go. Hmmm, there's that message about letting go.

I watched a beautiful 25-minute meditative film on waterfalls. Beautiful music accompanied the most amazing waterfalls I've ever seen. And Rainbows! It was the most calming half hour of my day. I felt hugged by Gregory the whole time. The peaceful rush of water is the most calming sound I know. So today feels better. I'm excited about everything my life holds for me once I've survived this loss. I looked at the bottom of this page of my journal to a Scripture from Ecclesiastes 3:11: *"God has made everything beautiful in its time."* Oh, yeah.

Chapter 22

Loosening My Grip

November 13, 2015

This part of my grief journey is starting to feel quite amazing. I can't explain it. *I feel at peace.* About everything. Today my reading talks about how little by little we need to loosen our grip on the past so that we can more fully embrace the life we have now. I'm grateful that this process seems to be happening automatically. The reading reminds me that in dealing with all manner of grief it's most important to keep the process going.

November 19, 2015

I've scooched over and am sharing the driver's seat with Gregory. Back behind the wheel with him still right beside me. It's the best of both worlds. Perhaps I will always need him to share the seat with me. I just can't believe I was lucky enough to have him in my life for 30 years. To have been loved by him. It's a blessing I'm only beginning to fully grasp as my grief turns to pure love.

November 23, 2015

As soon as I sat down with my tea at 4:20 a.m. and turned on the Weather Channel there it was, *Rainbows Caught On Camera*. All kinds. Moonbows. Fire Rainbows. The smiley face Rainbow like I saw in my dream! One after the other amazing home videos of beautiful Rainbows. Tears rolled down my cheeks. I felt Gregory everywhere. I thanked him. Not only for an amazing life together, but for the Rainbows and everything he has done for me since he died to help me through this. Showering me with Rainbows because he knew it was going to be the darkest period of my life.

November 25, 2015

I cried looking at Gregory's picture when I sat down here. The strong feel of the new guy getting closer has me near trembling with joy and fear. *"I hope I can be the brightest—funniest—light in someone's life,"* I cried. *"Was I enough of that for you? Was I worth it, Honey? Was I worth all I put you through while I grew up?"* I had the muted TV on the music channel and expected a song to comfort me. To let me know he hears me. A Rainbow maybe? Something, anything?

I looked up to see *Boulevard of Broken Dreams*, just beginning. *"Oh, is that what I get? Very funny, Dr. Jones…. I walk alone now?"* In that moment I got it. He loved my sense of humor. I loved his. Over the years—anniversaries, birthdays—we would tell each other the things we loved about the other. He would often say, *"You're smart, you're funny, you're hot!"* Lol! Or he would say, *"You're beautiful."* I remember always loving that he thought I was funny. That's important to me.

I was always a bit surprised that he thought I was smart. Not sure why. Maybe small-town girl partied through High School and barely graduated….. And, of course, I loved that he thought I was hot or sexy or beautiful. All the words he used to describe me over the years. I knew the teasing, *Boulevard of Broken Dreams*, was his way of playing with me the way we did. Letting me know— *reminding me*—about the fun, beautiful, playful relationship we shared. And then I got a Rainbow!

December 1, 2015

I dreamed about Gregory! I dreamed about Rainbows the past few nights. They always wake me up! I see Rainbows and I wake up smiling! I dreamed a lot about Gregory. Nothing specific other than he was just there with me. He looked great. He had a full beard and I kept running my fingers through it. I was soaking him up. I was in heaven.

December 3, 2015

I had a Gregory thing happen. I had cried for a moment during my workout. Those fairly new, happy/sad tears. Missing him so much yet so grateful for all that time with him. Excited/scared about my future and all its beautiful possibilities. I moved into the last relaxation feeling exuberant. I raised my arms in the air and shouted out, *"I did it, Gregory! I survived! I'm excited about my life again!"* Just then the upbeat music seemed to get louder as I heard, *I can't believe it! I never thought I'd see you smile again!* Are you kidding me? I sat there stunned.

December 4, 2015

I've had several Rainbows already this morning! Gregory, so close in my heart, filling it to overflowing. I miss him. I also can get very excited about falling in love again. It's so magical anyway, but now that I'm older—and perhaps a little wiser—I look forward to cherishing every exciting moment. I wonder where I'll find him? My life has me preparing for my own beautiful destiny.

December 9, 2015

This morning—before 4:30 a.m.—I got a beautiful double Rainbow on the TV. If that wasn't enough I got another a few minutes ago. Last night I got a Rainbow reflected from the camera lens on a program. I can't count how many times I get those. Flashes of a Rainbow across the screen. Dim, faint sometimes, and other times bold and seeming to blink at me. The one I got last night was the full upside-down arc. The smile. Its colors faded dark to light, vibrating, flashing at me before fading out. It stayed much longer than my normal flashes of Rainbow light. *"I got it, Honey!"*

December 10, 2015

The tears roll down my face and my sweater is wet from all that have fallen this morning. No weeping, no sobs, no cries. Just tears flowing endlessly. Missing Gregory with my entire being mixed with gratitude for 30 years with a love like that. I ordered the Firefall CD and listened to it while doing Yoga yesterday. The first song really threw me. It's called, *Livin' Ain't Livin'*, and talks about life being pretty easy when you have someone to love and share it with. But livin' ain't livin' on your own.

Later in the workout I found myself sobbing through yet another Firefall song that felt like encouraging me—giving me permission—to move on. It's called *Goodbye I Love You*. It's encouraging me to find love again when it says that our love is not enough now because he's not here. That I'm going to need someone who is. Someone who'll never say, *"Goodbye I love you."*

I know the goodbye it speaks of. I cried the words, knowing I was letting go. Not of the Gregory that sends me Rainbows, but the man that was my husband. My person here on earth. The one I shared meals with, rode bikes with, and went to Mackinac Island every year with. The man I slept next to every night who is no longer beside me. I sleep alone.

December 12, 2015

As soon as I came into the house after my meeting two days ago I realized one of my earrings was gone. Heartbroken, I called on my dad, who believed nothing was ever lost. I retraced my steps back to the car in hopes of finding it. They're my favorite pair. No luck. I searched the car. Nothing. Once upstairs I put the lone earring on the dresser and tried not to feel heartbroken. I said the usual, *"Nothing is lost in the kingdom of God,"* and affirmed the earring is right where it's supposed to be. I let it go. The next morning when I went to put on earrings for the day there lay *both* earrings. Right where they're supposed to be. That's my father's doing. *"So, thanks Dad!"*

December 16, 2015

I'm meeting Greg's sister at the nursing home this morning to set up hospice for Mom. She went downhill just in the past two weeks. Makes me so sad. I've cried a lot about Gregory too. I told him I need a message, a sign, a Rainbow, to reassure my grieving heart. A few minutes later I needed to look up a word in the dictionary. It's usually right on the nightstand but I couldn't find it. I found it under the nightstand, along with his journal. It's been three years since I've looked at it. His words stole my heart and I sobbed big tears. *"Thanks for a good day—for no injuries to my fellow workers—they're really not a bad bunch. For LoriJean the Love of my life.... Megan and the joys she brings to me—Thanks again."*

December 19, 2015

I woke up, sat up in bed, and looked at the clock. It said 4:20. I turned on the TV to the Weather Channel. As soon as the picture came on I saw a big Rainbow! *"Good morning, Honey."* Before I got out of bed there was another one. I had a glimpse into another way of looking at things yesterday as I sat in silence. I saw something through Gregory's eyes. *His* life and the plan for it. Contrary to my vision 30 years earlier, I believed Gregory was it for me. I'd found the love of my life for the rest of my life. Grow old together. I see now that was exactly the plan for *Gregory's life* not mine. I was the love of *his* life for the rest of his life and we were together when *he* grew old.

In that moment I was filled with peace and I fully understood the part I played in Gregory's destiny the last 30+ years of his life. He had me loving him all the way to the threshold of the Other

Side. I can see that beautiful plan perfectly. It was an Aha! moment of the very best kind. It gave me strength. That, coupled with my clear vision 30 years before, and it all came full circle.

Lol! I went into the kitchen to warm my tea. I was stretching while it heated and talking to Gregory. As I stretched my arms over my head my sweater came up to expose my midriff. I remembered Gregory's hands on my waist, pulling me to him. My senses could feel the memory as if it were happening in real time. I whined to Gregory that this is what I need, what I miss. *"Feel my pain, dude,"* I said out loud, *"Four years...."* I moaned, and just then, I heard Gregory say, *"No doinky-doinky?"*

OMG! I burst out laughing like you wouldn't believe! That's my Gregory! In his goofier moments that's what he called sex. Doinky-doinky. Lol! I haven't thought of that in years! Makes me smile even now and confirms exactly what I've been talking about. That my wild and crazy guy is still here. Still making me laugh.

December 20, 2015

I had a sad cry this morning. Really sad. I miss that man so much. I miss everything about him. He was fun. I watched *Long Island Medium* last night and a wife and daughter were there to connect with their Dad and Husband. The wife said when he died all the fun left their lives. I could relate to that.

December 24, 2015

Oh that husband of mine. He's very funny. It's Christmas Eve morning but I hadn't really thought about it yet. I sat in the peace of my tinted blue bedroom while the winds howled outside and the chimes on the front porch clanged wildly. My thoughts—my heart—turned to Gregory and in a flash my memory scanned the past. In every bit of it I'm wrapped around him. My mind and heart began to think about the future. About being in love again. My eyes filled with tears and I said out loud, *"I can't imagine kissing anyone but you, Honey."* To which he quickly replied, *"Oh, you're gonna want to kiss this guy!"* LOL!

December 26, 2015

As I sat down to write, *Crazy* came on. I got up, as required, and danced. As always I felt my Gregory there with me and my heart overflowed with love and gratitude. My vision in 1982 frequently haunts me now. Something I conveniently put out of my mind for thirty years is now playing like it was yesterday. My steps in this foreign land continue to be hauntingly familiar.

Now I want to write about my experience in the basement. I found myself going through a couple of tubs and thumbing through stacks of cards I'd saved over the years. The first thing I came across was a little card that comes with flowers. It said, *"Happy Anniversary,"* and he'd written, *"You're the light of my life – Greg."* Then another and I remember this one. I had to hide it from the kids because it's X-rated. That's all I'm going to say. That's my Gregory.

Then a beautiful card. Water colored with a couple walking together along the beach holding hands. I opened it and it says, *"Happy Birthday,"* and he writes, *"And many more to share with you, Heart and Soul, G."* Then another birthday card. Blank inside he writes, *"Trees grow tall, a leaf will fall, but my love is deep like the roots. Greg."* Then I saw a Rainbow on the next card and, *"Happy Birthday."* It says, "We create our tomorrows by what we dream today." Inside it's from Greg's mom. She writes, *"Have a Happy Day!"* I felt like I hit the jackpot. I know there's more to find but this was enough for today.

December 28, 2015

I had a few sad conversations with Gregory yesterday and one already this morning. I miss being married. I don't want to let go. But how do you hold onto something that keeps getting further away? *I dreamed about Rainbows all night long.* Kept waking up. I love that. But I really want to see *Gregory* in my dream. I know it would help me so much.

December 29, 2015

I had a sad cry this morning then another a while ago. I realized I didn't get a Rainbow today. I let him know. Not long after that I got the most beautiful Rainbow when I turned on the TV to an Alaskan show. About an hour later I got another much more beautiful Rainbow, full, colorful arc. It made me cry.

December 30, 2015

I've been sitting in silence surrounded by the lights of the Christmas tree. I have memories of my life with Gregory and I hold onto them. I seem to be crying more sad tears as those memories play rather than gratitude or warm smiles. Last evening I felt the scary grief threatening as it has the past several days. The numbing, heart-stopping, breath-stealing grief that I'm surprised I haven't had all along. This is the reaction L.J. had to losing Greg. He died and it killed her. She couldn't breathe without him. She didn't want to.

He kissed me in the kitchen earlier. I was overcome with tears. I sat down and cried to him, looked up, closed my eyes, and kissed him. I felt his lips on mine. Ever so gently, ever so softly, I felt him kissing me! In a moment reminiscent of that day at Hospice House, he just kept kissing me over and over again in our kitchen. Tears rolling gently out of my closed eyelids, we just kept kissing, one after another. It was magical and heartbreaking. The tears flow now as they did then.

I've still been sick and have struggled to be well. My energy is low. I'm over it.

Chapter 23

One Rainbow At A Time

January 1, 2016

Wow.... What a morning already. I was the first to say *"Happy New Year"* when I woke up at 4:20 a.m. As I settled in the living room I turned on the TV and got bombarded with Rainbows!

January 5, 2016

I was sitting here in gratitude for everything. For 30 years with Gregory, for this house, for everything in it, for life itself. Ha! I turned to Gregory's smiling face and said, *"You gave me every-thing, Mr. Mister....."* Just then I looked up to the muted TV and *Broken Wings* was starting. By Mr. Mister! I love it! It reminds me that I need to learn how to fly again even with my broken wings. I miss him. I miss sharing my life, being in love. I will be ready for all of that again when the time comes. The light at the end of the tunnel. The pot of gold at the end of the Rainbow.

January 8, 2016

I got in the car yesterday and turned on the radio to hear my Rainbow in *True Colors*. That's more like it. I haven't been getting as many Rainbows lately and I didn't get any more after that. Kind of scary. I guess as long as I get at least one Rainbow a day I should be grateful. My first song this morning was Backstreet Boys' *Incomplete*. Beautiful song, but…. I just got a Rainbow! And then, *Crazy* came on and we danced! It is so amazing!

January 9, 2016

Woohoo! *I dreamed about amazing, beautiful, spectacular, colorful—like you've never seen—Rainbows! OMG! The colors were so intense and so vivid. The Rainbow was huge in front of me with other Rainbows behind and at the sides of it. Freakin' incredible! Woke me up!* I love that. Only thing better would be Gregory himself in my dream. But I needed that. The past two days I've only seen a handful of Rainbows. It was great for Gregory to say, *"Now this is a Rainbow,"* and give me all the brilliance from the Other Side.

I've cried sitting here this morning. Sad, sad tears. Missing Gregory so much and yet knowing….. Ugh. My word this year is *Completion. "I have to get over you, don't I? I have to accept that you can't come back and I'm still here."* My heart feels warm with his encouragement. My reading this morning talks about being able to loosen my grip on my grief so that it can be lifted from me. That my connection to Gregory is unchanged and can never be broken.

January 11, 2016

I had a few tears yesterday. Got my Rainbows too. I'm here without my Gregory in the physical and that's just the way it is. I have to accept it. I have to move toward the unchanged purpose of my life. And, as if on cue, I just got 3 Doors Down's, *When I'm Gone*. What do I do when you're gone? Love you when you're gone. Just love you. The other unchanged purpose of my life. And, in keeping with the theme of the day, my morning reading says that sooner than later we need to face the fact that things are different now and start living in this altered reality. Whatever.

January 12, 2016

I got my Rainbows yesterday! I laughed when I turned on the Weather Channel and heard, *"Now there's a Rainbow! A Double Rainbow! No, a Triple Rainbow!"* The co-anchor says, *"That's not a Trible Rainbow; One,"* and he circles the main Rainbow, then the second and he says, *"Two Rainbows."* Then he points out the wet pavement with the reflection of the Rainbow and says, *"Okay, it's not a triple Rainbow, it's a Bonus Rainbow!"* The word seems to shout at me and I was laughing at this point and giving Gregory *the weasel*, my heart overflowing with joy. Then they showed another picture of a double Rainbow and another and she said, *"We're just getting bombarded with Rainbows this morning!"* Lol! I'll take responsibility for that!

January 13, 2016

(Bedtime)—When I went to bed very early last night—not feeling well—I thought I hadn't got my Rainbow. Panic. Oh yeah, one little Rainbow. Whew. Still, it scares me and by this evening when I hadn't got a Rainbow *all day* I started to cry. *"Gregory, you have to keep sending me Rainbows, Dude."* I couldn't believe the emptiness I felt. I turned on the TV and *American Pickers* was on. Danielle called the guys from the shop. There it was, a Rainbow across her t-shirt! Ahhh, relief. A few minutes later another Rainbow. Whew! *"Not funny going all day and no Rainbows, Mr. Mister."*

January 14, 2016

I've had a miraculous morning already and I've only been sitting here for half an hour! It wasn't until I wrote the date that I remembered it's Gregory's birthday! He wins! He acknowledged it first. I turned on the music channel and Taylor Swift's, *Style*, came on. It made me want to move! So up I got and began moving to the music and feeling so free. Like with *Crazy*, I felt Gregory, only this was a much faster beat. The slow dances with *Crazy* we sort of melt into each other, our energies swirling together. This time it was different. No one would believe it. I'm having trouble describing it.

We were dancing, he twirled me, we danced toward each other, then out again but still touching outstretched hands. It was a great duo! An amazing feel of his hands on my waist, the feel of the twirl, of him pulling me back to him. I swear I could see the outline of his body, his energy, and I followed his lead. We were dancing a sexed up, jazzed up, waltz! I kid you not! My body was filled with goosebumps, the hair on my arms and neck stood up from the electricity. It was flawless.

And then I closed my eyes and opened my heart and I could feel someone that is alive for real. I could envision the new guy. My new dance partner. It was the most bizarre combination of relishing in this amazing dance with Gregory and then seeing my future dancing with someone else. *Can't Let Go* came on next. My heart felt so connected to the music and the feel in the room. Beautiful, amazing, indescribable peace.

When the song ended I recognized the music right away to *Endless Love*. That song will forever connect me to that moment in time when Gregory took his last breath and jumped right into my heart. The words sang in my head, reminding me that we are two hearts beating as one. Endless love. But this morning I heard something different right at the beginning. He starts out saying, my love and how there was only me for him. I found myself thinking, *"Yep, I was it for him, only me in his life."* Then the female verse says my *first* love. Wow, that's something to think about. No Rainbow yet today. *"Happy Birthday, Baby."*

January 16, 2016

I got three Rainbows by 5 a.m. On a commercial and the last one sort of pulsed at me. *"Thank you, Honey! That's more like it."* I've only got one little Rainbow a day for the past couple of days. Then not ten minutes later the Weather Channel was showing a photographer's work. It's hundreds of time-lapsed photos of the Boston skyline. One showed a Rainbow that moved across the sky.

After the slideshow the meteorologist said, *"I especially love the Rainbow seeming to dance across the sky."* Dang straight. This evening I turned on the TV and there was a *beautiful*, big bright Rainbow across the trees along the shoreline in Alaska. I needed a 'normal' Rainbow day. *"Thanks, Babe."*

January 17, 2016

Restless this morning, I tuned into a program and at the end the narrator sort of summed up the lessons and truths from the episode with words of wisdom. It resonated deeply within me and my mind wandered with the words. *It's hard to differentiate beginnings from endings. The end of something is not always painful and new beginnings may not be completely joyful. But letting go of the past brings its own serenity as life moves us gently toward a brand new day.*

January 20, 2016

Rough night. Still not feeling well, I decided to go back to bed after I fed the cats, something I rarely do. I knew there was a chance I would dream. Maybe even about Gregory. I didn't feel like I was going to be able to fall asleep. It felt more like just resting. Finally I decided to give it up. I got up and went down to the kitchen. As I passed the laundry room I glanced in and saw Gregory's boots, with him in them! I rushed in and there he was! His beard was dark and he looked so good. I couldn't believe he was standing in front of me.

I said, *"I knew you could do it! You're here and I'm not even dreaming!"* I put my hands in his beard then threw my arms around him! I was so happy! I said, *"Thank you for coming! Thank you, Honey!"* And then I opened my eyes and I was in my bed! I weep now only because it was so real and I was able to hug my Gregory again. I mean, there he was, exactly as he was in life. To be able to throw myself around him again felt so amazing. To have him standing here in our home again was the best. I needed that so much. And yet I weep because it's never going to be enough. Just like when he was alive. I always wanted to kiss and hug him.

January 21, 2016

I sat here and cried in my tea first thing. I'm struggling. I don't feel well. I have no appetite. I'm having a hard time breathing. I turned on the TV and heard that life isn't always unicorns and Rainbows. Whatever. And just now I heard that after a big storm comes a Rainbow. Well bring it on! I'm about ready for this storm to be over. Still, I got several Rainbows yesterday and I hugged my husband!

January 23, 2016

It's a beautiful thing to know you're doing what you're supposed to be doing. In life and in the day. The enemy attempts to make me feel useless—if not worthless—but I know I'm doing the best I can. When I feel better I do better. Period. I cried earlier missing Gregory so much and feeling like I'm never going to stop being so sad about it. Perhaps in those moments of letdown, where the tears overflow like a swollen river, I will always feel that sad. It's how I feel after a crying spell that's most important. To the degree that I mourn I also rejoice.

Chapter 24

Rainbows And More Grief

January 25, 2016

Greg's mom died yesterday. It was a quiet, peaceful day and I knew she was going to die. Every time the phone rang I figured it was the call. At 3:40 p.m. it was. Megan had just left and Greg's sister and two of Mom's granddaughters were there. They said it was so peaceful and I knew it was. I could feel it at my house. And I have felt that peaceful numb until just a few minutes ago and then I cried.

January 27, 2016

When I was going through boxes in the basement looking for pictures of Mom I found more cards from Gregory. I found a letter he wrote to me in 1990 when he was in Ohio at Line School. We were separated for three weeks, our longest ever at that point. We hated it. His letter expresses his love for me and the kids. *"Sat. 10-27-90—10:18 p.m.—Hi Baby, it's been just a few minutes since I talked with you and I miss you even more. I really miss just feeling you against me in bed at night."* He has messages in there for both of the kids, which I was thrilled to read. But he missed me so much and I felt the same way. *"It's time to go baby,* time to call it a night—*I miss you like I never thought I could—I love you so much—your forever Greg.*" Those treks down memory lane can be exhausting. I continue to feel poorly. Life feels like a blur as I struggle to get well.

Oh! First thing this morning I came down and turned on the weather before I went to the kitchen. Even before the picture came on I heard, *"Look! It's a circle!"* And just like I knew it would be, a Rainbow! Not just one, but a Double Rainbow! Oh yes! I went to the kitchen and the clock said 4:20. Of course it did! I'm so excited about the Rainbow book. You can't make this sh-t up!

January 28, 2016

I started my day at 4 a.m. with a Rainbow. I turned on the TV to check the weather. I heard, *"Cloud Rainbows,"* and was just in time to hear all about this amazing weather phenomenon. Then I turned to the music channel just in time to hear *Wherever You Will Go*. Tears rolled down my cheeks when I heard that perhaps he'll find a way to make it back to me. He sure did! The next song was *Unwritten*, by Natasha Bedingfield, and the words spoke to me. They say to open up those dirty windows and allow the sun to come back in.

I feel like that's how I've been looking at my life. Through a dirty window. All this illness and health stuff just has me feeling like all my windows are dirty. I sat here realizing that life just hasn't been any fun since Gregory died. His death, which could have killed me—and I would have been alright with that—didn't. The plan hasn't changed in the bigger picture. In fact, Gregory's death, like I saw 30 years before, should be confirmation that these visions of mine can be trusted.

And yet, beaten down with illness and injury, pain and discom-fort, the enemy gets in and says, *"You're too sick to ever do the things you're shown. Your hands are getting old and are over-worked and hurt all the time. They're going to give out on you. You'll <u>never</u> do cartwheels again."* Ugh. If I felt good I would kick the enemy's ass to the curb. I would see the lie. My God tells me to be still and know. Trust. Grieve. Heal. It all takes time. The enemy doesn't want me to know that.

February 1, 2016

For three days I did nothing but rest, eat, watch movies, rest, repeat. I didn't write because it was just too painful. I have to give myself a break for not feeling well. I need to stop judging myself for the way my body heals. For the time it takes. His mom dying has put a shadow over things, even as I'm happy as can be for her. As I linger in the in-betweens the scripture below helps immensely. *"Do not worry about tomorrow, for tomorrow will worry about itself."* –Matthew 6:34.

February 2, 2016

I dreamed about being surrounded by an aura of spirits and light. They were alive with movement and electrical lights that seemed to be attached to me. No matter where I went they were protecting me. It was really cool. Nothing could hurt me. I had spiritual protection. It was a powerful reassurance dream.

February 3, 2016

I got my Rainbows at 4:07 a.m. As soon as I turned on the TV to check the weather it was Rainbows and lightning! A fairly rare phenomenon. Double Rainbows and lightning! I'm so tuned in that even the word itself seems to reverberate every time I hear it. This morning it was *Rainbow, Rainbow, Rainbow,* as the meteorologist kept saying the word. It seemed to echo from the TV. The energy in the room changed and I can't stop smiling.

February 5, 2016

I got my beautiful Rainbow early this morning. Still, not a minute ago I had one of the saddest, most heartbreaking cries I've had in a long time. The kind where you can't catch your breath, like an inconsolable child. The saddest of the sad. I cried to Gregory,

"I told you! I begged you, pleaded with you. This is why." I was referring to his smoking and my periodic pleas over the years for him to think about what it would do to me if he died before his time because of cigarettes. In my pathetic state I cried to him, *"Your death nearly killed me. Truly. Almost four years later I'm still struggling to be well!"* I looked to the scripture on this page. *"For the spirit God gave us does not make us timid, but gives us power, love and self-discipline."* –2 Timothy 1:7

February 11, 2016

I had a few sad tears here this morning. I miss the playful interaction between Greg and me. This morning in the kitchen I remembered all of that. And then I felt him, felt his hands on my waist, his body behind me. I remembered everything. And in that moment I could sense a time when I would be *alive* in a relationship again. It's a strange sensation. The ghost of a man who isn't here yet, blended, or simultaneous with the ghost of the one who's gone but hasn't left.

February 16, 2016

Yesterday I turned on the TV and there was an animated squirrel prancing around a blank screen before stopping in the middle, arms folded to his chest, then with each paw unfolding like a fan, a Rainbow! *"Swear to God, tell you to your face!"* The commercial continued, having nothing to do with squirrels or Rainbows. It was a Rainbow just for me. I got several yesterday.

February 17, 2016

I turned on the music channel as soon as I sat down and turned the volume to low. I wanted to be able to hear when *Here Without You* started, which I somehow knew was going to play next. When the song ended I reached for the remote to turn it up just as I heard the familiar music. Tears filled my eyes to overflowing. I thanked my Gregory over and over. The song means so much. It is truly a gift to me every time I hear it.

When *Here Without You* was over I thanked him again and then turned the channel to the soft rock station where *Who Loves You?* was just beginning. My heart leapt. That's my Gregory! He would often say, *"Who loves you baby?"* He did. He does. It's an amazing feeling when he's sending me Rainbows or speaking to me through songs. The energy changes in the room. My heart feels light and full of life. My grief is lifted in those moments. Otherwise I have my honey heavy on my mind.

February 21, 2016

By 4:40 a.m. I'd received three Rainbows! Makes my day. I've had my tears too. I haven't written for a few days because my hands were hurting worse than ever.

February 22, 2016

I feel terrible, I mean truly. Mornings are so rough and I feel so sick I can barely stand it. A headache last night and now. Lungs clogged and body bloated. Hands nearly useless especially the left one. My liver area is swollen and hurts so bad. I am as beaten down as I've ever been. As unwell as my worst day. Another trip to my doctor and I have no answers and am beyond discouraged. Chest x-ray clear. She said it must be allergies. X-rays on my hands showed tendonitis in my wrist. Liver enzymes normal. Went to my Kinesiologist and my liver showed again. I knew it.

Thankfully a light shines in the distance and I move toward it. Trusting what I'll find when I get there. Today I feel down. My first song was *Crazy* and dancing is non-negotiable. I got up and danced. Moved this sick and tired body and knew that Gregory did that on purpose. I could hear him, *"C'mon,"* as he pulled me up, *"You can do it. You're never too sick to dance."*

February 27, 2016

I dreamed about my dad! Ahhhh. He walked in the room and stood there looking so handsome and so healthy. I ran over to him and gave him the biggest hug. I threw my arms around him. He looked so good. I told him I've missed him so much. Then he was sitting in a comfy chair and I went over and sat at his feet. I just loved looking at him. I asked if it was true, was he healthy? No pain? You can breathe? He said, "Yep, just like you told me." And I did! I told him he'd be able to breathe and would have no pain. It was such a great dream. I saw my dad! Reassurance dream. I needed it.

February 29, 2016

I just got *Here Without You* and didn't cry! It made my day. That sad grief I was feeling again hasn't hit me for days. I think I'm glad about that even as I feel a little lost. A quote from Plato in my Gratitude Journal says, *"The beginning is the most important part of the work."* I have made a beginning. I just got *Here Without You* again! Bonus!! But I cried all the way through this time. It's okay.

March 3, 2016

I have been so sick. I struggled to get to my Kinesiology appointment and was barely functional when I got there. Liver still showed and so did adrenals. Hiatal hernia was out and I felt really sick. Calcium was low which I also knew because I've been getting cramps in my feet and legs. Out the door with herbs and supplements and a new attitude! I should start feeling a lot better in a day or two when adrenals and liver restore.

March 7, 2016

Mom's funeral a couple of days ago was beautiful. I brought Gregory's ashes with me. It seemed fitting. I didn't cry yesterday. It's been a long time since I could say that. I got several Rainbows though and talked to my love but no tears. So far so good today too.

Chapter 25

Relief At Last

March 9, 2016

I laughed my head off when I turned on the TV and there was a Skittles commercial. Steven Tyler's image made out of Skittles. He sings, higher, higher, and his face of Skittles explodes! Then a big bright Rainbow shoots across the screen and it says, *"Rock the Rainbow! Taste the Rainbow!"* Love it! I smiled to my toes. I could feel Gregory there with me in that moment. It's such a gift. I feel kind of in-between. Not in my deep grief yet not really in life after all of that. In between. *The Hall*. It feels like a strange place to be. In transition. Becoming something new.

March 10, 2016

I dreamed about Gregory! I was standing next to him and we were sort of leaning on a big wooden bar or counter. I wrapped my arms around his and put my hands in his and just held onto him! It was so great having him next to me again.

March 13, 2016

I haven't written for a couple of days. I just haven't had anything to say. The *in-betweens* have required no dialogue. No processing of thought or feeling. No highs no lows. No excitement no sadness. Just am. A sort of crazy void. A lapse in time and space where life is okay. Needs are met and I feel content. As foreign and perhaps uncomfortable as that has felt. Especially journaling. Nothing to say.

March 16, 2016

I dreamed about Gregory and I'm not sure I like it. *He and I were walking in opposite directions. We walked right past each other. I had my head turned watching him as I went by but he was looking straight ahead. We both kept walking. The C.C. Power guys Greg worked with—who gave him his nickname—were off in the distance and they were hootin' and hollerin' at him, saying, "Look! It's Rainbow! Hey Rainbow!" Greg sort of smiled, amused, but kept walking and looking straight ahead.*

As I sat down to process the dream I turned on the music channel just in time to hear, *"I love you, but we should go our separate ways."* What?! I have cried most of this morning. I wept about the dream. I cried to Gregory. *"You can't be walking away; I'm still waiting for a sex dream!"* Lol! The gal on the weather channel just said, *"There are going to be lots of Rainbows today as thunderstorms move across the area."* Yes there will be.

March 18, 2016

This morning I turned on the music and heard something about moving along, moving along, in an upbeat dorky song that reminds me of my Gregory. It's like he's saying, *"Lighten up, life's not so serious, chillax!"* It's how we were. We were playful throughout our life together. We had fun. This is exciting for me to remember. To feel his energy all around me. This morning feels profound to me. I feel like I'm being pushed out of the hall. Ever since that crazy song first thing this morning. It's called, *Move Along*, by The All-American Rejects. Even if you've lost your hope, just move along.

I started watching *The Haunting Of (Harry Lennox)*, the night before last so it was still paused where I left off. As soon as I hit play Kim Russo is pointing her finger and says, *"Your dad just said get that book finished..."* and it went to break. I hit pause and stared at the screen in shock. From the energy in the room I knew that my dad took this opportunity to get that message across to me.

I hit play and the show came back on and I continued to watch. On the next break it says, *"Coming up—Your dad just said get that book finished."* It came back on and during the actual segment the message was reiterated a third time, only now with an added piece. *"Your dad just said get that book finished.... it's important."* The words seemed to echo as the message repeated its importance. *"I get it! I'm doing it!"*

March 19, 2016

I turned on the TV and Sheryl Crowe's, *Try To Love Again*, was on. *"Oh, Gregory."* The song after that was even more powerful. It was *Change*, by Kimberly Locke. So powerful to me in that moment. It gave me goosebumps head to toe. A woman came up to me after a meeting the other day where I finally talked about my hands and my fear and frustration about them, and she handed me a paper with *"Medical Medium"* written on it and asked if I'd heard of it. No, but I went right home and ordered it. I can't wait to read it. I feel good. I feel alive. Excited. Like a change comin' on!

March 20, 2016

I keep crying those amazed tears. I can't stop. I don't know how to even begin to tell the story and do it all justice. It's a feeling so strong I'm overcome and overwhelmed most of the time. How do you describe a feeling in the air? A change in the energy field all around you that had been previously undetectable? It feels too incredible to talk about. I'm only making myself attempt to do it justice here.

I got in the car yesterday and music began playing. There were no words as the gentle music played on, vaguely, eerily, familiar. I was lost in the energy in the car, in that residual swirling of Spirit that seems to be even stronger around me lately. Pretty soon my mind started to key into a long-forgotten, yet powerfully connected emotion and a chill ran through my spine.

I began to recognize a song I haven't heard in probably 20 years. A song that was such a favorite of mine I still have the video recorded on VHS somewhere in the basement. No way to play it but I still have it. As I realized what song was playing I continued to get goosebumps. It was Tesla's *Love Song*. As that distinctive voice began and a shiver ran through me, my eyes filled with tears and I forgot to breathe when the words spoke to me. *"Do I think that it's over?"* Maybe. Then it reassures me that it may take some time to heal my broken heart but that I don't need to worry because love *will* find me again.

Now the tears were flowing and the chill bumps tingled throughout my entire being. I sat stunned in the car as the words continued on, touching me to my soul. Then first thing this morning when I turned on the TV, I got *Second Chance*. Geesh. Okay, okay, I know that you can't have a second chance at anything without letting something go. Never before has this second chance been so evident. Never before has it felt so clearly part of the plan. Right after *Second Chance*? *Meant To Live*. *"I get it! I get it!"*

March 21, 2016

I've been crying deep, sad tears this morning. The loss is near unbearable in these moments. I looked up to the muted music channel. *Right Here Waiting*, by Richard Marx. It's a beautiful song. Beautiful timing. It says that no matter where I go or what I do he's going to be right here. In other words he's still saying to me what he said from the start, *"I'm not going anywhere, Babe."*

I got my Rainbow in a really profound way. Sitting here in silence I started thinking about that crazy little cartoon squirrel I saw on a TV commercial a couple of days ago. Hopping around before landing in the middle and paws to his chest he opens his arms like opening a fan and opens a little Rainbow! I sat in the living room staring at the muted TV and thinking about that funny little commercial. I had the thought, *"Now watch, I'm going to see that silly commercial right now."* Just then the little squirrel appeared and I couldn't believe it! He hopped around, stopped in the middle and opened up a Rainbow for me..... I just sat there.

March 23, 2016

(Evening) —A migraine has had me in a dark room all day. It finally let up enough to be bearable. My Rainbows came when I turned on the TV a minute ago. It was an Indian dance. The Instructor waved her arms one way and said, *"Rainbow..."* then the other way, *"Rainbow..."* It made me laugh. Seriously? When that was over there was a preview for the new season of *Life Below Zero* and the music was an eerie, slow, haunting version of *Somewhere Over The Rainbow*. Oh, and after feeling and sensing Uncle Steve the past few days I got in the car yesterday just as Autograph's, *Turn Up The Radio* was starting! He was the original keyboard player and sang background vocals. I can hear him clearly. I turned it up and rocked out all the way to my destination!

March 25, 2016

I've been literally bombarded with Rainbows here this morning. I just got a smiley face Rainbow! When I first turned on the TV I got the Steven Tyler Skittles commercial. *Rock the Rainbow! Taste the Rainbow!* Lol! Then I changed the station to the Animal Planet channel just as they were showing a dove snuggling with a cat. I heard, *"This is Rainbow the Dove..."* Seriously? I laughed. Rainbow, Rainbow, Rainbow. I hear the word and I smile. I need to smile. I need to laugh. I'm healing and no one ever said they were having fun while healing from anything.

All the Rainbows feel like extra encouragement from Gregory. I need it. I'm barely functioning. I've still been so sick. After reading *Medical Medium*, by Anthony William, I had my Kinesiologist test me for the Epstein Barr Virus (EBV) and it showed. It causes all kinds of health problems. I feel empowered and got started on all the supplements to eradicate it. It will take time but I'm willing to do whatever it takes. And the author says if I follow his guidelines I will heal from this.

April 9, 2016

After feeding the girls this morning and getting my tea I turned to *Weather Caught On Tape*. I was feeling pretty peaceful, it's Saturday morning and I'm home for the weekend so I can rest. I feel good. The segment showed an amazing shot of the sky exploding with lightning and hitting three skyscrapers at the same time as smaller lightning bolts exploded all around them. Just then the guy adjusted his camera ever so slightly upwards to capture a Rainbow fading into view!

This is the shift in my grief that I've been waiting for. To get over the part that just feels so devastating. To a place where life doesn't feel like a threat. Where love and laughter and fun are the biggest part of it. Life is beginning to look inviting again. Feeling safe enough to venture out. All I know is I feel stronger about Gregory. I was touched to tears this morning by the Rainbow. Amazed and humbled by the love emanating from him.

My *Writer's Digest* magazine came yesterday and my eyes fell to the word *Rainbow* on the cover. I couldn't believe it. It's actually someone's last name! I love the way the word seems to gently pulsate before me, putting an emphasis on it. I love my life! I love this magic, this extraordinary, mostly unexplainable—if not impossible—series of events that is my life.

April 13, 2016

I just got *Here Without You* and I can't tell you what it does for me. It's a beautifully sad, soul-soothing song that somehow puts me in a place where I'm nurtured in my grief. Comforted like a parent reassuring their wounded child. Songs have always had a way of softening the sharp emotional edges of life. I looked at Gregory's picture beside me..... a slight numbing chill ran through me. I haven't been so sad. I haven't cried a lot. I may not have cried yesterday at all.

This morning I said something that I'm not sure I've asked him before. Kind of like the question I had for my dad after he died before he answered me with the 'photo album' incident. I asked him, *"Are you good with where you are? Happy? Better than being here? Because I feel sad that you lost your life, that it was cut short."* In that moment I knew he was going to send me a message in a big way.

The music was on low. A song ended and there was a pause in between and I knew my love was going to speak to me. I could feel the energy in the room shift and my heart could feel Gregory everywhere. Then the song came on. *Photograph*, by Ed Sheeran. I love the song. How could I have never heard these words before? I know them, I sing along to the radio in the car. But not like this morning. It reminds me that love can hurt, that it can be hard sometimes, but that it's the only thing that matters. Then it says that I can keep our love like a photograph, that our memories are made for us and that they are the only thing we take with us when we die. The love. It's all about the love. It never dies. It only grows stronger.

It gives me great peace knowing he is, indeed, waiting for me to come home. It gave me goosebumps. I also know that he doesn't want me to wait to go home. He wants me to live. I'm still here. I'm still young. Love can heal. It's the only thing. When I was talking to him I also said, *"If you're okay, I'm okay."* Lol! *"Ha! Ha! Gregory, very funny."* Just as I wrote that a mellow song in the background ended and I found myself switching to another channel. Just as the channel was changing and a new song was starting I swear I heard an upbeat, goofy jingle that said, "Nah, nah, honey I'm good..." Seriously? He's getting pretty darn good with the songs, don't you think?

April 15, 2016

I had a moment here in the living room. A moment when I looked around at pictures of Gregory on every wall and at every age—especially our wedding picture—and I couldn't connect. I couldn't relate. For a moment I was lost in some kind of in-between place. Where my life with him seems too far from where I am today. *"It feels too far away, Gregory,"* I cried. And then I wept for a few moments. It's a feeling I've never had before. As if in that moment I could feel the shift in the Universe where everything in this moment moves ahead and the past moves further behind.

The swirling around me of his life in pictures—*our* lives in stages over thirty years—took my breath away. This journey without my Gregory—four years next Tuesday—has gone so fast, like I've been in slow motion and the world's on fast forward. I watched a movie this morning where a guy lost his wife. He was in a dark place for a year—mostly drinking—and I couldn't help feeling so grateful that I'm sober. If I'd have added alcohol to losing Gregory, I can only imagine how dark it would have been.

When he emerged from his isolation and stepped into the real world they showed the world around him going in fast forward while he was in slow motion! I couldn't believe it. It's how I've felt for a very long time. A month felt like a week for the first couple of years.

I was standing in Lowe's yesterday waiting to buy stuff for his mom's house. I thought about how this is the last time I'll have to do this since the house is going up for sale. Just then I heard, *"Rainbow after the rain,"* in the background music. I couldn't believe it and yet I smiled and said under my breath, *"I love you too, Babe."* He hears my thoughts. He hears my heart. Later, upstairs for the evening, I turned on the TV and there was that goofy little animated squirrel just as he positioned himself in the center of the screen, front paws to his chest, and opened a Rainbow!

April 17, 2016

I wish I could say I felt better but it's been rough. My body feels like it's fighting the battle of a lifetime. Gregory has sent me many Rainbows already today so no sense getting discouraged.

April 20, 2016

Rough night. At 12:30 a.m. I finally ran a hot bath, whining. Uneasiness and unrest taunted me. The bath soothed all the restlessness and pain out of me. Somewhere around 4:30-5:00 a.m. I reached for the TV remote saying, *"Okay, whatcha got for me on my birthday?"* Just then the picture came on to a beautifully haunting scene of a double Red Rainbow! The photographer said, *"OMG! Look! It's a Double Red Rainbow!"* Then they went on to say that Red Rainbows are rare, let alone a double Red Rainbow. There you have it. I knew my Gregory sent me a *Red* Rainbow as an added nod to me—to *Red*—his redhead. Also rare.

Chapter 26

Laughing Again

April 22, 2016

This morning when I looked at the pictures all around me I couldn't help smiling. *"We had a lot of fun, didn't we? So much fun."* Then I remembered this was something my grief book promised. That one day my sad memories would be replaced with all the happy times we shared. It was a time I've longed for. A time when I would feel strong enough to step into a new life.

April 25, 2016

I've had three beautiful Rainbows already this morning and also got them all weekend. I really need to write down every time I get my Rainbows because my writings do not come close to documenting the frequency of this phenomenal gift. Like last night when I turned on the TV and it was on Ghost Whisperer. A couple were dancing to a vinyl record on a turntable and I heard, *"You're beautiful... like a Rainbow."* Happens all the time.

April 27, 2016

I've seen several beautiful Rainbows already this morning. Including an amazing Red Rainbow over the Grand Canyon. *Incredible.* I laughed yesterday like I haven't since Gregory died. Twice. The second time I really let it out. It felt so good. I laughed a lot with Gregory. *He* made me laugh. It's been four years and I haven't felt like laughing. At least now I feel like I want to laugh. So go ahead, bring it on, make me laugh!

May 4, 2016

I was sitting here deep in thought, in feeling and memory. I turned to the Animal Planet channel to check in with a program about cheetah cubs being released back into the wild. It was a rainy scene and just then the camera panned the sky to a beautiful Rainbow. A most peaceful scene. Those quiet moments are filled with Gregory, with reassurance, with comfort that seems to always come at the exact moment I need to know that he hears my heart, knows my pain, feels my love for him. What a beautiful response. Health-wise I'm struggling. My hands ache. I want to cry but I think I'll make a smoothie and run a bath instead. Then if I need to I can cry in the tub! Just got *Lotta Love*! Sweet.

May 6, 2016

I had a special moment this morning. I was sitting here with my tea, switching channels between country videos and my usual music channel that plays *Here Without You*. I switched to that channel as a song was ending. Then that haunting, *Here Without You* music began and everything in the room changed. How his spirit can envelop every fiber of my being is beyond me. Like an amazing, incredible hug from him.

May 10, 2016

I saw my doctor again and she called with the results of my blood work. Everything looks great, especially my liver, even though it's not. After I hung up I had a flashback to my seven-year nightmare with being so sick—before discovering food allergies—and trying everything the medical field had to offer, only to get the continued and repeated message, *"Everything looks good. Tests came back normal."* But the worst one? *"There's nothing wrong with you."* It caught me off guard and made me cry for a moment. Then I was like, are you kidding me? The Epstein Barr virus didn't show! I kicked its ass! Woohoo!

May 13, 2016

It's one of those mornings where I can just feel that I'm going to hear a song that speaks to me. I turned on the music just as a favorite of mine was starting. *Miracles,* by Jefferson Starship. Love that song. As I listened to it I was shocked at what I heard. I guess I never realized what a sexual song it is. I printed out the words and blushed when I read them. Oh, my. But what surprised me even more than that was a line I swear I didn't realize was in there. The one that talks about being able to hear Rainbows when he talks to me.

May 18, 2016

I'm excited about my life. I know it's a beautiful life. I saw myself in the mirror yesterday and I was smiling. Kind of caught me off guard. Hmmm..... been smiling a lot more lately. And talking to Gregory and smiling.

May 19, 2016

I'm definitely smiling more. I feel lighter in my spirit, more playful in my soul! I talk to Gregory and I smile. I think about funny things he said or did and I smile. I'm smiling now! I guess I'm surprised because it makes me realize how much I *haven't* smiled since he died. I'm reminded of how much I smiled when he was alive.

May 26, 2016

Oh my, not sure how to feel about my latest song. It's one I'd never heard before and now I've heard it three times in the past three days. Every time I got in the car and turned on the radio it was starting. It's called, *Tell Your Heart To Beat Again*, by Danny Gokey. Powerful. It basically tells me that I can't live in the past anymore. That door is closed. I have to say goodbye to where I've been in order to move forward. It says that my story isn't over yet and my journey has just begun. It says that God is working everything out for my good so I need to trust in the plan for my life. Tell my heart to beat again.

Upstairs for the evening I turned on the TV and a movie was just ending. I was pulled to the next one starting. That gentle nudge from Spirit that I've learned to follow. The movie was called, *The Color of Rain*, and began with a video diary from a man to his young children that you knew he wouldn't be there to raise. The true story follows a young widow who goes to the same church as a man who lost his wife suddenly to brain cancer. He had three young children and she had two young boys.

As the story was unfolding I couldn't help but connect to those two. Feeling from early on that if I were to ever fall in love again I would feel safer with someone who had also suffered the loss of their spouse. It was heartbreaking when a scene showed her standing in the doorway of their bedroom, staring at their empty bed. It's such a personal loss. When the two began dating—too soon in the eyes of some—they were both worried that they were doing the wrong thing and she said she wished they could get a sign letting them know their spouses approved.

They took the kids to the woods. The children ran ahead on the path as the adults walked and talked. As they came around the bend he stopped when he saw something up ahead. He grabbed her arm to pull her back. He smiled and pointed. I just knew. I felt the hairs on my body rise as a shiver ran through me. He pointed and said, *"Look, there's your sign."* She turned and there it was, the most beautiful *Double Rainbow*. I couldn't believe it. I knew it, but I still couldn't believe it. Tears rolled down my cheeks.

When the credits rolled and the song began I knew, again, that this song I've never heard before was going to have Rainbows in it. I'm like, are you kidding me right now? Is this the sign for me that it feels like? And the chorus began. *"All the colors of the Rainbow... All the colors of the Rainbow."* Are you for real? Afterwards, I reached to shut off the TV and saw the Skittles commercial just starting. I smiled big when I saw Steven Tyler. Then the huge Rainbow at the end and the words, *"Rock the Rainbow! Taste the Rainbow!"* Love-love it!

(Bedtime)

I can't believe this. I was ready to shut off the TV and lights when I heard in my head, *"Turn to the soft rock station."* *Beautiful In My Eyes* was just starting. As the words sang out and the music played, I felt like I was being hugged by my Gregory. He says that I am the Rainbow in his skies. He says that we never have to say goodbye because true love lives forever.

June 2, 2016

OMG!! This is incredible. Ever since I had that dream in 2012 where I asked Gregory how long before I join him and he said, *"Twenty-two years,"* I've been talking to God about that. I asked if the twenty-two years is negotiable? Lol! But seriously, it's been weighing on me ever since the dream. That's not enough time! So last night at bedtime I reached to turn off the light and I heard, *"Grab your Bible."*

I wanted to ignore the voice and turn off the light but the feeling was strong. I grabbed my Bible knowing I was going to get a message and feeling a little unnerved. I shuffled the pages then let it fall open randomly, closed my eyes, made a circle with my finger, and landed it somewhere on the page. I opened my eyes and read the words under my finger. A numbing chill ran through me. I couldn't believe it.

I landed on II Kings 5-6: *"I have heard thy prayer. I have seen thy tears; behold, I will heal thee: And I will add unto thy days fifteen years."* I stared at the words. Tears rolled down my cheeks one after the other. Do you realize what that says? It says that I just got blessed with fifteen more years on top of the twenty-two years Gregory told me I have left before I join him! I'm excited. I'm relieved to know I now have thirty-three years left instead of eighteen! It's huge! It means I could have *another* thirty years with someone! Woohoo!

June 5, 2016

I've been in the best place—in my mind and heart and with my grief—since Gregory died. I didn't cry for three days! I didn't feel sad or anything. I felt normal. Yesterday afternoon I stopped at the video store. I started looking for a thriller but then said under my breath, *"I shouldn't be looking for a thriller when I'm trying to be open to God's messages."* I rounded the corner and there it was. I was pulled to it like a magnet. *God's Compass.*

The backstory was about a woman my age whose husband also died too young. She went into the closet and there hung all his clothes. My heart sank. They looked just like Gregory's. Then there it was, a Hawaiian shirt. Gregory loved to wear Hawaiian shirts. I started to cry. So did she. When she started pulling clothes down and laying them on the bed my heart skipped a beat and I began to cry. She folded the Hawaiian shirt then folded it again and stared at it. She was me in that moment and we were in a club no one ever wants to be in. *The Widow's Club.* She woke up lying on the bed with his Hawaiian shirt laid out next to her where he would have been. I cried some more.

She stared at their boat covered in a tarp..... The message was all about God having a *true north* for each of us, and He already knows we can handle it. The movie ended with the widow driving the boat, aptly named *Dreamchaser*, cruising across the water wearing the Hawaiian shirt! The song, *What A Wonderful World*, by Louis Armstrong, was playing as the end credits rolled. I had a big smile on my face and felt really good inside when I heard the part about how beautiful all the colors of the Rainbow are. Don't I know it! What a wonderful world we live in.

I've been smiling a lot lately. I mean genuinely burst out smiling like I haven't done since before Gregory got sick. It feels really good. I know he's happy about it. I feel light in my life for the first time in years. I just heard Gregory excitedly saying, *"There's my girl!"*

June 14, 2016

Mama was hospitalized and had to have emergency gallbladder surgery. My sister and I went to the cafeteria. It was full so we ended up sitting in a section in the back where we never do. She set her purse down and I went to heat my coffee and to go to the bathroom. When I got back Sis asked where the bathrooms were. I told her and she picked up her purse and there it was. My Rainbow! A Country magazine lay on the table with a big Rainbow across the cover. I knew Mama was going to be okay. It was my sign.

June 21, 2016

I had a moment coming up the picture wall last night. All the pictures are looking dated. The ones of Greg and I look so young, the backgrounds—if not the clothing—reflecting the decade we were in. My life with him is feeling in the past. I'm not sure how I feel about that. Ahhh, I just got Keith Urban's, *Making Memories of Us*. We can follow the Rainbow… When I crawled into bed last night my mind was full of him. I turned on the TV to a beautiful Rainbow on an Alaskan show. It was such a peaceful scene; a Rainbow set gently against the grassy green hills.

Chapter 27

Relying On Faith

June 22, 2016

When I got in the car I heard, *"Beautiful like a Rainbow...."* I haven't been wearing my wedding rings and that feels okay. Just for today I'm good with that.

June 29, 2016

This morning I got, *I'll Be There*, by the Spinners. It's a beautiful song and a familiar reminder. I'll take all I can get. It reminds me that I'm at a fork in the road. That can be a scary place to be if you don't trust the future. But as always he reminds me that all I have to do is call on him and he'll be there. I was watching a show last night and there was a love scene. My mind wandered over thirty years of beautiful lovemaking and I wept. Straight-to-the-heart grief. Missing Gregory so much I could barely stand it. Crying to him and telling him how much I miss us. How much my life is missing. I looked up to the muted TV. *We Found Love.* "We sure did, Baby." After that, *Dare You To Move.* "I am, Babe." After that, *Forever In Love.* "I hear ya."

July 1, 2016

I finally caved in and took a pain pill to get relief from the pain in my hands. For the first time in a long time I was pain free for about 8 hours. But when the pain med wore off the pain was worse, it seemed, than what I was dealing with before. And my liver does not handle meds, so I'm really sick today. I won't be doing that again. I've cried more these past few days and already this morning missing Gregory so much. Megan called to say Kadyn told her, *"Papa Greg is my friend."* She asked him what he does with Papa Greg and he said, *"He plays toys with me."* She asked him what he looks like and he said, *"Like that picture,"* and pointed to Greg's picture. I love that so much.

July 2, 2016

I turned on the radio and heard, *Just Remember I Love You*. I love that song so much even if it's a bittersweet Rainbow for me. It made me cry but that's how it's been lately. I've cried a lot again. Sad, sad, missing Gregory tears. Heartfelt communication with my love. Right after that I got *Here Without You* and the energy I feel in and around me during that song is indescribable. It's such an amazing sensation. The beautifully painful reality of being *here* without him poured out in a love song, all while feeling his presence *everywhere*. It's quite magical.

Tears rolled down my cheeks at one point, but by the end I was smiling ear to ear. Just in time for *Crazy* and I got up. I danced and cried and danced some more. I danced *for* Gregory and I cried. There is something so amazing about dancing. It says I want to live. In the midst of my sadness I choose life. I choose joy. I dance.

July 4, 2016

The Scripture on this page of my journal from, *Exodus 33:14*, makes me tear up. *"God said, 'My Presence will go with you. I'll see the journey to the end.'"* If I held onto nothing else, this would get me through. I'm feeling more alive than I have in a very long time. I'm tired, make no mistake, and not at all where I want to be with my health, but in my mind and heart I am so excited about my life. Gregory is happy to see me like this. He sends me Rainbows every single day.

July 6, 2016

Before I turned off the TV for the night I switched to the music channel and said, *"Let's see if I get a Rainbow before I go to sleep."* I did not get a Rainbow in the song that was playing but when I flipped back to the Weather Channel there was my Rainbow! *"High five! Weasel! Love-love you!"*

July 8, 2016

Last night at bedtime, just before I shut off the TV, I got a beautiful Double Rainbow! And the Meteorologist kept saying the word, which almost shouts at me. I smiled as I heard, *"Rainbow, Rainbow, Rainbow."* Love it! I shut off the TV and picked up *Imagine Heaven*, to read a couple of pages before going to sleep. The first thing I read was a recounting of a Near Death Experience. He said he could see all the colors of the Rainbow. I stared at the word, also with a boldness so it stands out from every other word on the page. I smiled and gave Gregory *the weasel* again.

Oh, at the meeting.... Lol! Gregory and I used to have this goofy thing with Idaho. He'd hear the word and say, *"Idaho? Who da ho? You da ho?"* then point at me. Or I'd point to myself and say, *"Idaho?"* and he'd say, *"No, you da ho!"* At the meeting there was a guy sitting straight across from me. He had on a dark t-shirt with the state of Idaho on it and it says, *"Idaho? No, you da ho!"* I practically burst out smiling through the whole meeting! Remember, we're in Michigan!

July 10, 2016

Last night I was watching *Alone* and all of a sudden the guy says, *"It's a Rainbow!"* Then turns the camera to show a beautiful Rainbow. Early this morning I picked up where I left off watching a show OnDemand. The scene was a woman listening to a recording of her late sister leading a Bible study. It starts out, *"Did anyone see the Rainbow on the way to church?"* I smiled. Then she said, *"When I saw the Rainbow I thought the Lord is definitely looking out for me because today we're going to talk about a story from the Bible that ends with a Rainbow!"* Hmmm, a story that ends with a Rainbow.

July 11, 2016

Last night at bedtime I was watching *American Pickers*. I reached for the remote to shut off the TV just as Mike was negotiating the price of a Model T. He says, *"I'm at the very end of the Rainbow..."* I smiled as the word echoed through my body. Now I seem to be getting messages about the end of the Rainbow. Still, what's at the end of the Rainbow? A pot of Gold!!

July 16, 2016

Last night at bedtime I checked the Weather Channel just as they were showing the top five pics for the day. First up.... Double Rainbow!! Beautiful. This morning I turned on the TV and *Firework* was already playing. When the sound came on I heard my Rainbow. Kaylee dreamed about Papa Greg and it was amazing. She told Meg right away and they both cried. Then Meg called me and I cried!

She said he had his dog Clancy with him. He teased me at one point and called me a pet name that she can't remember now but she told Meg, "It was cute, Mom." She said she knows we've all told her he's in Heaven, but she needed to hear it for herself. She said he told her he is in Heaven and that when she listens to the choir the loudest one is the one he's in. She said he told her that everything is going to be alright, that there's going to be ups and downs—that's the way life is—but everything is okay.

I cried hearing it and it makes me cry as I'm writing this. But it's a good cry. So grateful to him for coming to our Kaylee. She was only seven when he died and four years later she got to see him again! Now her memory is refreshed!

July 18, 2016

I've been crying again every day. I feel traumatized all over again. It was happening before Kaylee's dream, but I seem worse since then. I cried at 5 a.m. yesterday while out in Gregory's over-grown garden. I felt lost. I felt overwhelmed. I felt so much love and life and yet I cried to him, whispering through silent tears in the middle of the backyard, *"Help me Gregory, help me."* I felt like I didn't know where to start to take care of his garden. I heard him say to start cutting out anything dead.

I began pulling brown leaves off otherwise green plants. Crying, I kept at it. *"Like this, honey?"* Sniff-sniff. Tears pouring out of me like crazy. *"This one?"* *"Yes, you can pull the brown ones,"* he chided. I heard him perfectly, just how he would say it. I smiled. I kept cutting and weeding and feeling him there with me and pretty soon I wasn't crying and my heart was filled with joy. I shaped up the yard in record time and it feels manageable. It looks beautiful.

July 19, 2016

I got my Rainbow first thing this morning. I turned on the TV at 4:20 a.m. and as soon as the picture came into focus it was the most beautiful Rainbow. It made me cry. In a good way. I just got another Rainbow! Beautiful at the end of my show.

July 22, 2016

Last night at bedtime I changed the channel just before shutting it off. A commercial for crayons. A little girl is coloring away, making.... yep, a Rainbow! Then she holds up the picture to the camera! I gave Gregory *the weasel* and smiled ear to ear, eyes welling with tears. Rainbows! He sends me frikken Rainbows! I'll never get tired of that feeling.

July 23, 2016

I turned on the TV a few minutes ago and flipped to the music channel. Big, colorful Rainbow across Mariah Carey and the white wall she stood against! I smiled big, surprised as I always am when he sends me Rainbows. *"Hi Baby...."*

July 28, 2016

Last night I was watching a program OnDemand at bedtime. When it was over I went back to normal TV before shutting it off to go to sleep. I couldn't believe my eyes. Just then there's a family in a car, six of them wearing bold tie-dye Rainbow colored t-shirts and across the front in big letters it says, *"Rainbow Runners."* I just stared at it, big smile on my face. They were headed to do an obstacle course challenge.

Before each challenge they would do the 'all hands in the air' and shout, *"Rainbow Runners!"* I had to laugh. These Rainbows at bedtime have been amazing. Then this morning I turned on the TV to a CMT video. All different scenes. Then there it was. A waterfall and, you guessed it, a beautiful Rainbow. When it ended I muted the TV then turned it to the music channel and saw *Firework* was playing. I turned it up just in time to hear my Rainbow. After that was Santana's, *Why Don't You And I*, and I *had* to dance to it. There was a pep to my step and a lightness to my twirls. Happy! *"I'm feeling alive and so happy, Gregory!"* He said, *"You go, Girl!"*

July 29, 2016

When I passed under the bridge on the way back from watching the sunrise, I could see our boat there at the dock. Gregory in it, helping me step down, then messing with the motor and untying us so we could head out on the bay. Precious memories that seemed so ordinary at the time. Walking back to the house holding hands, both of us so grateful for where we live.

August 3, 2016

Twice yesterday when I turned on the TV this is what I heard. In the morning, *"...and his riding horse named Rainbow..."* I smiled. Then later on a home improvement show, *"...and we can stain it any color under the Rainbow..."* Every time I hear the word I hear it in bold. This is an amazing life I'm living. Ups and downs like Papa Greg told Kaylee in her dream, but so amazing.

August 9, 2016

Little Kadyn Gregory fell and broke his arm. Megan brought the kids over so I could love on them and sign his cast. I put a Rainbow on it!

August 11, 2016

I just got a Rainbow! As soon as I turned on the TV there it was. An ad for cable with a colorful Rainbow. Just as I was thinking about Gregory and how much I miss him.

August 19, 2016

I can't tell you how many times I turn on the TV or the radio just in time to hear the word Rainbow. Last night I turned it on and heard, *"We're at the end of our frikken Rainbow."* Lol! Then a few minutes later, *"No Rainbow here."* Hmmm. Wanna bet? I've done well for a couple of days. No sad tears.

August 26, 2016

I've continued to be really sick. I saw my Kinesiologist and my liver still shows. I'll keep taking my supplements and hope I turn a corner soon. Even so, I find myself smiling a lot, thinking about love. Remembering how I felt with Gregory. Knowing I get to feel that way again.

Chapter 28

One Day At A Time

September 23, 2016

I dreamed about Rainbows! There had to be fifty or more. They were small and so colorful. It woke me right up! Made me smile.

September 24, 2016

After feeling so much better the past few weeks, I had a rough day yesterday. I was caught off guard when I didn't feel well when I got up. Ugh. Hangover without the party. Headache, nauseated. Liver. Sh*t. I wanted to jump off a ledge. I went from feeling well, the light getting in, processing the darkness I just came out of, to boom! Feel like crap. I'm tired. I'm worn out with the pain and limitation. It throws me into despair. *Fear.* I sent the *Sick Girl* away, don't you know?

September 27, 2016

I wish I'd write down all the ways I get my Rainbows every day. Like how many times I turn on the TV or walk back into the room when it's on—no matter what channel—and there's a Rainbow or a Double Rainbow or a beautiful picture of a Rainbow in the background. Like earlier. It was on the soft rock station when I went downstairs. When I walked back in the room there was that brightly colored Rainbow splashed across Mariah Carey and a white background.

September 28, 2016

This morning on Oprah's, *Super Soul Sunday*, two things struck me deeply. One from Joseph Campbell when he said you must be willing to let go of the life you planned, in order to be open to the life lined out for you. Just think about that for a moment. And then today's guest, Mark Nepo, made Oprah cry when he said that to be broken is no reason to see all things as broken. Amen!

October 2, 2016

I've been getting some amazing and beautiful Rainbows today. Three in just a few minutes on *Breathing Space* following *Super Soul Sunday*. I needed them. The enemy has been at me. Fighting for my very soul it seems. Holding me hostage in my own body, in my own darkened bedroom. Brutal headaches and hands so sore it's hard to write, do laundry, make the bed, let alone change sheets. A standoff between me and the enemy in front of me, blocking my path, making me feel weak and useless. Tomorrow is our anniversary.

October 3, 2016

Gregory wins! I thought I did when I woke up at 4 a.m. and said, *"Happy Anniversary, Baby."* But then I remembered earlier. *I woke after midnight having dreamed Gregory was standing there all smiles surrounded by Rainbows! Lots and lots of Rainbows! The most colorful display imaginable!* And then I woke right up! He wins! *"Thank you, Gregory, my love."* He is so amazing still. He gave me a bouquet of Rainbows with him in the middle! Woot! Woot!

I have a guarded heart this morning. Afraid of the feelings and memories resonating just beneath my skin. And here are the tears. So sad. I look at our wedding picture and remember back. It was a fun day. Hard for me to think what we would be doing today, how we'd be together, share our meals and our day. Ordinary moments in an ordinary day. Precious. *"I miss you, Babe. Happy Anniversary."*

October 4, 2016

Yesterday when I turned on the music in the car it was Phil Collins' version of *True Colors*, right at the end where it says not to be afraid. This morning when I turned on the TV it was Cyndi Lauper's version and again was right at the same part. I got the message. Be brave.

October 7, 2016

I'd put my wedding rings back on after only having them off for a couple of days. But then my finger started itching and once again my body is acting allergic to them. So today I'm forced to take them off because I can't stand it. I feel irritated about it.

October 9, 2016

I dreamed about Gregory. He was sitting up in his hospital bed at Hospice House. I went over and crawled into the bed and snuggled right up next to him and just held onto him. He didn't look sick. He had his long hair and beard and looked really great.

This dream is powerful. Hospitals in dreams represent *a place of healing*. I feel in my heart that Gregory is showing me that in order for me to hang onto him—curl up in bed next to him and snuggle—I would have to remain sick, represented by the hospital bed. I can do that, there's nothing wrong with it. I think what he's showing me is if I do that, I'm not going to go anywhere. Ouch. It also shows where I am, consciously and in my heart. I'm back at Hospice House where Gregory is still alive. I crawl into bed and curl up next to him just like I did then. This dream is showing me that my mind and heart are still back there, hanging onto a time that is no more.

October 12, 2016

I turned on the TV and it was on the country music station. A beautiful song was playing called *Suitcase*, by Steve Moakler. I couldn't believe my ears. It made me cry when it talks about how everybody is searching for the pot of gold at the end of the Rainbow but all he wants is me and if he had one more chance to make me smile that's what he would do.

I love that! When I went to the gym with Mama we came out and there was the most beautiful Rainbow spreading out across the entire sky. As soon as we stepped out we were like, OMG! It was breathtaking! I followed that Rainbow all the way home!

October 14, 2016

I'll call this entry *Food Grief*, and I'm practically sobbing as I write. I've been so emotional lately when I see people eating, like on TV commercials or in a movie I'm watching. People ordering up anything they want, taking big bites of a cheeseburger or a turkey, cheese, melted sandwich—*whatever*—and not get sick. I guess I'm grieving the loss of being able to eat like a normal person and feeling like it's going to be so hard to be in a new relationship. Like I'm going to be no fun around the whole eating part. Like how I have to eat is a pain in the ass.

Okay, so I just let myself sob for a few minutes. I feel better. I couldn't figure out why I was crying every time I watched people eat. Gregory knew how I had to eat and he was used to me. It makes me nervous about meeting somebody new. Unless he's a gourmet chef, vegan, health nut, ready to take me on as a happy challenge. Big sigh.

October 15, 2016

I've already heard Rainbow three times in songs. It happened every time I turned back to the music channel after watching a show. The last one was *True Colors*. I get several Rainbows every day. I cried out to Gregory earlier, *"Help me do this life alone. I don't expect to get over you but help me start feeling stronger in my grief and in my life. Help me not be so scared and not miss you so much."* And then he sends me Rainbows! Like here I am!

October 16, 2016

I dreamed I was going downtown to a festival. There were tons of people. I made my way through the crowd and there was Gregory! He had his guitar and was laying down a platform so he and a couple of other musicians could stand and perform for the people gathered there. I ran over and gave him a big kiss and hug. It was awesome!

October 25, 2016

When I walked out of a meeting yesterday after talking about Gregory and his Rainbows, there was the most beautiful Rainbow in the sky! It was magnificent! The whole way home I enjoyed this *huge* Rainbow that filled the sky! The biggest, most perfect arc from one end of the sky to the other! Incredible! I was giddy happy!

November 6, 2016

OMG! I just got the most beautiful, colorful Rainbow appearing across the pillow I'm writing on! The light from the stained-glass window shows me Rainbows all the time but *this* is amazing. This is a dancing Rainbow! I stared in awe at the perfect row of vivid colors—deep purple, incredible aqua blue, yellow, pink, green, red—dancing on my pillow! Pulsating its colors at me as goosebumps and a smile washed over me. Are you kidding me right now? This followed tears missing him, even as I feel him so close. Gregory is dancing Rainbows all over the room now! They are everywhere! Tears are streaming down my face. There's even Rainbows on the ceiling right now!

November 8, 2016

This morning, feeling good, feeling happy because I'm feeling good, I turned on the music channel and got Switchfoot's, *Dare You To Move*, to which I chided Gregory by saying, *"Oh you shut up."* To which he replied, *"No, **you** shut up."* Then I laughed, *"No, **you** shut up . . . No, **you** shut up."* That's what we used to do! I'd forgotten all about that. It makes me smile.

November 23, 2016

My dream last night was all about God working in mysterious ways and basically that everything is working out behind the scenes regardless of how things appear. Then a part about an old standard TV set. This one was on legs and stood alone. The TV was in an isolated area for healing. I had the feeling the TV somehow represented my liver. Crazy, I know.

This felt like a reassurance dream for me. A reminder that God is working in mysterious ways and that I am being healed, regardless of how things appear. The part about the old TV representing my liver feels super important. The dream shows that the liver stands alone. This tells me that it's separate from the rest of the house (self). It's *isolated*, which means it's the only issue. I knew this, but with liver issues causing so many different symptoms it's taken a long time to pinpoint the one first cause of everything. Good news is the '*TV*' is in an isolated place for healing. Woohoo!

Chapter 29

Thanksgiving

November 24, 2016

I won this morning! I wished Gregory *"Happy Thanksgiving"* first. So far he's been a no show and I've let him know I'm expecting something here. I cried at bedtime and I always hate that. I'm thankful it doesn't happen often. This morning I cried too. I told him I was safe in this world, strong when he was my husband. Now I'm being made to stand strong alone. I'm gonna do it. I am doing it. But I miss my love. I miss sharing my life with him. And now, as the years go by, I just miss sharing my life. And I get darn excited when I think about it. It's going to be amazing.

November 25, 2016

When I wrote yesterday about winning this holiday, I didn't write about how I was really feeling because I didn't want to influence the day. It was later than usual when I thought to wish Gregory *"Happy Thanksgiving."* I felt emptiness around me when I did, and I was surprised that I hadn't heard from him by that point and was somehow feeling like he hadn't heard me. Something just felt different. *Empty.* I couldn't feel him. I talked to him throughout the day, expecting a response, searching for a Rainbow, and reminding him that it's *Thanksgiving*.

Back home from Meg's early evening I felt the change. I couldn't feel him. I searched the channels for Rainbows, songs, anything. The music channels were all off. Blatantly *not* my songs. There was nowhere I could go to connect to my Gregory. This can't be happening. Not on Thanksgiving. Not ever, actually. I turned off the light at bedtime with a tear in my eye and an emptiness in my heart that was borderline scary. When I woke up this morning I couldn't believe it. For the first time he didn't send me Rainbows. *On Thanksgiving.* Was that his gift to me? Detach because I wouldn't?

I guess it was bound to happen, eh? There was a quiet inner knowing deep inside accompanying the realization that something had changed. I felt a subtle numbness all over my body. That feeling of shock and denial as one processes a sudden change in life. I didn't want to believe what I was feeling. What was actually happening. I mean, after four and a half years, Rainbows every single day, feeling his presence all around me, why would I think it could end one day?

This morning feels like a mixture of sadness, shock, stunned disbelief and yet, a quiet, fragile strength. I can't actually process the information that Thanksgiving—my fifth one without him— is the day he chooses to stop sending me Rainbows. To stop speaking to me through songs. To pull back enough that I can't feel his energy around me anymore. *"That's harsh, Dude."*

November 26, 2016

I put on my wedding rings and I don't care. I'm still trying to process the past couple of days. When I wrote yesterday I wasn't crying. That's the stunned part I think. It was like I didn't want to cry or didn't need to cry. That must be the quiet strength. I turned on the music just as *Chances*, by Five For Fighting, was beginning. It talks about all the chances of things happening one way or the other. That no matter how I'm feeling today nothing lasts forever.

It says that chances are we're going to find two destinations. My mind wandered with the words. So this is it. I'm witnessing my own letting go. My own spiritual growth. Feeling myself getting stronger. There is beauty, sadness and pain in that.

I went to the office—his Man Room—and grabbed my calendar from under Gracie. I haven't rehung it since putting up my miniatures shelf a couple of months ago. I held it in my hands and there was the most beautiful Rainbow. A double one in fact. I could feel Gregory again. I smiled as I set it aside and turned on the computer for music and began my Yoga.

My mind wandered to all the times over the years—doing Yoga early—that I'd sense I was being watched and I'd turn to see him leaning in the doorway just watching me with a smile on his face. Other times, depending on the pose I was in, he'd attack me out of nowhere! Lol! My mind continued to play the tape. Sunday mornings waking to Van Morrison on the stereo, the smell of breakfast and fresh coffee under my nose, awakening my senses. One plate with breakfast for two, shared with one fork.

I smiled as the beautiful memories played. In the kitchen, him standing with hands behind his back then boom! out came roses from the garden. He was the best. I continued my meditative workout. The words from a song called *This Time*, by Jonathan Rhys Meyers, broke through my silence. It talks about sitting on the sidelines and watching life pass you by. It says I wonder what will happen if I let you go? Will I ever get you off my mind? It really got to me when it talks about the things I've left behind. I understand the 'leaving all this behind part.' Not going anywhere physically but leaving this; my life with Gregory. My grief.

Everything resonated with me on a deeper level. I could feel a change in the air around me. After my workout I got my Rainbow on TV. It felt like a relief. And yet, I understood what Thursday was about. I can see Gregory doing it to get my attention. To jolt me forward. Now he can reassure me. It's so him. I turned on the computer to FB and up pops a smiling, bright, healthy picture of Greg and me. It was a sunny day and we were all smiles. It was one of the last pictures taken of us.

November 27, 2016

So, as always, I continue to process Gregory's jolt of reality on Thanksgiving. The lack of that constant spiritual connection—my bubble I see now—felt like it *should* have been terrifying, that I *shouldn't* be able to breathe, and yet I could breathe and it wasn't terrifying. It was new. It was unfamiliar, uncomfortable even, but there was that quiet strength that shows me I'm stronger than I think I am. I was forced to see my world without Rainbows and constant communication with him every day.

When I went to the indoor Farmer's Market yesterday I couldn't help but continue pondering how it feels to *not* get Rainbows or songs or Rainbows in songs. Feeling strangely capable in this unfamiliar territory, I gladly entered the market and was instantly engulfed in a healthy consciousness. I got what I needed and was headed out of the building when I took a moment to set my stuff down on a small table along the wall so I could readjust my load.

I looked up and there was the most beautiful photograph. Big, full-arced Rainbow perfectly centered above Building 50 on the old State Hospital grounds. The sun also shone on the amazing architecture. I could feel Gregory all around me and goosebumps shot through me. I smiled clear to my heart. Then I heard him say, *"See….you'll always see me in Rainbows but live the rest of your life."*

There is something very freeing about this new space I've entered. Gregory was right, I needed to be jolted out of Rainbowland. It's been amazing and I wouldn't trade it for the world. I hope he keeps sending me Rainbows and speaking to me through songs. But if he doesn't? The void is not going to feel like it did when he first left. He's in my heart. He's in my mind. Nothing can take that away.

December 1, 2016

I've changed since Thanksgiving. I'm stronger. I know I don't *need* Rainbows and confirmation from Gregory. I learned from his gift that day that I am stronger than I knew. It makes me smile. I'm not crying when I talk to him. It's pretty amazing. A reading from *Daily Word* in mid-November has stuck with me. *"Inner wisdom leads to new perceptions, and I begin to see a greater picture of my life. With determination and purpose, I strive to get out of my own way and allow divine wisdom to guide me on my path to good."*

When I got on my knees and prayed this morning—something I find myself doing more and more—I acknowledged where I'm weak, who I am, and that I know God knows all of that and loves me anyway. *"I know I can do this,"* I cried, *"I know I have all the information I need at this point. I just don't know how to get there. Help me get there."* *"You are getting there,"* a quiet voice said, and an inner knowing acknowledged Wisdom's voice. I breathed a little deeper. My train is right on time.

December 3, 2016

I can feel my husband strong this morning and I've already had three Rainbows. I cried when I talked to him. A good cry. Grateful, accepting tears. Stronger since Thanksgiving. Since I was pushed out of my bubble. It's been pretty amazing since then. I had the music on low, somehow knowing the next song was for me. I heard the familiar upbeat music of *Firework* and tears rolled down my cheeks through the whole song. My cheerleader song. And my Rainbow. After the Hurricane.

Yesterday morning as I was getting ready for Yoga, *Change*, came on and I listened to every word as goosebumps covered my body inside and out. A rush of that familiar energy that fills me up with endless possibilities. I was overwhelmed with the feeling and the words. So powerful.

I can feel a change washing over me, like a breath of fresh air after a long winter. Like sunshine bursting through the windows after days of rain and cold.

My tearful conversations with Gregory over the weekend were all about the intimacy, the touching, melting into each other. I'd watched a movie and there was a brief love scene. I cried and cried. I was spoiled for thirty years with that man. I told him so. My mind replayed precious moments. I had the music on low, certain the next song would also be mine. When the music started I could barely contain the sobs. *Finally Home*, by Mercy Me. Such a beautiful, hopeful, reassuring song. When I *finally* make it home. I like the sound of that.

Right after that a beautiful melody began that I knew I'd never heard before. It was Nora Jones', *Carry On*. The message was strong. Carry on..... you're still here. There is the most beautiful piano in that song. Still feeling Gregory's spirit all around me, I felt Uncle Steve playing those keyboards and I felt his spirit in the room. Goosebumps covered me inside and out as I could see him playing his heart out like he always did. This was such a powerful morning. After that was, *The Climb*, and that's another powerful cheerleader song. Perseverance even when my faith is shaken and I'm unsure of every step.

December 7, 2016

This is my fifth Christmas without my Gregory. He's as close as ever though and I'm still getting my Rainbows. I got one already this morning. My reading talked about where I am now. It says that perhaps I can start to trust life again and settle into a new day.

December 13, 2016

I lost four days to the flu. *Brutal*. I made it to the Kinesiologist and my liver showed. No surprise since I've been hurting in that area along with everywhere else. It was clearly overtaxed by whatever bug I had. I've had my tearful cries of grief over the past few days—always seems harder when I'm sick—but I got a lot of Rainbows the whole time. He's so close. Still, my heart is broken missing the man. I appreciated my reading a few days ago when it talked about it being a well-known fact that our bodies are more vulnerable to illness and injury after suffering a serious loss. It's so validating to me.

I'm not weak. I'm not a hypochondriac. I don't want to be sick or to die. I'm grieving. When you lose half of who you are it leaves you in the most vulnerable state. Fragile. Good thing I didn't know how sick I was going to be all these years. I may have curled up and died with Gregory. I remember how he filled me up after he died. So full of love and life I couldn't even cry in those first few days. That was his way of keeping me alive.

December 19, 2016

It's been a long time since I've heard *Here Without You* and I've waited to hear it. This morning I heard familiar yet new music as a 3 Doors Down song I've never heard began. This one is called, *It's Not My Time*. Clearly one of them lost a love. This song talks about the plans we made and the dreams we had. But *it's not my time*. I'm still here, right?

December 20, 2016

I got Rainbows in my dreams last night! Like the other times, lots and lots of Rainbows. Colors unmatched here on earth. Absolutely brilliant colors like you've never seen. Woke me right up! Amazing! Woohoo!

December 26, 2016

I've spent the past half hour or more with my husband. Tears roll down my cheeks still. I miss him. I miss us. He sent me a Rainbow first thing this morning. A Rainbow in a big storm cloud. My heart skipped a beat as it always does when I see my Rainbows. I felt him so close... like normal. He was everywhere. I must have needed him more than I realized because I felt relieved and I relaxed into his presence. Into his love.

December 27, 2016

Oh, those morning readings have been speaking right to my heart. She talks about how every bone in my body is sore, tired and weary, crying out for a warm oil of honey to be poured over me, seeping into every aching joint and muscle. About wishing for anything to relieve the pain and wanting them all. Anything to heal me, to make me new, to forget who I am for even a moment.

Powerful for me to hear. Especially because I'm coming up on five years. Sheer time alone is on my side now. Still, the reading was very validating when it says that even when we are distracted by sleep or other activity, the return to the grief can be so painful that we'll wonder if the diversion was worth it. Don't I agree. It's best to just be in it and heal through it. That day's reading ends with the promise that even though it's going to take some time I will feel good again. I've done it one day at a time. Five years was impossible.

December 28, 2016

I turned on the music and got, *Dare You To Move*, and I smiled. *"I'll take your dare,"* and I scrunched up my nose at Gregory. Life feels lighter.

December 30, 2016

Yesterday ended up being a great day. I went to Gordon Foods and as I pulled in, I saw the C.C. Power bucket trucks blocking the first entrance to the store. Two more trucks were in the parking lot. I waved at one bearded guy moving a truck and went into the store. When I came out that guy was walking toward me. Then two more behind him. Greg worked with all three of them.

They all gave me hugs and we talked about Greg and Rainbows. They're the ones who gave him the nickname. I could feel Gregory right there with us. I know they felt it too. It was a serene calm. It felt surreal. When I got in my car and drove out of the parking lot I was crying and talking to Gregory. *"It was the guys, Honey. They hugged me."* It felt like a gift. I rarely go to that store so what are the chances? Even though I was crying it was so good. It made my day.

Chapter 30

Everywhere And Nowhere

January 2, 2017

Where do I start? How about Rainbows?! I got one first thing on New Year's Day. I said, *"Happy New Year!"* first so I won, but right after that I got a Rainbow! I turned on the music just as Cyndi Lauper's, *True Colors* was beginning. *"Of course,"* I smiled at Gregory, *"It's New Year's Day."* It's a relief. Several times during the day I got my Rainbows and I felt Gregory with me all day.

As soon as I sat down I picked up my new Daily Word for the first time. It fell open to a beautiful Rainbow with the words, *"Happiness Lives"* across it. What a gift. Gregory and my Rainbows... it's so beautiful. Watching TV last night I flipped to the Weather Channel to check the temperature and as soon as I did I heard the guy say, *"Liquid Rainbows..."* and he went on to talk about this amazing phenomenon. The colors were spectacular. In the water! I'm the luckiest girl on the planet.

January 13, 2017

I hugged Gregory in the night! I wanted the hug—Gregory's hug—the way we melted into each other and I got it! It felt like home and I embraced it for all it was worth. Woohoo!

January 14, 2017

Today is Gregory's birthday. I've had some tears this morning missing him and wrapping my mind around my own reality. He died in 2012. It's 2017. Through my tears I heard, *"You knew this was how it was going to be."* Another deep sigh of acceptance. There is great peace that comes with acceptance. I've decided *Intention* is my word for this year. Let's do this.

January 17, 2017

Yesterday's Daily Word was *Dream*. A line stuck out to me that reminded me of Intention. *"I am dedicated and purposeful toward achieving my goal."* It doesn't say goals. One goal at a time is what will lead me to my dreams. I went to the grocery store before the sun came up. I didn't turn off the car right away but instead listened to a song I'd never heard before. It was really nice. Then out of nowhere it seemed, Rainbows! I wish I would have written down the words because now I can't remember a one. But there in a dark parking lot at 7:15 a.m. I got bombarded with three or four Rainbows in a song that otherwise didn't have a thing to do with Rainbows. I felt Gregory right there with me saying, *"Happy Monday, Baby! Have a great day!"*

January 18, 2017

I never feel like I can adequately describe these powerful, incredible encounters with Gregory. Perhaps no one would believe it anyway. But I can tell you this, I am blessed beyond measure to have them. This morning I sat down with my tea and turned on the TV. The music began as one song ended. I could feel the change in the air around me. It was *Wherever You Will Go*, and I settled into the words as I felt my whole body sort of firm up. I felt I was being hugged, held, from head to toe!

Hand on my heart, I could feel a subtle vibration throughout my entire being. My hand seemed to be one with my heart. It's so hard to describe and yet so incredible I have to try. The words themselves vibrated into me somehow. I could feel Gregory everywhere and my heart was so full of him. He seemed to speak the words straight to my heart. After that was *Second Chance*, and my reminder that after this heartbreaking goodbye I'm going to get a second chance to embrace life and love again.

January 25, 2017

Yesterday I heard a song by Lukas Graham called, *You're Not There*. It talks about the only place I have him is in my stories. Isn't that the truth? It talks about how he used to lead the way and now I'm terrified on my own. This one made me flash to being glued to Gregory's side, holding his hand but wrapped around him. I felt safe tucked into him. It talks about trying to remember how he looks and what his voice sounds like and how sometimes I think I see him in a crowd.

January 31, 2017

Time to start putting together the Rainbow book. One more walk through my life with Gregory. See how I feel when it's done. The years since he died are mostly a blur. I'm ready to remember what all went down. How I've survived 1747 days without my love. One thousand, seven hundred, forty seven days. Are you kidding me? Good Lord, I am single!

February 5, 2017

I've already had my Rainbow. Like the past two days, I got it as soon as I turned on the TV. On Friday it was around 4:30 a.m. when I turned on the Weather Channel and there it was, a beautiful and rare sight. A Rainbow next to a waterspout! Yesterday morning I turned on the TV and there was a beautiful Rainbow and more to come! It was a whole segment on Rainbows. It was one I haven't seen. I saw footage of rare and beautiful Rainbows. Blood red Rainbows, rare and magnificent. For a full fifteen minutes I was thrilled and delighted by Rainbows.

When I got one first thing this morning I gave my Gregory *the weasel* and thanked him for all the Rainbows. My mind wandered to the shock of losing him and how hard it's been to survive that loss. How hard I've had to fight not to go down. And how I *wouldn't* have survived had it not been for the Rainbows. For the music, giving voice to the words I needed to hear from him. Keeping me going, bringing color and music to my world so I could breathe another day.

February 10, 2017

Yesterday I turned on the TV and a woman had just caught a fish. She held it up to the camera and said, *"Look! It's a Rainbow!"* I laughed out loud.

February 15, 2017

Yesterday was Valentine's day and I remembered first. When I said, *"Happy Valentine's Day, Honey,"* I didn't feel him. Like Thanksgiving he wasn't there and I knew it. Not wanting to believe he would go AWOL on Valentine's Day, I said to him, *"Okay, Honey, it's early. But it's **Valentine's Day**...."* This time I didn't tell him I expected to hear from him. I went about my day with an open mind and heart and a hope that at some point I *would* get some amazing little (or big) acknowledgement. I stayed busy and didn't give it much thought after that.

This morning I realized that he was a no show. On Valentine's Day. Yesterday I told a friend that I miss getting flowers. Miss having a sweetheart. I realize now that I spent more time thinking about having that again and how fun it will be, than I did about Gregory and the fact that he was gone. I see what's happening. I can't get the interaction from him that I crave as a human being. He's kept me alive with a connection to his essence and I wouldn't have survived without that lifeline. But nearly five years later he knows I need more than he can give.

I need to share my life and love with another human being. The tears of loneliness I cry at times are, for the first time, not about Gregory. They are about yearning to be in love again. So, he made me feel alone this Valentine's Day. How else am I going to know how that feels? His songs and Rainbows have carried me through the darkest of my days. Maybe I don't need to be carried now.

I'm okay with his no show yesterday. I've yet to feel him this morning. I can do it. I feel like I should be scared, should feel the emptiness, and freak out, but I'm holding my own. I have been dependent on him. I haven't walked alone because he's been with me. I don't know that I could have made it otherwise. But now? Dang. I guess I'm strong enough.

February 16, 2017

Gregory was a no show again yesterday. He showed back up the morning after Thanksgiving and didn't leave me again. But I can't feel him. No Rainbows. Songs are all wrong, no magic around them. It's so strange. I feel like I should be in a panic, full of fear. But I'm strangely okay. I'm breathing just fine. I know what he's doing. This is the only way to know that I'm okay without his strong presence all around me.

I thought of something else. I know where I can find him and feel his essence all around me. In the pages of my journals. In the book of Rainbows. So there you have it. He's giving me the motivation I need to put the book as a priority. To go *there* and do the work. If this keeps up I'll be running to the work. My living room feels empty. The house, the air, feels flat. It's so strange. Even stranger that I can breathe in it. Feels like they cut off life support and I started breathing on my own. Miraculous.

February 17, 2017

I got four Rainbows yesterday! I was starting to protect myself. Brace myself for Gregory being gone, the Rainbows with him. The fourth one made me laugh. I was in the waiting room at the tire place when a gal came in and sat down. She's a bubbly, energetic woman around my age. She started talking about precious stones and began describing an amazing one she saw. It was an angel's wing on the side and when she turned it she saw the other wing.

She held it to the light and she could see the whole angel in there. *"Then,"* she said, *"I could see a Rainbow above the wings. It was so amazing!"* You're telling me!

February 20, 2017

Gregory sent me Rainbows all weekend and I feel him around me again. He was testing me. Making sure I know that I can live without him. He also wants me to know I can't hide forever. I thanked him for coming back. I get what he's saying and I do know I'll be okay. But I'm really excited to dive back into him for a while and put our book together. Wear my wedding rings and just snuggle into Greg and L.J. one last time.

Yesterday I was in the backyard and I could feel his strong presence. The sky was blue with scattered white clouds here and there. A big white cloud surrounded the sun above and around it, but it was so bright I couldn't look at it. I cupped my eyes to see what appeared to be colors in the cloud around the sun. I squinted.... OMG, a perfect upside down Rainbow filling the white of the cloud. A perfect smiling Rainbow! At bedtime I turned on the TV and heard, *"It's like you can't have a Rainbow without rain."* I laughed out loud. *"Oh yes you can!"* In my world anyway.

February 23, 2017

I've been getting Rainbows like I used to. I turned on the Weather Channel and there it was, a blood Red Rainbow. Then I could see it was a double Red Rainbow. The ten-minute segment was just beginning and was all about *rare* Red Rainbows. It blows my mind. Later I turned on the TV and it was on a commercial. A woman knelt down in front of an open dryer. She pulled out a folded piece of paper and opened it. Wait for it.... it's a child's crayon drawing of a Rainbow. Then I had the TV muted and was working on my laptop. I looked up just in time to see a gorgeous Rainbow. Beautiful. Amazing.

Before I left the house yesterday I told Gregory how happy I was feeling, how close I feel to him, how much I love him, and how relieved I feel to have weathered his death. *"I'll be listening for you in songs today, Honey. Ready to hear whatever you think I need. I trust you so much."* I got in the car and turned on the radio. There it was. The very beginning of *Tell Your Heart To Beat Again.* It's very powerful.

March 2, 2017

I dreamed about Gregory! Just for a moment but he was sort of crouched over goofy, moving from side to side playfully. Big smile on his face, to which I immediately smiled back and then woke up, with a big smile. It still makes me smile. Ah, dang, now the tears as I thanked him for coming. Just that one little piece of him, so vivid, so clear, so real. My Gregory playfully smiling at me! Just to see him again did so much for me. *"Thank you, Babe. More."* The dream reminded me of a picture taken of him at the cottage on 4th of July our first summer in Michigan. He had just lit fireworks and backed off as it took off. He was crouched down playful like that. He was so much fun.

March 6, 2017

I was starting to feel better but then my liver took a dive and I was sick all weekend. Trying not to add suffering here. Feeling really sick right now. Fatigue, nausea. I just want to cry in despair but I won't. A light of hope attempts to remind me that nothing has changed. This is a tiny setback not a roadblock. My hands make it even more difficult because I struggle to clear my mind through writing when just holding the pen is painful.

The morning after I dreamed about Gregory I was searching for something in the office. I picked up a box in the closet and under it was a bag of pictures. The first bag I picked up said, *"The Cottage,"* and right on top was that picture of Gregory on 4th of July that my dream reminded me of! That blows my mind! Later that day I turned on the TV just in time to hear, *"Pretty excited to see what I'm going to find at the end of the Rainbow..."* Lol! *"Yes, me too!"* Woohoo!

March 9, 2017

The woman sitting next to me in the meeting yesterday was wearing earrings that were a bright sun with a Rainbow hanging from it. I miss Gregory. My reading this morning spoke to the love being worth the loss. *"Tis better to have loved and lost than never to have loved at all." –Alfred Tennyson.* The reading also spoke of a man who lost his daughter. He told his pastor that they are so grateful for the time they had with her but there was a time when grief was all consuming. The reading ends with beautiful words to remind me that I hold my loved one close in my heart and that their life was a gift.

March 14, 2017

I saw the most beautiful Rainbow over the weekend. Not just one. I got them all weekend. I turned on the Weather Channel and heard, *"Rainbow rocks surround the lake..."* Lol! Another time I turned on the TV to a commercial just as children are walking from the bus. One little girl was holding her treasured drawing of... you guessed it, a Rainbow! I continue to be thrilled and delighted every time it happens. Then for it to happen so frequently just blows my mind.

March 15, 2017

(Crying) Here's my reality and then I'll quit feeling sorry for myself and get on with my day. I haven't felt well and knew it was my liver. Kinesiology confirmed. Ugh. Nausea is back. I feel like crap. Then my hands. It hurts to write and that's after I rested them all weekend. Ugh, ugh, ugh. Waaa, waaa, waaa. W... T... F...?! I'm over it.

March 16, 2017

I turned on the TV and before I could change it to the Weather Channel I noticed the crazy sweater a woman was wearing. It had everything going on, like a kid's shirt. I noticed a colorful arch across her upper arm and chest. Kind of looks like a Rainbow. I followed it to the end. Yep, pot o' gold! It's a Rainbow! Lol!

March 28, 2017

Today is my twenty-third anniversary sober. It's also seven years since we lost Dad. Hard to remember the woman I was before these past seven years. After I finished writing yesterday I read my Daily word. *Let Go and Let God*. The scripture—from Proverbs 3:5—says, *"Trust in the Lord with all your heart, and do not rely on your own understanding."* The reading was all about affirming spiritual truth. Relying on denials and affirmations. *"We deny thoughts of lack or limitation. We affirm that we are strong, positive, wise, loving, fearless, and free beings of Spirit."* Today I celebrate me and Dad.

April 1, 2017

Last night as I was about to go to bed, I turned on the TV to check the weather. There was a commercial and a *beautiful* Rainbow! A Jimmy Dean ad about a man who didn't get excited about anything. He saw a beautiful Rainbow and was like, *"Eh, no big deal..."* But after his breakfast he was playing hopscotch with his grandchildren, wearing a t-shirt with a Rainbow and two kittens on it! Lol!

April 3, 2017

I remember my dream! It was another one of those dreams with all the Rainbows in it! Spectacular colors! Rainbows everywhere! Then, just like always, it woke me up! Love that!

April 6, 2017

Wow! My dream! I walked into a big room and saw Gregory on the other side of the room! I sprinted toward him with everything in me, running as fast as I could and dove into his arms and gave him a big kiss and just held onto him. He looked so good. He had his dark beard and that smile on his face that he had when he looked at me and was happy that I was his.

Woohoo! *"Thank you, Gregory Roy Hunt,"* I said out loud, *"That's what I'm talking about!"* Made my day! I hope I'm going to dream a lot more about him while I'm putting together the book. It will be a long, sweet good-bye. Until I see him on the Other Side and I sprint into his arms and never stop kissing him.

April 12, 2017

I dreamed about Gregory! Woohoo! All I remember is kissing him! We had our ten second kiss! He looked so good! He had his dark beard and looked young and so healthy! This makes me so happy.

April 13, 2017

Woohoo! I dreamed about Gregory again! But this is weird because it's the exact same dream I had six months ago, almost to the day. I was going downtown to a festival. There were tons of people. I made my way through the crowd and there was Gregory! He had his guitar and was laying down a platform so he and a couple of other musicians could perform for the people there. I ran over to him and gave him a big kiss and hug. Talk about déjà vu! I guess he really wants me to know he's hanging out at a festival, playing his music.

Chapter 31

Lonesome Lonely

April 19, 2017

First thing this morning I pulled up a cartoon image of a Rainbow against a black backdrop with two swings hanging from it. One has a lonely little rabbit on it, looking at the empty swing next to her. She says, *"Wish you were here..."* It's such a powerful image and couldn't be more perfect. Today is five years since Gregory went to Heaven. I woke up at 1:30 a.m., which is the time he left. I got two nice birthday cards in the mail. One has a big RAINBOW—the word—on the cover, each letter a different color and says, *"Ignore the Rain, look for the Rainbow."* It's very cool and very colorful. Inside it says, *"If anyone can find it you can."* I'm still not feeling it—my birthday—but maybe tomorrow I will. All I know is today I feel like that little rabbit on the swing.

April 20, 2017

(My birthday)—When I was getting out of my car at the theater this afternoon I locked the door then glanced to the car parked next to me as I walked away. My eye caught something in the backseat so I stopped and went back. There it was, a big

Rainbow heart, colored on a big piece of construction paper. *"Got it, honey!"*

April 25, 2017

Ha! I turned on the Weather Channel to see, *"Can lightning and Rainbows happen at the same time?"* Oh yeah! Then they showed an amazing shot of a lightning bolt happening right next to a Rainbow! *"Good morning, Baby!"* Four different times yesterday when I turned on the TV or changed the channel there was a Rainbow. I've been thinking about my Gregory a lot lately and seeing Rainbows to remind me he's thinking about me too!

May 5, 2017

I haven't written about how I've been feeling about Gregory. I'm back to crying when I talk to him, missing him, and just holding onto him through my grief. My heart feels newly broken. I heard it said perfectly yesterday on a program. Basically about when the memory of our loved one starts to fade it's like losing them all over again. I realized that's what's happening.

May 7, 2017

It's my baby girl's birthday! It's beautiful and heartbreaking. Meeting someone new at every stage of their life while losing who they were. My 3-year-old is gone. So is my 10-year-old and my 15-year-old and my 20-year-old. Left to memories and in pictures. And yet, I look into my daughter's eyes and I see the same heart and spirit that has always been there. I feel a deeper love and a greater love because I know all of who she is, the infant and the little girl, the young lady, and the blossoming young woman. I see the wife and the mother, the teacher, and the friend. I see the grieving child who lost her daddy. And she is all beautifully wrapped into a precious package that I'm lucky enough to call, *"My daughter."*

May 13, 2017

I'm still getting Rainbows every day. I forget to write about them but they always seem to come as an endorsement. When I'm making a right choice for myself or I'm focusing on the positive. When I'm daring to have fun in my life, to laugh even, and see that storms really do pass and the sun shines again. Then he sends me a Rainbow. This has been one long hurricane season.

May 14, 2017

I dreamed I was walking next to Gregory, holding onto him. I smiled, remembering how good it felt to walk with him and hold his hand. I'm so grateful for that little dream.

May 19, 2017

My face is wet with tears. I've been crying with my Gregory and crying because I'm alone..... At first I was feeling and sensing the new guy and I was excited. Then my energy shifted back to Gregory and I settled right into my now familiar comfy zone with my loneliness and his spirit. The Rainbows have changed. More like little Rainbow winks. Before he was having to make a big production of the whole thing. Changing the energy in the room, feeling him in my heart and soul, and drawing my attention to the Rainbow.

These little Rainbow winks here and there throughout the day have been perfect. I always give Gregory a quick *weasel* and I feel him in my heart and then I carry on. That's progress, right? So, as I'm sitting here thinking about these Rainbow winks, my heart sank and I started to cry, telling Gregory how much I miss him. I knew I was going to get a song. I could feel a change in the energy all around me. The hair on my arms stood up. The beautiful melody began, but I wasn't sure what song it was. I just knew this was it. This was my message from him.

The words made me cry right away. They say that he doesn't want me waiting. The words faded in and out, bold and louder the ones I needed to hear. It was Default's, *Wasting My Time*. I knew exactly what he meant. He meant it in the nicest way. He lovingly said I'm wasting his time now. He has stuff to do! Lol! It hit me hard, but real.

It says there are no more reasons for him to stay. Those reasons would be that on some level I don't want to face reality. I'm still wearing my wedding rings and acting like I'm married. When the song talked about me being too scared to feel, that this isn't real, I had an Aha! moment. I owned it. On some level that's been me. Gregory and I used to say, *"This can't happen here!"* Denial. This can't be real and I'm too scared to feel.

There's no denying I've been feeling and grieving all along, that's the crazy part. I realized that I've been on guard anyway. Perhaps waiting for the other shoe to drop? Waiting for *unbearable* grief to hit me? Wow. There's the lie I didn't even see. There is no unbearable grief about Gregory that's gonna hit me. The worst has already happened. I can't lose him again.

This morning he made me realize that to hang on to what used to be isn't helping me heal. It's time. He says that he's already gone. It hit me in that powerful way that only a true awareness can. Then I heard that there's no reason for me to stop my feelings. I heard that in a powerful way too. ***There isn't any reason...*** The part that says let's take it all, is all that life has to offer. Jumping back in, daring to have fun, be in love with life again, like I was when Gregory was alive. Like I was before I even met him. Time to be..... me again.

The good news is that I've been building a life for myself without him whether I like it or not. When I look around and think about moving out of my comfort zone I realize that I'm already safe. If I let go a little more of the life I had with Gregory I'm not going to find myself in a scary life. I know what all this is saying and I get it. I know I still have the book so I'll be close with him until it's finished. But the rest of the time I don't always have to hold onto him so tightly. Just the fact that saying that didn't terrify me is progress.

He's shown me a few times that it's time we went our separate ways, that things are different for us now and I'm still here, still breathing. I can't live in Rainbowland forever. As beautiful as it's been there's a lot of pain that goes with holding onto something that is no longer there. It also prevents new experiences from getting in. That's the stalling, lonesome, lonely part. I feel empowered. I'm not all full of zest, but I am committed to the book and I'm working my way through it one page at a time.

May 22, 2017

The realization that I was holding onto Gregory tighter than I knew has been hitting me hard. I wonder what letting go would look like? In what ways am I still hanging on? Is it all the pictures of him and us everywhere? One could argue there's nothing wrong with mementos, but I look around and I get it. I'm a single woman living mostly alone with my three cats. There are pictures on every end table, dresser, and nightstand of the two of us, or just Gregory. It looks like a happily married couple lives here. Ugh. This crap is hitting me hard. His clothes still hang in the spare closet upstairs and I hear him say, *"Take them to Goodwill."* Hmmm.

And then there's my little shrine on the side of the fridge. Time to take that down? I couldn't see it before but it's practically glaring me in the face now. I looked at his ashes and I heard him say, *"I don't want them in a box on a shelf in the dining room. Put some out in our garden, put some in my mom's garden, and put the rest over at the bay. And about those wedding rings..."* Alrighty then. Wow, now that I'm seeing it, there's a lot of stuff that I haven't dealt with. Closets and rooms that I can utilize. Spaces I can clear out – I just got my Rainbow wink! – tells me Gregory approves of my line of thinking!

May 28, 2017

I'll be working all day today which I'm excited about. Just got my Rainbow! I've been getting Rainbow winks all morning. Four in the first hour I was up. It's so powerful to me. I've let go a little more, I can feel it. *I dreamed I was being healed on every level. There were three levels and two of them were healed and then*

I was focusing on the third level which seemed to be the "symptoms" of everything. It was very powerful. This dream tells me that the symptoms are going to be the last to go. They are on that third level – the mind, the thinking – and that everything else has been healed. *The Sick Girl* lives in my mind so this was powerful for me. I keep getting my Rainbow winks! I know it's because I'm working on the book. It's his way of encouraging me to keep going.

May 29, 2017

I continued to get Rainbows yesterday like I haven't had in a long time. At bedtime I turned on the Weather Channel just in time to see an amazing segment on Rainbows that I had never seen before. I smiled all the way through it. I also took off my wedding rings. For now.

May 30, 2017

I became aware of something I hadn't realized. Loyalty and commitment to Gregory are ingrained deep in me. That's why he had to be the one to tell me it's time. I wasn't going to do it. I wasn't going to take off my wedding rings or take down some of the pictures. I wasn't going to deal with his clothes in the spare closet. It wasn't even on my radar. That's how you get stuck.

I didn't see this part. I was feeling guilty at even the thought of moving on. To make the choice to take those wedding rings off felt like a betrayal, let alone allow myself to think about being with someone else. And maybe part of it's the kids. Feeling like letting them down by 'cheating' on their dad. Wow. This is unreal. I suddenly see how I've been thinking. That on some level, no matter when it happens, I felt like I would be cheating on Gregory..... Long pause. *"It's okay, L.J., you've shown your loyalty. Your heart will always have Gregory in it."*

June 2, 2017

I got my Rainbows right at bedtime last night before I turned off the TV. Then first thing this morning when I turned it on I got another one! He's never going to let me forget he's here.

June 3, 2017

I dreamed that Gregory sent me a private message on FB. The little window popped up and it was an explosion of mini Rainbows. They were like fireworks shooting little Rainbows. Heart Rainbows, splashes of Rainbows, little fireworks. Brilliant colors. I immediately woke up just like I always do when I dream about Rainbows. It's so crazy. I love it! It shows me that I can 'message' Gregory anytime I want, like a loved one that lives far away. And he will keep sending me messages as well. I don't need to keep him with me 24/7 anymore. He can be on call. I think I can live with that. I bagged up his clothes and will take them to Goodwill.

June 8, 2017

I came home and Greg's brother had mowed the lawn. He had an adapter in his hand for the hose. I came inside and then noticed he was looking around in the backyard. I went out and he said, *"Either Greg is f-ing with me or I'm losing my mind! I just had that adapter in my hand and now it's gone."* We both searched everywhere, but he said he hadn't gone anywhere but right there, pulling the hose out of the big box it rolls up in. I said, *"Greg is known to hide things and you watch, he'll set it right here,"* and I patted the hose box. When I left to go to the chiropractor Brian was gone. I got my adjustment and, as I was pulling into the garage, he was pulling into the parking space.

We came into the backyard at the same time. A flash of light caught my eye like a beacon shining right at me. It was the adapter sitting on the hose box. I said, *"So you found it, huh?"* He said, *"No, I even looked again, I'll have to get another one, they're cheap."* I stood pointing to the box..... We couldn't believe it. I couldn't believe it because of what I had said Greg would do. Brian was in shock and I started laughing. *"Welcome to my world, Bro!"* Lol! *"Good one Gregory!"*

I dropped off his clothes at Goodwill. It felt strange, somber, but it was okay and I did it. I took a deep breath as I drove away. Moving forward. Looking up. When I turned on the music channel a minute ago it was a song I don't care about so I muted it and went about my morning. Then I moved the remote so Riley could jump up and I must have hit the volume and it came on. It was *Tattoo* by Jordan Sparks. I almost muted it until I started hearing the words. I couldn't believe it. I heard something about needing to let my spirit be free. I stopped then turned up the volume.

It talks about living every moment like it was the last and not looking back because there's a new direction I need to be heading. It says that I'll always have him and he'll still be a part of everything I do. His life is imprinted on my heart like a tattoo. The words soothed my wounded heart like a healing salve. I can do this thing. I am doing it. I can make a new start, a new life without Gregory. I can do that with someone new. It's what he wants for me. He doesn't want to see me waiting. Lonesome, lonely. That's the truth of it.

June 10, 2017

I found a pile of cards and letters from Gregory. I sat here yesterday and went through everything, ending with his journal, before I put everything away for safekeeping. One entry dated August 25, 1998, he writes, *"Thanks for a good day, for no injuries to my fellow workers—they're really not a bad bunch—for LoriJean, the Love of my life, Megan and the joys she brings to me—Thanks again, GR Hunt."* That makes me smile. He always mentions me in those lists of gratitudes. Another entry he ends with, *"I love you L.J. – I miss you too – and can't forget about Mega-boo! – Thanks for a Good Life."*

These journals were before, during and after his father's death. He would always write when he was working out of town, away from the family. I'm so grateful he found this outlet. I didn't realize how much he was using it. I thought I knew my husband, but his journal has shown me even deeper into his heart and soul. The part of him he didn't always share. Now that he's gone—and someday I will be too, the one who knew him best—this is a priceless gift.

His letter to me when he was at Lineman school really got to me. He misses me so much and tells me everything he misses about what we have. He talks about how much he loves and misses Megan and Jeremy. His heart was with us. He ends the letter with, *"I miss you like I never thought I could—I love you so much—yours forever Greg."*

June 11, 2017

This morning when I turned on the TV to watch a movie, the first scene was a Smiley Rainbow! It was really bold too. It dipped down over the water and back up. A big, beautiful Rainbow smile first thing in the morning. A few minutes ago I looked at the muted TV to see a cereal commercial and a Leprechaun throwing his arms up to spread out a Rainbow! It was magical.

June 13, 2017

I'm getting used to not wearing my wedding rings. It hasn't been easy. Some days I stand in front of my dresser looking at them, tempted, and I hear Gregory yell, *"Don't do it!"* I smile because I know everything he says is to help me heal. I want to put them on, but I don't have to.

Chapter 32

Dare To Dream

June 18, 2017

This morning I needed to talk to Gregory and I cried. I told him he was so safe for me. So familiar, so wonderful. The tears came when I found myself saying, *"I won't be betraying you by falling in love again, right Honey? I'm still here, over five years now, and you're not coming back. I get to move on. Thank you for thirty years, Babe. It was a wild ride!"*

June 22, 2017 (Evening)

OMG! I love it! I turned on the TV and switched to the channel I wanted. The remote didn't take all the numbers and put me on a different channel. As soon as it changed over I heard a woman say, *"Like Rainbows! Who doesn't like Rainbows?"* And the husband says, *"They're just colors in the sky! I don't hate them, I just don't know why we have to pull over and take a picture every time you see one."* Lol! I love that! I can't tell you how many times over the past five years that this happens and I don't write it down and then it's lost. So yay for me!

June 27, 2017

I feel lonely. I long to share my life again. I long to share my bed, go to sleep and wake up with someone next to me. I long to feel alive in love again. Lol! I looked up to the music channel and it's, *Show Me The Meaning Of Being Lonely*, by the Backstreet Boys. *"Very funny Dr. Jones."*

July 2, 2017

I've been getting beautiful Rainbows every day. They are my Rainbow winks from Gregory. He lets me know he's always with me and that he's proud of me for learning to let go more and more. It hasn't been easy but I know it's necessary and I want to do it.

July 9, 2017

I've felt alone this morning. Here's the thing, now I feel alone even when Gregory is right here with me. He's not enough anymore. Ugh. That's a realization for you. It just isn't enough to live with a ghost; with a memory of a life that's gone now. How it feels to be alone has changed. I long for someone in my life. I don't feel like I'm searching as much as I'm waiting in faith. I'm open and feeling ready to fall in love again.

July 15, 2017

I was sitting here and had a flash of regret, I can't even remember now, but I always wonder why it is that, if I'm going to recall something it has to be negative? I was aware, as I tried to recall a good memory, how difficult that seems. Then I said to my dad—knowing that he was one to regret things—*"Why do I always recall something sad?"*

Just then, from the street below, I heard someone shout, *"Robert Palmer! Wooooo!"* followed by a R.P. song blasting from the Pedal Pub as they strolled past the house. My dad *loved* Robert Palmer and my mind immediately went to him rockin' out to his music. I smiled as the memory played and then realized that my dad just responded to my question with a happy memory! As if to say, *"I also knew how to have a good time! Remember this?"* It makes me smile clear to my heart. *"Thanks Pop, Me Love You!"*

July 17, 2017

I got a Rainbow yesterday and I was so happy. It made me realize that I haven't been getting them every day and it's okay. I didn't think I'd ever hear myself say that.

July 23, 2017

Yesterday I got two beautiful Rainbows and was so excited. I gave Gregory *the weasel* and I smiled with my whole being.

August 7, 2017

Gregory was in my dream last night and I woke up sad. I couldn't see him clearly but he was there. To wake up and know that I was with him felt a little heavy. I don't think I would have been sad if I'd been able to see him more clearly. I want a ten-second kiss, a hug that lasts forever, a good look at his beautiful face. I just want more. *"God, I know you're going to send my new guy when the time is right, but I'm just so lonely. Help me do my part to get ready for him."*

August 11, 2017

My grief has changed. Now I find I'm crying about how far away our life together is. I'm grieving about the healing. It's crazy, but there's a sadness about missing the grief. That early grief is like a warm blanket. Life is all emmeshed with the one who has died. The relationship is on a different plane now, but it's all encompassing, nonetheless. There is comfort there. If done properly, in the worst of times, grief is a safe place to be. Where it's all about me and my loved one.

All I know is, for five years in the midst of my deepest grief

I received Rainbows every day. Not just one a day either, lots of Rainbows. And music, wow, powerful messages through song. My connection with the Other Side—with the world of the spirit—was strongest when I was grieving the most. It was unbelievable. I'm grieving the loss of that.

(Later)
When I turned on the TV to check the weather after journaling there was a beautiful Rainbow and the guy spread out his hands and said, *"Now there's a Rainbow!"* Lol! I love that!

August 12, 2017
I sat down and turned on the TV and it was on the music channel. I heard something about living together even when we're ghosts. The song is, *Say You Won't Let Go*, by James Arthur. I took a deep breath. Then I heard the words that he wants to love me until his lungs stop working. Deeper breath. *"Yep, that's what you did. You loved me til your heart and lungs gave out."*

I know what the words were saying. *"Say you won't let go,"* says that we will always be connected, joined at the heart. I can never let go because he is so much a part of who I am now. The Rainbows will always be my connection and my communication with him. Beautiful, loving reminders of what we've shared. A lifetime of memories left in my care. But I miss him. My life will feel lonely until I fall in love on this earth once again.

(12:45 p.m.)
I came in just now after mowing the lawn and realized I'd left the TV on. I picked up the remote and pointed it at the TV to shut it off and there it was, a beautiful Rainbow. Are you kidding me? I shouldn't be surprised when this happens because it happens all the time. But I am! What are the chances? I know I say that a lot, but seriously, what are the odds? Love-love.

August 15, 2017

Woohoo! I dreamed about Rainbows! So amazing. In the middle of the night I dreamed about the most breathtakingly beautiful Rainbow and then woke right up. I went back to sleep, dreamed about a different, brilliant Rainbow, and woke right up. I went back to sleep again, dreamed about a third, magnificent Rainbow then woke right up! I love that! I love that every time I dream about Rainbows it wakes me up. It's awesome!!

(4:40 p.m.)

I turned on the TV and there it was, a Skittles commercial just ending. A colorful Rainbow and it said, *"Contract the Rainbow! Taste the Rainbow!"* Lol! This makes me laugh. It's been happening for five years and still it just tickles the heck out of me! *"Thank you Baby! I will always love the Rainbows!"*

(6:50 p.m.)

I was sitting here thinking about the Rainbows earlier and smiling. I looked up at the muted TV and it was a commercial for Hershey's bite sized candy bars. Just then a bunch of little candy bars exploded out into an arc, which I didn't think anything of until I saw the smiling clouds that joined the arc at each end and that's when I realized it was a Rainbow made of chocolate bars! Seriously. Lol!

August 19, 2017

My husband has been speaking to me in songs all morning. One after the other. It's been kind of funny. Let me just say that my connection to him is so strong and he's here with me, close in my heart always, but even more than that. Now that my grief has lessened, my hope has increased and my relationship with him becomes less dependent. And yet there he is, sending me Rainbows, encouraging me, reassuring me, excited for me. My hope for the future is off the charts.

August 27, 2017

When I was crying the other day, talking to Gregory, telling him how much I miss him and how ready I am to find love again, a beautiful Rainbow came on the muted TV and I couldn't believe it. He's been sending me Rainbows every day again and I'm surprised. I guess I had myself adapting to the idea that one day they might stop altogether. But then, as I'm struggling this past week with no energy and feeling kind of useless, if not self-sabotaging, I kept getting Rainbows. I know he doesn't want the enemy to get me down so he's helping me.

August 29, 2017

I woke up this morning to Johnny Lang's, *Missing Your Love*, playing in my mind. It played over and over in my head all through my morning routine. It says that every day and in every way I miss your love. And when it said that even though he's still here I'm missing his love, the words couldn't be truer.

August 31, 2017

I've been crying a lot lately. Missing Gregory more as he feels further away. And yet, yesterday while I was crying I kept getting Rainbows on the TV. His reassurance that all is well. I had to order new checks and I struggled to take his name off. But I did it and the new checks came with just my name on them and that was hard. Maybe by the next time I order them they will have two names on them again. "Oh, funny Gregory," I just got, *You'll Never Find Another Love Like Mine*. I guess we'll see about that.

September 1, 2017

I turned on the TV and immediately got *True Colors* by Cyndi Lauper. It made me smile. My singing Rainbow song first thing in the morning. When it was over, *Hold On My Heart*, by Genesis and another reminder that he's always going to be there for me. I keep feeling amazed. I just can't believe the way Gregory communicates with me. The songs and the Rainbows, well, it's indescribable really. At least my words don't seem to do justice to how the whole thing feels. It's pretty spectacular. Thank goodness because I haven't felt well the past few days and that makes life feel harder. My grief has always felt heavier when I don't feel well. Plus it's Mackinac Island time. We'd be getting ready to leave. So there's my heaviness. I can deal with the dark cloud as long as I know what it is.

September 2, 2017

This morning I turned on the TV and Ronnie Millsap's, *Wouldn't Have Missed It For The World*, was already playing. It talks about how all good things must come to an end but that he wouldn't trade one experience, one memory, one moment that we spent together and that given the chance he'd do it all again. He wouldn't have missed it for the world. *"Ditto, Baby."*

September 3, 2017

When the weather is good I want to take some of Gregory's ashes to the Bay. I took off the bottom of the box and pulled out the bag of what was once my husband. I held it to my heart. *"I know this is no longer you, Honey, but it used to be."*

Chapter 33

Rainbows In The Dark

September 6, 2017

I dreamed I was walking toward my car. All of a sudden a very big man, well over 6', was behind me and threw his right arm firmly around me, pinning both arms to my body and his left hand covered my mouth. He lifted me off the ground and took off running with me! I thought, "Oh my God, this is it. This is the thing I thought I was pretty aware of—my surroundings, strangers getting too close, etc.,—but here I am caught off guard and in a terrible situation." I knew I was in big trouble.

I woke up startled. The most frightening thing was how quickly and securely he had me. I always thought I could put up a fight, scratch, bite, scream, but in an instant I was totally incapacitated. I'm happy to have remembered a dream because it's been so long, but really? It doesn't surprise me actually. The darkness seems to have a bit of a hold on me this past week. I didn't think it had me incapacitated, but I knew it had me. I'm in a fog. A darkness that reflects the dark, stormy weather and pouring rain we had all day yesterday. I loved it.

September 7, 2017

I just turned on the TV to check the weather and there were two Rainbow pictures in the background! Oh yeah. And then, oh my goodness, I just turned the channel and got a bunch of Rainbows on another commercial! Fantastic! The new Lucky Charms commercial. *"What's more magical than a Rainbow? A bunch of Rainbows!"* And then it was Rainbow after Rainbow! Woohoo!

September 8, 2017

Lol! I turned on the TV, changed the channel and it was Hoda Kotb with Kelly Clarkston and her little daughter. They said to her, *"Are you going to sing with us?"* They started singing—and the baby joined in—*Somewhere Over The Rainbow*!

September 10, 2017

First thing this morning I got *Pieces*, by Rob Thomas. Let me just say that I've been haunted by my dream the other night. The idea that the darkness I've been feeling lately is worse than I thought and that the bad guy has run away me, is unsettling. Then I got this song and felt Gregory speaking straight to my heart. He said he warned me that I was going to break down. He says that I need to start believing in myself. That even though the pieces of our life are scattered at my feet I must look for the light in the darkness and I'll find my way.

Then I had a flash of that life together and it was good. I mean, ups and downs, struggles and hardships, it was so good. I gave Gregory *the weasel* and then I held onto his hand. I could feel him. It was so strong. It was so powerful. It gave me goosebumps. It's Sunday and we would have been home since Friday night. We'd have been resting up from a fun-filled, major bike riding, walking, eating, playing week on the Island. We would be so happy. I feel a weight lifted now that the week is over.

I often smile now when I think about Gregory and our life together. I got Rainbows all weekend. Two were even real ones!

A double Rainbow even! I realize I've been trying to push myself to be somewhere I'm not. Maybe that's been making it worse; making me feel sadder, more alone, lost without him. I just took a big cleansing breath. I know that Mackinac Island week is tough and that our anniversary on October 3rd sort of looms ahead of me after that, so I attribute a big cloud to that. But I also see that I've been pushing myself to get over this, move on, start living, be happy again.

That's all fine and good—and is certainly what I'm striving for—but what made me think it wasn't okay where I am? The five-year mark? I think that's what it was. That's when I felt Gregory's loving suggestions to take his clothes to Goodwill, spread his ashes, take off my wedding rings. I still want to be wearing them. So maybe I have been pushing myself and it hasn't helped. I feel a little relieved.

September 15, 2017

I have to write about this. I made some lunch and was watching something on TV while I ate. Greg's brother was in the basement. Just then the table saw fired up. My heart sank. I haven't heard that sound since Gregory was alive. All at once the memories came flooding back and I got that sort of chilled numb race through me. I was catapulted back in time where my husband was in the basement cutting trim for whatever room we were working on.

It took my breath away for a moment. Just then I looked at the TV and there was a beautiful scene. Clear blue water and a most beautiful Rainbow! The scene seemed to stay for several moments as I just soaked it in. I gave my Gregory *the weasel*. He feels my every emotion. He sends me Rainbows so I remember that everything is going to be alright. I believe him.

September 16, 2017

I took some of Gregory's ashes over to his mom's yesterday and spread them in her garden. That was enough. Later I can do the same here and then take the rest over to the bay at sunrise.

September 22, 2017

After a rough few days I'm feeling better. I guess I didn't antici-pate how hard it was going to be putting together this book. What did I think? Geesh. Seems pretty obvious now, but somehow I thought it was going to be simply amazing. Rainbows and butter-flies. Well, it is that, but it's also a lot of gut-wrenching grief and loss.

October 3, 2017

Today is our anniversary. Seems strange. Six now without him. I don't feel sad or heavy about it and I think this is the first time. It just seems a little strange. Like this day always had significance and now, well, it still has significance, but it doesn't feel as relative to my life today as it always has. And the grief surrounding it is not there. I'm thinking about the new guy now more than ever.

I turned on the TV last night and it was a children's dance class. The instructor said, *"Do the Rainbow!"* and everyone swayed their arms from one side to the other as they said, *"Rainbow! Rainbow!"* I love it! Later I looked up to the muted TV and saw a child's drawing of a Rainbow on a commercial. You just can't make this stuff up. It thrills and delights me every time. *"Thanks, Babe."*

October 4, 2017

I miss Gregory. I miss my dad. I've been seeing Dad every-where. I'd like to see Gregory everywhere, but that probably wouldn't be good, right? I might want to follow him. I turned on the TV and a crowd of people had their hand over their heart for the National Anthem. I could see a Rainbow on the t-shirt of a young girl, peeking out from behind her hand. I smiled. Then later there was a woman with earrings that were the moon and stars on one, a cloud and a Rainbow on the other!

October 10, 2017

Carly Pearce's, *Every Little Thing*, has been heavy on my heart lately. I turned on the music first thing this morning and there it was. More about those scattered pieces on the floor. It says that his ghost still haunts me but that I can't sleep with a ghost. Oh, I remember every little thing and I miss it all. But my Gregory is a ghost now. I'm making peace with that. I'm beginning to feel whole. Complete. Like the empty space inside of me has built up scar tissue and no longer hurts the way it did.

I've known this was an amazing journey from the start but nothing like hindsight to bring the full impact to the forefront. Nothing like the feeling of having made it through an ordeal. Makes you want to shout to the rooftops. Do cartwheels. I got Rainbows all weekend. Every time I turned on the TV there was a Rainbow. I got the Jimmy Dean commercial three times.

October 18, 2017

I woke up to Sarah McLachlan's, *You're In The Arms Of The Angels*, playing in my mind. *I also dreamed about a big, beautiful Rainbow and it woke me up.* I love that. I put on my wedding rings yesterday and told Gregory that I wasn't taking them off until I dream about him. And then I got a Rainbow. *"Nice, but that doesn't count, Dude, I want you."*

October 20, 2017

The tears are rolling down my cheeks non-stop. It's been happening for a couple of days. This morning I turned on the TV and there was a beautiful video on CMT called *Sunday Morning*. My mind went back to my own precious memories of Sunday mornings. Van Morrison playing on the turntable, steaming coffee on the nightstand to wake me. The smell of breakfast wafting from the kitchen.

I could feel him right here. I closed my eyes and I was in his arms again, the love between us all encompassing. My mind and body savored the feeling and the tears began to fall. What a gift to be transported back to a place where I felt so incredibly safe and loved. My hands touched his face, I kissed him, held him tight, swaying to the rhythm of each other.

And then, in mere moments, my mind scanned over every embrace, every kiss, every hug, every intimate look into each other's eyes. The tears rolled down my cheeks like a waterfall and I felt so much love. I miss it so much. My heart longs to be with someone again. To share my every thought. To hear his every thought. To be there for each other in this life and make it better. But for now I've put on my wedding rings and I've moved back into Gregory until I finish the book. It's my process.

October 24, 2017

I took off my wedding rings and then couldn't get them back on. Dang. I must say, it felt kind of weird anyway. Can't really explain it, but it didn't feel all warm and fuzzy when I put them on again. It almost felt foreign. Sad to say I'm getting used to not wearing them.

October 25, 2017

I just got my Rainbow! A music video is playing and all of a sudden there was the image of a man sticking out his tongue with a big Rainbow on it! Seriously! Lol! I continue to get Rainbows most days even if I don't always remember to write about them. They are as special now as they've ever been. My love's way of giving me a wink, a smile, a message that he's always with me and that brighter days lie ahead. I love him for that. I miss him.

October 26, 2017

I just turned on the TV to the Weather Channel and got the most beautiful Rainbow I've ever seen! It was a *Red Rainbow,* or as the locals in an area of the Philippians called it, the Unicorn Rainbow, because it resembles the flowing mane of the Unicorn. It was fantastic! Woohoo! Yesterday when I got in the car and turned on the radio it was the tail end of a song I really like. I switched the channel, tail end of another great song. This went on for about five songs, so I realized something was going on. As yet another great song was just ending, I said to myself, *"Watch me get a song especially for me right from the beginning."*

And there it was. I started to cry. It was the familiar drum beat and introduction to my favorite version—the one we played at Greg's memorial—of *Somewhere Over The Rainbow.* Tears rolled down my cheeks through the whole song and I had goosebumps! I could feel my Gregory right there in the car with me. Magical. I know I got that Rainbow first thing this morning to encourage me. I had a migraine yesterday and woke up feeling rough. – Just got another Rainbow!

November 3, 2017

After being brutally sick for a few days with some freaky flu thing, life is good again. I did cry some yesterday and the day before, missing Gregory. But he's been sending me Rainbows like crazy! Seriously, every time I turn on the TV lately there's a Rainbow! Love it!

November 9, 2017

I've been getting several Rainbows every day. Yesterday I got like five and I wondered, *"Does everyone happen to catch these commercials with Rainbows as often as I do?"* I was able to get my wedding rings back on but they just don't feel the same. I'm wearing them anyway.

November 11, 2017

I dreamed about Gregory last night! There he was and he had his full dark beard. We were talking and interacting. It was awesome! I didn't feel sad when I woke up and remembered. I know it was his way of affirming about the wedding rings and holding me to my deal to take them off when I dreamed about him. I needed it because yesterday I told God to f—k off.

I've been feeling so sick again. I told God he doesn't listen to me. He doesn't answer prayers—at least not mine—and that I'm just so sad. I've tried everything I know to get well. I cried and sobbed and cursed at God. I told Him I don't trust Him anymore. I even said I hate you. Good thing I know my God can take it, but it was a rough day. That's probably why I've been getting so many Rainbows. And Gregory in a dream! Trying to reassure me that all is well. That the future looks bright. That there is hope. I continue to need the reminders because I feel like I'm going through hell right now.

November 13, 2017

I had a wedding reception to go to just down the block even though I didn't feel well. In hindsight I shouldn't have gone. When I got there they hadn't put the food out so for the next hour and a half I felt like a fish out of water, despite my best efforts to smile and look like I was engaged. I wasn't. I sat by myself in a comfortable chair and watched everyone.

The alcohol on the counter when I got myself a tonic water continued to grab my attention, as well as everyone who was drinking. Not many, by the way, social drinkers to the extreme, I kid you not. But this is the part that surprised me. I looked around at every face in the room and realized that no one there knows that I'm an alcoholic. *No one would know if this tonic water I'm holding right now had vodka in it.*

Wow, where did I think that thought was going to take me? What I see in hindsight is that I wasn't in fit spiritual condition. I haven't been for a while, so why did I not see the slippery slope in front of me? I mean, after all, I had just told God to f--k off the day before. *Danger, danger, Will Robinson.* What the hell? So it was extremely uncomfortable for me and I know it's because I haven't felt well. I need to be spiritually fit going into an environment like that. I never gave it the slightest thought.

All I know is I haven't felt that out of my element in a long time. Everyone was a couple. I felt like I was the only single person there. I found myself trying to fit in, trying to be a part of what was going on. But all I could do is look at the alcohol on the counter and think that a little something in my tonic water sure would make this situation more comfortable. *Yikes!* It's sad to me that my association with fitting in and being a part of—at least with that group of people—was to drink. I came home after the reception and took a hot bath and went to bed!

November 17, 2017

Well, I made it to the Kinesiologist, lungs so full I could hardly breathe, and it showed mold. He tested on three different points and it showed mold. Dang. It's my bedroom I was sure. I came home and looked and OMG, there was a lot of black mold growing all around the window where the A/C had been and the window-sill was completely black. WTF? Can a girl catch a break here?

Chapter 34

Holy Rainbows!

November 22, 2017

Our grandson is here for Thanksgiving from Idaho and he was asking me about some of the signs and stuff from Papa Greg and about the Rainbows. I rattled off a few examples and it got me excited about the book and Grayson said he can't wait to read it. I thought how cool it would be if Greg did something while he was here.

This morning when I went into the office I couldn't believe it. There was the little Rainbow card lying on the keyboard. It's the one I printed off after Greg died and then later found propped up on my keyboard. Now he did it again! I don't even know where the little thing has been, but there it was this morning, right in front of me. It says, *"I am not afraid of tomorrow, for I have survived the storm of yesterday and that has made me grateful for today."* Oh yeah. I couldn't wait to tell Grayson.

November 23, 2017 (Thanksgiving Day)

On my way to Meg's I was thinking about Greg and missing him even more on days like today. I turned on the radio and my heart melted into the beautiful music I recognized right away. It was Firefall's, *Just Remember I Love You*. I can live with that.

November 25, 2017

Grayson and I got my Christmas tree yesterday. When we got back I asked him if he wanted to walk over to the bay with me to spread Papa Greg's ashes. He did. I spread some in our garden and then we walked over to the beach and spread the rest of them. I could feel Gregory with us and I was so grateful to be doing this with our grandson.

November 29, 2017

I've had Gregory on my mind a lot. I talk to him all the time. He keeps sending me Rainbows. I went down to the kitchen for a snack. When I came back up and walked into the bedroom I heard, *"How do you connect with Rainbows?"* Are you kidding me? I love that so much! It happens all the time!

December 1, 2017

Yesterday when I got in the car and turned on the radio I heard a woman say, *"Come join us at the Rainbow of Hope Farm..."* and it went on to talk about this farm in Kingsley. I had to smile. Then, I'd lost one of my favorite earrings last week and I've been really bummed about it. I ran errands and when I got home I noticed I was only wearing one. This morning the lost earring was on my dresser..... Um, that would be my dad. He did that last time I lost an earring. *"Thanks, Pop, Me Love You!"*

December 2, 2017

I was watching a movie this afternoon and the song toward the end had the chorus of, *"I'll fill the sky with Rainbows..."* It made me smile like the Rainbows always do.

December 3, 2017

I was watching a program and on the commercial I turned the channel to check the weather. As soon as I did there was a double Rainbow. I couldn't believe it. How does this continue to happen? How is it possible to have that kind of timing? Does everyone see Rainbows as often as I do? Do their hearts swell with joy and does the energy in the room change with every Rainbow? I wonder? Even as sick as I've been I can see a light at the end of the tunnel. That long-ass tunnel.

December 26, 2017

I haven't written since Saturday and it's been rough with my health. But I have to write about the Rainbows yesterday. Gregory outdid himself. Every movie I watched someone said something about Rainbows. It was the music in the background of one of the movies, something about painting Rainbows in the sky for you. The first one came when I turned on the TV to a show about an artist who painted ceramic tiles and has done murals. They showed one big mural and it was a countryside scene with a beautiful Rainbow spanning the entire sky. I had goosebumps and I knew that was my *"Merry Christmas"* from Gregory.

Then all day long I got them. I'd walk back in the room with my coffee or something to eat and just then, whatever channel I had it on, they would say something about a Rainbow. One time it was, *"...every color of the Rainbow."* Another time it was a commercial with Rainbows or a Rainbow light would just move across the screen during a movie or show I was watching. I bet I got 10-15 Rainbows yesterday. I was laughing as the day went on. It was truly the highlight of my day!

Otherwise it's been rough. Maybe I need something else for my liver or maybe I need to up the one for my adrenals. Usually I would rebound much quicker, but my body is also fighting this fungus and my lungs have never felt worse and I've never coughed so much. My body is fighting the good fight and winning! But I'm going through hell in the process.

Oh, and about Christmas morning. It was unlike any I've had since Greg died. I didn't have the energy to open my presents. I didn't have the enthusiasm or the excitement I would normally have and that told me how sick I was. The stairs have seemed monumental for weeks, but yesterday they seemed nearly impossible. I take two steps and stop to rest. So that's my sad, sad tale for the end of a really tough year. A year that all I did was fight one thing after the other and struggle to be well.

December 28, 2017

I feel like my year with the word *Intention* was a waste. I intended to get well and was sicker than I've ever been. I intended to finish the book and didn't work on it for months. I intended to meet Mr. Wonderful and barely left my house. It does not feel like a successful year with my word. I guess we'll pray about it and see what comes up. In terms of my health this has been my worst year since Greg died. Oh, but the Rainbows! They have continued. Yesterday when I walked back in the room a movie was playing and I heard, *"It's time to stop chasing Rainbows."* Um, I think not!

January 8, 2018

I think I've picked *Purpose* for my word this year. My life's purpose—the vision—has been playing clearer than ever. I can feel myself being moved closer. I got my Rainbows all weekend. One time I turned on the TV and there was a sea of hot air balloons dominating the sky. There were hundreds and so colorful. My heart leapt, as it does when I'm getting Rainbows, so I was sure there would be a Rainbow amongst the balloons. I didn't see one, but then suddenly realized that the hot air balloon closest to the camera was named *"Rainbow Rider,"* big across the balloon. Love it!

January 15, 2018

Yesterday was Gregory's birthday and I didn't realize it until Megan mentioned it. I didn't write in the morning so I didn't write the date. Still, it was a good sign that my first thought was not that it was his birthday and bummer he's not here. I think I'm getting better. I did think of him a lot and I got my Rainbows all day, but there wasn't such grief attached to it. Progress. Healing. His death didn't kill me, but it sure could have.

January 19, 2018

The last time I wore my wedding rings they felt foreign, but I wore them anyway. I took them off, as promised, after I dreamed about Greg, and I haven't been tempted to wear them again. Before when I wasn't wearing them it was a daily struggle not to put them on. So that's progress. *The wedding rings no longer fit.*

January 20, 2018

OMG!! I just can't believe this! I'm actually laughing. It's early afternoon and I just turned on the TV to check the weather. A guy was filming these amazing clouds and then zoomed in as he said, *"And what's in the middle of this amazing cloud? A Rainbow!"* The remainder of the segment was about Rainbow Clouds and Fire Rainbows. Not only did I see Rainbow after Rainbow, but I heard the word—which hits my ears like a beautiful chime—again and again and again. Love it!

February 20, 2018

While I was making dinner a song came on that made me dance in my kitchen! Dance like no one's watching! I felt Gregory and I danced for him, to show him that I'm getting happy again, playful, goofy, carefree, the way I was all my life before he died. I could feel him smiling at me with that smile I loved so much. The one that said how happy he was that this goofball was his wife. Just then *Who Loves You?* came on and I smiled ear to ear. *"You do!"* Then I danced around the kitchen to that whole song! He sent me beautiful Rainbows today and my connection with him is strong.

February 25, 2018

This morning I was watching a music video for Scotty McCreery's, *Five More Minutes* and I found myself thinking how true that is. I thought about my dad, feeling his presence as my eyes welled with tears. I thought about everyone I've lost, and I said out loud, *"What I wouldn't give for five more minutes with each and every one of you. But, unfortunately, I get to wait, don't I?"* I turned my attention to Gregory. *"But I can't wait for love, Babe. I'm so lonely, Gregory. To go from what we had to....."* Before I could even finish that heartfelt thought he said, *"He'll be worth the wait."* Deep sigh of relief.

March 5, 2018

I have to write about the Rainbows. I continue to get them every single day. There was an ad for Blue Kitty Cravings cat treats with a smiling cat and a big bright Rainbow one time. Then I came back into the room and the Weather Channel was on. I heard, *"It's a full circle Rainbow!"* and then I saw a couple of incredible, double, full circle Rainbows that were just amazing! Another time I walked in the room just in time for this little segment on Rainbows. Welcome to my world!

(Evening)

When I turned on the TV and went to OnDemand I was thrilled to find the first episode of the new season with Tyler, the *Hollywood Medium.* I'm no stranger to receiving my own messages when I'm watching these shows. The very first reading Tyler did he said, *"I see a big Rainbow,"* and he swept his hand up and around like a big Rainbow. A subtle chill ran through me and I burst out smiling. Then he talked more about the Rainbows and the woman he was reading said that was the connection she had with her loved one. That they would always run out after the rain to look for Rainbows. I was so happy just to hear the story, hear the word, and know that no matter what I'm doing in my life

I will always have this amazing connection to the most beautiful symbol anyone could ever ask for. He said Rainbows are about hope for the future, new beginnings, fresh starts. Oh, yes.

March 11, 2018

I don't know if there are just so many Rainbows and references to Rainbows in this world that you can't help but turn on the TV and get one every time, but it still delights and amazes me. Just a minute ago I turned on the TV to watch a program about Angels and in the very first segment the woman said, *"...I contacted the angels of qualities, which are to me, the breakup of the energies of God, into love, into various qualities, like the Rainbow is broken up from the white light."* It makes me smile to even hear the word.

March 16, 2018

In the car yesterday I was thinking about Gregory and it was good. I was thinking about all the beautiful years and everything we went through. I was feeling so grateful and so full of love for my life and for him and for how strong I'm feeling now. Just then I looked at the license plate in front of me and it says "LOVE86." I smiled. After four years together, '86 is the year we got married.

March 17, 2018

I turned on the TV yesterday morning at 5 a.m. and it was on *What Not To Wear*. Just then I heard, *"She really loves Rainbows,"* and then they talked about how the woman has Rainbow socks and Rainbow sweaters and just loves Rainbow colors. When they were going through her clothes Stacy said, *"How many Rainbows do you need?"* Lol! Then, during a particularly emotional moment talking to Gregory and crying about how lonely I am, I got a beautiful Rainbow on the muted TV. *"Thanks, Babe."* When I was at a friend's we were talking about Gregory and all of a sudden there was a beautiful Rainbow on her muted TV!

April 1, 2018

Life just keeps getting better. I can feel the winds of change. I can see everything changing in my favor. I turned the channel to 70's music, which I rarely do. Beautiful music started, keeping me there. The song was by The Brothers Johnson and is called *Strawberry Letter 23*. I listened to the beautiful words and smiled when it talked about Rainbows running through my mind. And my life!

April 4, 2018

My husband continues to send me Rainbows and they come when I'm thinking about him, reminiscing about our life together, or missing everything about being married. Then boom, there it is. I look up to see a beautiful Rainbow on the muted TV or I walk into the room to find one waiting for me on the screen. This morning I went on FB, thinking about Gregory. Then there it was. On the right side of the screen popped up a picture of a beautiful Rainbow at the end of a path, with a small child running toward it, arms open wide.

It's so amazing to me. Like a kiss from Heaven, a touch of the divine, a reminder that he's still here. Not only hasn't he left me, he hears my thoughts, knows my heart. He sends me Rainbows to remind me that brighter days lie ahead. It's pretty miraculous. I wish I would stop, like now, and write down every time he sends me Rainbows, because he never stops.

April 9, 2018

I had a sad meltdown about Gregory yesterday and just missing him so much and remembering what a great life we had. I got a double Rainbow on the muted TV and I thanked him. I've been getting Rainbows several times a day and I know it's his way of reassuring me that everything is going to be okay. I know he knows how sick I've been and how hard it's been, so I appreciate his colorful kisses from Heaven. They keep me going.

April 13, 2018

I came upstairs with my tea for the night and when I walked into the bedroom there was the trailer for an upcoming movie with The Roc, and a gigantic gorilla was busting through a humongous Rainbow banner. I couldn't believe it. Lol! For sure!

April 19, 2018

Tomorrow is my birthday and I still don't have back my special connection to it. Perhaps I won't until I have someone special to share it with. This year, perhaps more than last, I thought about standing in the funeral home, looking for the last time, at the lifeless shell of what used to be my vibrant, energetic husband. Then something kind of wonderful happened. Something I don't usually think about on April 19th. His passing was amazing. It was unreal and my mind took me back to that precious moment when there was no one there but me, Gregory, and the angels. When he took his last breath and jumped right into my heart, and I felt a peace like no other.

May 6, 2018

Gregory continues to send me Rainbows every day but hasn't really spoken to me in songs for a while. My tears have changed. More often they are out of loneliness and my longing to be in love again. Crying to Gregory now about how hard it is to be alone and how I don't want to do it anymore, instead of just crying because I miss our life so much. My sadness has turned into the desire for more in the here and now. More love, more companionship, more adventure. Those are hard tears too, but I will take them over the grief of loss.

May 23, 2018

I sat down with my tea and turned to the music channel. I recognized the music to *Here Without You*. I could feel Gregory right here. I started to cry. I cried just like I used to, and I felt my love everywhere around and through me. I've been practically bombarded with Rainbows the past few days. Every time I turn on the TV there's a Rainbow. On commercials, clothing, in pictures, words, you name it.

June 7, 2018

I've been bombarded by Rainbows for days now. If I wrote about all of them it would fill this journal! It's unreal!

June 9, 2018

I sat down this morning and turned on the music channel just in time to hear *My Immortal,* and the part I tuned in on was about being alone even though he's still with me. It hit me as truth in a way it never has before.

June 17, 2018

I just sat down and turned on the TV and there were Rainbows everywhere! A commercial for Mike's something or other. It shows several Rainbows! Woohoo! Love that. I did the same thing yesterday. Turned on the TV and there was a Rainbow! It helps so much because I have not been feeling well at all.

June 27, 2018

I saw Gregory in my dream!!! I was driving, heading toward home. As I crossed our street to turn into our alley, I looked down and there was Gregory standing in our front yard! I was so excited and I honked the horn and waved! When I turned down the alley he had walked to the back and was standing there waiting for me. I was so excited as I approached and then I woke up. Still! I was so happy just seeing him! I'm flying high on the memory! Now I'm crying, but in the best possible way. I saw my Gregory walking around in our yard again, waiting for me to come home.

June 29, 2018

I was watching a program OnDemand called, *Health & Happiness*. At the end there was a quick segment on the benefits of coloring. I went to shut it off but was kept from it. I thought that was odd but then I heard the woman say, *"My favorite thing to color is Rainbows. They're so easy and so beautiful. I like the quote; 'In the rain look for Rainbows, in the dark look for stars.'"* Oh yeah.

July 1, 2018

I just turned on the TV and there was a double Rainbow! It was a whole segment on Rainbows—one I've never seen before—and showed the rare and beautiful sight of a tornado and a Rainbow! It was magnificent! The most beautiful Rainbow arced near the ground with a white funnel twirling right down the middle! It was incredible! Rainbow after Rainbow. Woohoo! I've been getting a lot of Rainbows but this takes the cake!

Chapter 35

Reassurance From Heaven

July 24, 2018

Well, it's been nearly a week since I've written and I've been sick the whole time. I finally started feeling better on Friday. On Saturday I realized that I hadn't seen any Rainbows for a couple of days. That's the first time in a long time. Then Sunday I turned on the TV and got one of my favorite Skittles commercials. *Contract the Rainbow! Taste the Rainbow!* Lol! Love it! I got two more beautiful Rainbows right after that and yesterday was the same. I probably got five Rainbows yesterday! Then this morning I turned on the TV and saw three beautiful Rainbows. I felt my Gregory strong around me.

August 17, 2018

I opened up a magazine that came in the mail and there was my Rainbow! It still amazes me that I get my Rainbows just like that. Turn on the TV and there's a Rainbow. Turn the channel and there's a Rainbow. Turn on the radio and hear Rainbow. Open a magazine, boom, Rainbow. It's phenomenal! *"Thank you, Baby. I don't know how I would be doing this if it weren't for your Rainbows."*

August 18, 2018

Last evening I came down to make a cup of tea and was stopped in my tracks when I entered the living room. There in my path was the little stack of fake books that sits on my coffee table. It was right in the middle of the room sitting upright like it belonged there. *"Why are you there?"* I said out loud, just a little freaked out. No way the cats could have knocked it off. It was way too far from the coffee table. I stared at it. I was just down about a half hour before and it wasn't there. I got goosebumps. *"What does it mean?"*

August 24, 2018

This morning I had a session with a psychic medium! I don't even know where to begin so I guess I'll start at the beginning. First of all it was incredible. Much more than I could have ever imagined. Gregory did not disappoint. *She said there's a beautiful man standing by your side. He's always there. He's never left and he never will leave, but you already know that. He loves you so much and he is so proud of you. He says you are so beautiful. He said, "I love you, I love you. You're beautiful."*

He loves it when you talk to him and he hopes you always will. You can hear him, do you understand that? I do. Everyone thinks he left too soon, but he didn't. He left so you could come into your own. He said you've come a long way. Now he's standing behind you and has both hands on your shoulders. He supports you and he's guiding you and helping you, but you already know that.

At one point she said I see a camera. He has a camera around his neck, but so does someone else and she's an amazing photographer. I said that's our granddaughter, Kaylee. He's very connected to her and he's helping and guiding her as well and she knows that. She's very intelligent and she's going to do amazing things.

He knows that this has been very hard for you, but he had to leave as part of your evolution, do you understand that? Um, yes. You are truly soulmates and you have lived many lives together.

You have so much more to do and you're here for many years without him so you have to move on... Do you understand that? Um, yes.

The holidays are important and you need to celebrate them. Especially Thanksgiving and Christmas. There's one in particular that you have a hard time with and in fact you don't celebrate it. He wants you to celebrate it. He wants you to light a white candle on that day and celebrate. He wants you to laugh again. I told her that he died the day before my birthday and I haven't celebrated since then.

You're a writer; I see books, books, not just one, you have books. The one you're working on now is going to be a bestseller so get it finished. I see lots of travel for you, I see speaking and working with others and it's time for you to shine. It's time for you to spread your wings. Then she said, "I see Rainbow colors all around you, it's quite incredible. I've never seen anything like it." Tears rolled down my cheeks. You are being healed now and you don't have to worry about your health. You have struggled without him, but all that is about to change.

August 27, 2018

Woohoo!!! I dreamed about Gregory! OMG! I walked into a restaurant to meet the kids for dinner. I looked to my left and there was Gregory standing as close to me as he could get. I was practically in his arms. He had his beard neatly trimmed and a big smile on his face. He looked amazing. I burst into a joyful smile and turned into him and threw my arms around him for the biggest hug ever! He pulled me close to his chest and started dancing with me in the middle of the restaurant! There was no music but we didn't care and I held him tighter as we danced to our own music! I heard collective "Ahhh's" from people in the restaurant and I've never been happier!

September 1, 2018

Woohoo! I dreamed about Gregory! It was amazing! It seemed to be the house I grew up in. I looked outside and there he was! I was so happy to see him and I ran out and threw my arms around him from behind and sort of laid my head against him and held him tight. I held onto him like I would if he walked in the door right now. Then we were in the house and I was following him around. I couldn't believe how young he looked, like my 30-year-old Gregory. His beard was dark and neatly trimmed and his skin looked so smooth and there were no lines on his face. I just couldn't get over it and couldn't quit staring at him.

It was a beautiful dream! Seeing Gregory makes me so happy! When I dreamed of him early on I would always wake up sobbing. Now I can't stop smiling! I'm excited about everything! I just turned on the TV and it was a commercial with flying Unicorns sneezing Rainbows!

September 3, 2018

I just turned on the TV to a commercial for Lucky Charms and guess what? Yep, Rainbows! Lots of Rainbows! Then I changed the channel to a movie and just then a guy said, *"Rainbow food has always been my favorite kind of food,"* and he took a bite of a brightly colored rice crispy treat! Seriously? Oh, yeah.

September 7, 2018

I dreamed about Gregory! Just a little snippet, but we were walking across a lawn or park and he just grabbed me in his arms and started dancing with me! I love that so much!

September 12, 2018

I'm sobbing like I haven't done in I can't remember when. I've been in that heartfelt conversation with my husband and remembering the day we met like it was yesterday. Then a seemingly impossible quick scan of thirty years full of love. Tears rushing down my face, I remembered how often I was in this place after he first died. How comforting and spiritual and heartbreaking it was. My Gregory is close in this place and that's what makes it so comforting. But I realized this familiar place is becoming not so familiar and the grief of that hit me hard. I cried out, *"I'm forgetting to remember our life together!"* and then I sobbed and sobbed. Gregory was right here with me, feeling every heartbreaking emotion.

September 13, 2018

I turned on the TV and heard, *"It's a really big one, a Rainbow!"* It was a father helping his young son reel in a big fish! I will never get tired of this happening. It's unreal! Woohoo! *"Love you, Baby!"*

September 14, 2018

I turned on the TV and heard, *"Play She's a Rainbow."* Are you kidding me? It was a car commercial and sure enough the music began playing a song I didn't even know existed! Woohoo! I love this so much! *"Keep 'em coming Baby!"* And it's a Rolling Stones song! *She's a Rainbow!* Lol!

September 20, 2018

A week or so ago I wrote about coming down to the living room after I had just been in there and my little stack of fake books was sitting in the middle of the floor. I came home yesterday and there they were again in the exact same spot, right side up like they belonged there. I stood there staring at them in disbelief and this time I tried to recreate how they could have landed there.

I put them back on the table where they belong and tried to push them off the side like might happen if one of the cats were responsible. First of all they didn't scoot easily and were not sitting near the edge to start with. But I pushed them over and off the edge and three times in a row they hit the ground and toppled over, landing on their side, *under* the table! No matter what I tried I could not get them to land how and where they were. Suddenly it dawned on me. The books! *Don't forget about the books!* Duh! This is phenomenal stuff here and it kind of freaks me out. In a good way.

October 3, 2018

"Happy Anniversary Gregory!" Hard to believe. No tears this morning. And I just got two Rainbows as soon as I turned on the TV. He wins! *"Happy Anniversary to me!"*

October 8, 2018

I've been having a lot of disturbing dreams lately. This one woke me up. I was standing in front of the health food store where I shop. It was a gray, stormy sort of scene that I love so much. Cloudy and slightly windy with ominous dark clouds all around like a storm was brewing. I could see myself standing there in a long white gown and cape and the cape and my hair were flowing in the wind. It was a very cool scene and it almost looked like I could have been filming a video or something.

Normally in dreams we see through our own eyes but in this dream I was watching myself from a short distance. As I was looking at myself—hair and cape flowing in the wind—the me I was watching creepily turned and looked at me and she was wearing a spooky black mask! Her eyes were white and it was the most frightening face! Like death itself! It was so freaky. Then, scary-faced me looked in a mirror, and while the rest of me looked amazing in a very cool way, my face was most disturbing. Sends chills down my spine even now. I began walking home. It's about seven blocks and I hoped I could hide my face on the way. My steps seemed slow and arduous, every step labored and in slow motion.

WTF? I felt tired when I woke up and didn't want to get out of bed. I was feeling so good yesterday. But this morning I feel like I've been hit by a truck. Tired, groggy, headache. Is that the scary face? Illness? Fear? Grief? A *mask* covers up who you really are. To see yourself in a dream is a call to *look at yourself*. I believe the dream is showing me the power this mask of fear, of illness, of grief, has over me. We never want to hide our face in a dream. That's all about hiding who we truly are. The dream shows I'm not going to get very far in that state, and every step I do take is going to be labored. It shows the dark shadow that fear casts over an otherwise very cool life. Duly noted.

October 12, 2018
Ugh. I don't feel well this morning and didn't feel well yesterday. My Kinesiology appointment showed, as suspected, my liver. Dang it already. I'm crying again. It's because of this headache. I can't take it. I was doing so much better. I know this is just temporary, but it makes life so hard and I'm worn out with hard. I asked for a song, adding that I didn't think he could send me a song that would help. I turned on the music and it was Colbie Callat's, *Bubbly*. I said, *"F-you"* and turned off the TV. This is no way to start my day. I'm frustrated and irritated. I can't seem to stop crying.

October 15, 2018
I was talking on the phone to my niece about signs from the Other Side. She's been getting her sign from Dad—her Grandpa—by finding dimes in random places, and she has quite the stories to tell about them. I was standing in the living room looking out into the front yard. A big truck came down the street and my first thought is, *"We have a 5-ton weight limit, what are you doing?"* But as he went past my house there was a big Rainbow on the side trailer! Woohoo! I love when that happens!

October 17, 2018
Yesterday morning I started crying and talking to Greg and telling him how much I miss him. It was a little moment of letdown and the tears flowed out of me like they used to. When I got in the car I heard him say, *"Turn on the radio."* So, of course, I did.

Just then, *Sea of Love*, by The Honeydrippers, started and with the first words he asks me to go back to when we first met. It's a beautiful memory and I was grateful for the reminder. I felt Gregory in the car with me. My eyes filled with tears as my heart overflowed with so much love for the magic that is my life. I'm working on the book and remembering all the times he spoke to me in songs, and yet it doesn't seem to happen as often now. It was magical.

October 21, 2018

Woohoo! I came into the bedroom and the Skittles commercial was on. It ends with a big Rainbow and a shout to, *"Contract the Rainbow! Taste the Rainbow!"* My hands went up in the air and I smiled at Gregory and said, *"I love you!"* Next was an Allstate commercial talking about natural disasters and how we've had more 500 year storms just in the past decade. He's reassuring us that Allstate is there so that when the storm passes... and he turns to his left with a nod to a beautiful Rainbow in the sky! My arms went up in the air again and a big woohoo! *"Are you kidding me, Gregory?"* I love this!

October 23, 2018

Ugh. I didn't want to get out of bed this morning. It's my liver. Medical Medium's new book, *Liver Rescue*, comes out the end of the month and I can't wait to get it. I just need to heal my liver and all of my symptoms will be gone. I dreamed a lot but this is the only part I can remember.

Greg was here and it was like he was getting ready to go out of town for work. There was a car parked across the street with a small trailer behind it that had windows on the sides and I could see Greg's suitcase and other stuff stacked inside. He walked out to check on something and I just watched him from the window.

Hmmm... Perhaps I'm letting go of him a little bit? He's packed and headed out of town! I was quite accepting of this in the dream.

I didn't run out to him, I didn't want to hug him and wrap myself around him. I just let him be. I wasn't sad. I had acceptance. He was leaving.

October 27, 2018

I came upstairs and turned on the TV. It was a scene at the zoo and a woman came in with a beautiful bird and the man said, *"This is Amy and Rainbow."* Amy said, *"This is Rainbow. Rainbow, can you say hello?"* He said hello and then she said, *"What's your name?"* The bird said, *"Rainbow."* She asked the bird a few more questions and a little girl said, *"I love Rainbow,"* to which the trainer said, *"I love Rainbow too, he's pretty special."* Then a man said, *"Can you say goodbye to Rainbow?"* and all the kids start saying, *"Goodbye Rainbow, goodbye Rainbow."* I was laughing out loud! You can't make this stuff up! Not so sure about the *goodbye Rainbow* part, but I'll take it.

October 31, 2018

I got a double Rainbow right off the bat this morning. It's Halloween so Gregory wins. I decided to buy candy this year. It's the first time since he died.

November 1, 2018

Last night was so much fun! I could feel Gregory here with me and I was excited. The little ones were so adorable and I remember how much he loved that. I felt like I was channeling him! A group of older kids in great costumes came up and said, *"Trick or Treat."* I gave them candy and then I heard, *"Hi Grammy,"* and it was Kaylee! I didn't recognize her! Big hugs and it made my night! I was so grateful I'd made the decision not to hide upstairs again this year.

Chapter 36

Hope In The Midst Of Despair

November 5, 2018

I got the new book, *Liver Rescue*, and started on all the herbs and supplements, teas, you name it to begin detoxing and healing my liver. He said it could take three years. I'm feeling worse than ever. I'm still getting Rainbows every day but I don't always write about them.

November 11, 2018

I'm giving myself the day to rest and it's just what I need. I don't feel well. I cried a few minutes ago but promised myself and God that I am not going to lose faith. I walked into the bedroom and there it was, a beautiful Rainbow on the TV. And that is, after all, God's promise to us all, is it not? More tears only this time tears of gratitude.

November 14, 2018

I did more reading in *Liver Rescue* last night. I was encouraged about how much better I'm going to feel when my liver is finally healed. But in the meantime are you kidding me? This is bad. Detoxing is never a pleasant experience. Especially years and years of toxic build up.

November 15, 2018

Yesterday when I got in the car I turned on the radio and heard something about I can't get you off my mind because I'm seeing all these Rainbows. Isn't that the truth? I smiled clear to my toes. Yep, with all these Rainbows it's hard to get you off my mind. And that's a good thing.

November 22, 2018 (Thanksgiving Day)

I turned on the TV and saw a Rainbow! Gregory wins! I changed the channel to a Christmas movie while I wrapped presents and as soon as I did I heard, *"Rainbow!"* from a woman motivating the crowd. I missed what the Rainbow was about, but after she shouted *"Rainbow!"* the crowd echoed, *"Rainbow!"* I just can't believe this stuff. It's so amazing and it just warms my heart. My wink from Gregory, letting me know he's still with me. What a gift.

November 29, 2018

I dreamed I was in my bedroom and was cutting out a small heart out of felt. I had scraps and stuff strewn on the bed. I heard Gregory come home so I went to the top of the stairs and was surprised that the stairway was blocked with a big stand of some sort that had all the pictures from the picture wall on it like they had all fallen. Gregory was standing at the bottom of the stairs.

I woke up. Well, you don't have to be a dream interpreter to understand this dream. Clearly Greg and I are on different levels. He's still in the house, but on a different level. There are a mound of memories between us. The part about cutting out a felt heart touches me. Like I'm trying to somehow make something I can hold onto as the scraps lay scattered around me. Feels like another layer of acceptance.

November 30, 2018

I was heating my coffee just now, ready to sit down and write out some Christmas cards and suddenly I could feel Gregory fill up the kitchen. My heart and the room warmed as if I were sitting in front of a fireplace. I stopped what I was doing to just soak up his loving energy. In that moment he showed me not only accep-tance, but an inner knowing; a sense of peace and understanding that this is exactly the way it's supposed to be at this place in time. Exactly.

"Hi, Honey... So this is where we find ourselves, eh? I miss you. But I know... I know." Then I saw the premonition again. 36 years ago now. It played as clear as day. Thank God I had that vision. Acceptance at this level would not have been possible I'm afraid. This amazing, peaceful, inner knowing certainly would not have been possible. So I'm grateful. Grateful is a really nice place to be.

December 3, 2018

I came into the bedroom and turned on the TV. I felt the energy in the room shift ever so slightly. I knew I was going to get my Rainbow. I just knew it. The picture came on and there was a handsome man with long braids and he had a big smile on his face. He popped a couple of Skittles into his mouth and his whole face lit up and he laughed out loud! Then... wait for it... Boom! Beautiful Rainbow! Then a big Skittles Rainbow and the announcer says, *"Discover the Rainbow! Taste the Rainbow!"* Woohoo! I was so excited!

December 4, 2018

Three days in a row now when I got into the car and turned on the radio a song called *"Consequences,"* By Camila Cabello, was already playing. I couldn't relate to the whole song but the part that was playing all three times I turned on the radio touched my heart. It talks about being young and free, and how being together was a safe place to let down our defenses. But there are consequences to a love like that. The consequences for me was his death. Oh, yes, loving you was wild and free. It was a safe place to be... and then you died. Those were the consequences of loving you; having to lose you. But I wouldn't trade a moment of it.

December 11, 2018

I dreamed about Gregory! I was on a couch and he came over the back of it to kiss me! I woke up feeling like I'd been with him. It was so familiar and yet so foreign. Still, I feel a warmth in my soul like I've had a visit from my long-lost love.

December 17, 2018

Woohoo! I dreamed about Gregory! I woke up to the smell of bacon and Gregory's music playing just like so many weekend mornings. I headed downstairs, the smells and the sounds were so familiar! I could hear him in the kitchen making breakfast and I hurried a little faster. I got to the kitchen and there he was! He looked amazing. We met each other in the middle of the kitchen and I hugged and kissed him and didn't want to let go. Then we were in bed and I had my eyes closed. He was right next to me. Until I woke up and he was gone.

But it was amazing! Just having him in the house was so special. I still get Rainbows every single day even if I forget to write about them. I got a couple yesterday and one time I turned on the TV and it was on the Weather Channel about volcanos. I was just about to change the channel when I saw a Rainbow on the right side of the screen as molten lava was bubbling up and running over! It was amazing!

December 18, 2018

Last night when I settled in for the evening, I turned on the TV to watch a Christmas movie. I hadn't thought about it but suddenly realized that I hadn't got a Rainbow all day. What the heck? I searched through my memory of the day and no Rainbow. I talked to Gregory. *"I need a Rainbow, Honey."* The movie went to commercial and.... wait for it.... the Skittles commercial and a big, bright Rainbow! *"Contract the Rainbow! Taste the Rainbow!"* That's what I'm talking about! *"Thank you, Baby!"* Whew! Scared me for a minute.

December 28, 2018

The first thing I pulled up on FB this morning was a hippy looking Waldo sitting cross legged with his hands in a meditative stance, eyes closed. He has a long beard, glasses, and hippy beads around his neck. It's priceless. It reminds me of Gregory. I could feel him all around me. It says that when all is said and done Waldo finds himself.

I had to laugh. It's his funny way of telling me what I need to hear. Helping me sort out the unrest in my heart and soul right now. Wrestling with the enemy and reminders of past hurts. There is no good purpose for it. It holds me back. All of it; regrets, mistakes, injustices, you name it. They hold me back. They are weight in a backpack I don't need to carry. Gregory reminding me to *find myself*, is the simplest message I could have been given.

January 1, 2019

Every time I turned on the TV or changed the channel yesterday there was a Rainbow. One after the other and it made me smile. Scene after scene after scene—in a movie or on a commercial— there would be a picture of a Rainbow hanging on the wall in the background. Children's colored Rainbows just taped on the wall. I changed channels one time and a woman was thumbing through a stack of CD's and pulled one out that had a Rainbow sticker on it. I bet I got fifteen or more Rainbows yesterday and I've continued to get them this morning. Apparently he's not going anywhere.

January 14, 2019

Today is Gregory's birthday. I'm trying not to acknowledge the dark cloud I feel around me. I think I'm going with *Explore* for my word this year. Willing to go into unfamiliar territory to see what I can learn. I got several Rainbows yesterday.

January 18, 2019

Sitting here this morning I'm feeling nothing but peace and gratitude and love. In one of my tearful moments I thanked Gregory for the Rainbows and songs and told him from my heart that I would have died without them. That there is no way I could have made it through if he had not carried me with Rainbows and beautiful music. I truly believe that.

January 26, 2019

I can't believe this! First, let me say that I've been getting a lot of Rainbows the past few days and it's been so nice. I've needed the reassurance. I haven't felt well and I injured my foot. The Rainbows kept coming and helped me so much. This morning I got three Rainbows before 7 a.m. and I told Gregory I was going to count how many Rainbows I get today. In an attempt to keep track I put up three fingers and said, *"So far, three Rainbows, Honey, three."* Then I gave him *the weasel*. A few minutes later I got two beautiful Rainbows on a commercial and I started laughing. *"Way to go, Honey! Woohoo!* **Five** *Rainbows,"* and I held up one hand, *"Five."* Then I gave him *the weasel* again.

By Noon I'd gotten four more and I was laughing. I held up fingers every time and with weasels and high fives I could feel Gregory everywhere in the room. I told him how much it helps when I'm feeling down. Then I teased him that he was going to have to make the tenth Rainbow really special. I went about my afternoon and didn't think any more about it. I decided to watch one of my top favorite movies, called, *Déjà Vu* (*not* the Denzel Washington one). It's a supernatural love story. I pulled up the movie and hit play and couldn't believe it!

There was an old magician-looking, gray-haired robust man with a small orangish box in one hand, held up close to the camera, and with the other hand he reached in and began to pull something from the box. I couldn't believe it. His eyes were piercing into mine and drawing me in. Am I seeing what I think I'm seeing? Sure enough he pulled out a Rainbow! And then the letters appeared across the screen, one at a time, to spell out, *A Rainbow Picture.* I paused it and stared at the screen, slightly in shock. I've owned this movie for probably twenty years. It's a Rainbow picture? And then I smiled big. *"Good one, Honey! Really good one. TEN Rainbows! This is spectacular! Woohoo Weasel!"*

January 27, 2019

Holy cow, that Gregory! First let me say that I was completely satisfied with my ten (!) Rainbows yesterday—especially the tenth one—and didn't expect any more that day. I had the TV off, but just before I shut off the lights I wanted to check the weather. As soon as the picture appeared there it was, a beautiful blood red Double Rainbow! A segment was just beginning on Red Rainbows and for the next several minutes I was bombarded with amazing, surreal, Red Rainbows. And the word! Every time I hear it it's like it echoes or almost shouts at me. I added another fifteen Rainbows to the day! Making it a grand total of twenty-five Rainbow sightings in one day! Woohoo! I think he was showing off.

It's Sunday morning and I was deciding on what movie to watch. One caught my eye called, *A Time To Remember.* I hit play and as soon as the movie began there was an icon for the publishing company. It's a Rainbow running through a piece of film and the words, *Rainbow Restoration, New York, New York.* I stared at the screen. I paused it and stared some more, the word itself seeming to emanate some sort of magic. *"Weasel!"* and I blew him a kiss. I think he's helping me with the Rainbows because it gets me back to writing for the book. He's like, *"Here, take this, top that, better write it down!"* He's right, you know.

February 2, 2019

I dreamed about Rainbows! Lots of Rainbows. I woke up in the middle of the night and they had been floating all around me. Spectacular colors! It was amazing! I needed that! When I turned on my laptop a few minutes ago the screen came on and there was a Rainbow! It was the Rainbow from the beginning of the movie *Déjà vu* that I watched the other night. I know I shut it off so it was a surprise when it popped up on my laptop first thing.

February 4, 2019

This morning I was sitting in a feeling of complete acceptance. A flash of the vision in 1982 and more confirmation and acceptance washed over me. And Gratitude. *"Thanks, Dude, for 30 years. Amazing. Truly."* I looked up to the muted TV. Rainbow! *"How do you do that, Babe?!"* Deep in thought I looked up again and saw, *Boulevard of Broken Dreams* and turned up the volume. The part about the only one that walks beside me is my shadow and how I just wish someone would find me. I know it will happen but in the meantime I'm walking alone.

February 11, 2019

I miss my Gregory. I cried off and on over the weekend and overall I'm just feeling the loss of all that we had. But he sends me Rainbows every day and I got them all weekend. It helps. I can't tell you how much it helps. I will always feel him when I see one and know that he's still with me.

February 13, 2019

I dreamed I was looking out through a mask that was on crooked, like it was ready to fall off. My vision was partially blocked as I sort of peered out from behind the corner of a building where I was standing back out of sight.

Masks hide who you are. The dream shows I'm still hiding— keeping safe—but I believe the mask is starting to come off. I believe this to be my mask of grief. My mask of protection. I see that I'm still cautious, still hiding around the corner to make sure the *coast is clear*. That there are no dangers lurking. It's kind of sad to me, but I have to be grateful to know that at least I'm peeking out, ready to take off the mask and venture out once again. Just me. The me I am now, without my husband, without my grief.

February 14, 2019

I got two beautiful Rainbows right off the bat this morning. I turned on the TV and there was a cereal commercial. About six boxes of cereal lined next to each other and then, wait for it, a big Rainbow appeared above them. Beautiful. Gregory wins! *"Happy Valentine's Day!"*

February 16, 2019

Last night I dreamed I was holding hands with Greg as we were running off. It was like the scene after a wedding and the bride and groom take off running for their honeymoon (their future). I was thinking about how excited I was to be holding his hand again and how I couldn't wait to hug him and kiss him. It was one of those dreams where I was watching myself. It was a view from behind and I was watching us run away in slow motion, my beautiful dress flowing.

Ugh. I'm watching Greg and L.J. float away. It's always important to note when I'm watching myself in a dream as opposed to seeing things through my own eyes. To see myself means to *"Look at yourself."* It puts a stamp of importance on the message in the dream. As if to say, *"Look here, what do you see?"* And it feels like a sock to the heart even though I know it's okay. Greg and L.J. will always be. But they have left the building. They have a whole different life now. The time I've been alone has made me eager to be in love again.

(3:45 p.m.)

Just now, when I turned on the computer, there was the most beautiful scene of a little village centered smack dab in the midst of a small island, with rolling hills and lush greenery everywhere. Across the horizon was a Rainbow. I can feel Gregory here with me. He wants me to know that letting go of him doesn't mean he goes away and I never feel him again or get another Rainbow. Quite the opposite he assures me.

February 19, 2019

I had a strange dream. *It was about the coffee strainer for my espresso maker. It was huge and there was a part that was clogged or wasn't straining properly. I was able to take a bigger basket and cleaned it out so it would work better. I knew that now everything would strain through easily and nothing would get clogged.*

It just felt like it was symbolic of my liver. The connection in the dream was obvious. I was excited that a problem had been discovered and could be fixed. I keep feeling like I'm getting to some really deep-seated toxins in my liver and breaking them up. I'm hurting in that area most of the time but that's nothing new. I know the herbs and supplements are doing their job. But, alas, right now I'm trudging. I'm hurting and I'm sluggish. I didn't want to get out of bed again this morning.

February 23, 2019

I'm sad this morning. I didn't feel like turning on the music and I'm not sure why. In the kitchen while making my tea, I had the strong urge—push—to turn it on. As soon as I did, Seal's, *Don't Cry*, was starting. Beautiful song. I turned up the volume and sat down on the couch, feeling Gregory all around me and not sure if I was going to cry. I knew I needed to listen to the words. The energy in the room was overpowering. It talks about those memories, so long ago now, and my mind searched to retrieve them. Through my tears I heard that I'm not alone and that I'll always be loved. I can't hear it enough. It made me think about time being a great healer. I would add that so is music.

Chapter 37

It Isn't Raining Anymore

⌐

March 1, 2019

OMG.... This has been the most incredible morning I've had in a long time. I don't know that any of Gregory's Rainbows have ever hit me this hard. I'm still vibrating from it. I turned on the music on the way to get my laptop and it played in the background. On my way back there was the most beautiful song playing that I'd never heard before. It sort of slowed my step and there was a feeling in the room I can't describe, but it was palpable. I set down my laptop, feeling mesmerized by the music and the feel in the room. Then the words seemed to penetrate my soul.

It started out with a saying familiar to all of us. When it rains it pours. I found myself thinking, *"Isn't that the truth?"* but then I heard it say it isn't raining anymore and I didn't notice. Okay.... And when it suggested that I was stuck in that old familiar storm my heart slowed for a moment. Wow, there's so much truth to that. *The storm* has probably become too familiar to me. Then it says that I can hold onto my umbrella if I want to but there's something I may not have noticed. There's been a Rainbow above me the whole time.

I couldn't believe it. My heart started beating faster as I looked to see the name of this beautiful song that has Rainbow in the lyrics. My heart skipped a beat and tears filled my eyes when I saw that the name of the song is, *Rainbow*, by Kacey Musgrave. I was on my knees and I fell forward and laid my head on the carpet and sobbed. An indescribable numbing chill raced through me and held me as I wept. Gregory was everywhere. A powerful mixture of intense feelings, emotions, and vibrations filled the room and penetrated my soul. I couldn't stop crying. I couldn't speak, I couldn't move, I just sat there, big tears rolling down my cheeks one after the other, in a state of awe and disbelief.

And then it says that if I could only see what he sees that the colors would be blinding. Millions of colors the likes of which we've never seen here on earth. At the end it gently suggests that perhaps I can let go of my umbrella now because after all, not only is it no longer raining—that the storm has passed—but under that protection I can't see the Rainbow. The song ends with reassuring words that tell me everything is going to be alright.

When it was over I turned off the TV. I knew there was nothing that could top that and I needed a minute to sit in this feeling and process the Rainbow that just rocked my world. The tears continued to pour out of me and I just immersed myself in the feeling. Time seemed to stand still and the energy I was feeling in and around me was nothing short of miraculous and I just wanted to soak in it.

I talked to Gregory and couldn't really say enough to thank him and to be amazed by him. Gracie jumped up on me like, *"What are you doing, Mom?"* I looked at her and said, *"You gotta give me a minute, Dad hit me with a Rainbow and I'm still trying to recover."* Seriously. I kissed his picture. I love that throughout the song it says that I can hold onto to my umbrella (even if it's not raining anymore), but at the end it says to let go of the umbrella. The words played over and over in my head. Let go of the umbrella, honey, it's not raining anymore.

March 2, 2019

I dreamed about Rainbows! OMG! Twice! Incredible. Beautiful, vibrant, indescribable Rainbows everywhere! Floating all around, all different sizes and then a big, bold one in the middle. It woke me right up! Just like it does every time I dream about Rainbows. Then I fell back asleep and had the same dream again! And woke up again! Smiling! I love it! This blows my mind. The night after my amazing Rainbow morning where the song says that if I could only see what he sees the colors would blind me, he showed me!

March 4, 2019

I got Rainbows all weekend! I mean, seriously, every time I turned on the TV there was a Rainbow or I heard the word. It was incredible. One time I turned on the TV and there was a gorgeous Rainbow across the screen and it was an advertisement for a new Hallmark Movie called, *Love Under The Rainbow*. Seriously. Tee-hee.

March 5, 2019

Woohoo! I turned on the music channel just now and got *Rainbow*. I can't believe what a beautiful song it is and so perfect for where I am in my life right now. Gregory has continued to amaze me on a daily basis since he died. It's incredible. Someone should write a book about this stuff.

March 7, 2019

I came upstairs after working on the book and turned on the TV to find the cereal commercial. Love it! Five boxes of cereal lined next to each other and then a big, beautiful Rainbow appears above them. So cool! I changed the channel to a movie and there was a beautiful Rainbow! Then, across the bottom of the screen was advertising for the Saturday night movie. Yep, *Love Under The Rainbow*.

March 8, 2019

Woohoo! I turned on the TV and heard, *"There's always a little rain... before a Rainbow!"* Then the most beautiful Rainbow I've ever seen on a commercial for the Rainbow movie premiering tomorrow night. Beautiful scenery and, of course, a love story. I can't wait to watch it!

March 11, 2019

I couldn't wait to watch *Love Under The Rainbow*. I was in my element the entire movie! Talk about Rainbows from start to finish and everywhere in between. It was so much fun for me. My eye is pretty trained to see Rainbows so it was like Christmas to me with all the Rainbows in this movie. Beautiful, real Rainbows, but also everywhere else to be seen. The little girl in the movie had lost her mother and Rainbows were her mom's thing and became her thing when her mom died. She had Rainbow sheets on her bed, pictures on the wall, a throw pillow, you name it. Rainbows everywhere!

She did her science project on Rainbows and made a beautiful display with a bright and colorful Rainbow presentation across a big white board. She had round crystals hanging from a holder and had light to reflect Rainbows everywhere. It was just incredible. I heard the word throughout the movie and it echoes in my ears and brings a smile to my face every time I hear it. I was smiling through this whole movie! It's on Saturday afternoon and I'm watching it again!

March 15, 2019

I had an amazing encounter and conversation with Gregory last night. I talk to my husband all the time but those really heartfelt, incredible connections where I can feel his energy all around me don't happen as often as they used to. The energy in the room changed and I swear I could see and feel a soft glow all around me. Gregory's presence was so strong I almost expected him to materialize! It was our spiritual connection I was remembering and feeling. Tears poured down my cheeks as I talked to him and told him how much it all means to me. I gave him *the weasel* and I could feel his energy; his fingers touching mine and connecting the way we always did.

March 18, 2019

Hmmm, I didn't get a Rainbow yesterday. Not sure how I feel about that. Maybe it's because I watched *Love Under The Rainbow* the day before and got like a zillion!

March 19, 2019

Yay! As I sat down here I was a little sad thinking about not getting Rainbows again yesterday and not knowing how I feel about that. But then I turned on the TV and heard that it's not always unicorns and Rainbows. I'm beginning to see that. Lol! *"Thank you, honey, I don't think I'm quite ready to stop getting Rainbows every day."* Ha! I just got another Rainbow when I looked up at the muted TV! I know the time will come when perhaps I don't get Rainbows every single day, but for now I'm embracing them.

March 20, 2019

I ended up getting four more random Rainbows yesterday and by the second one I was smiling. Every time I turned on the TV or changed the channel there was a Rainbow. This morning when I turned on the TV, *Rainbow* was just starting! I think he was testing me. I think he wants to wean me off the Rainbows because I'm kind of needy about them. But they're back and I'm grateful. I wasn't all devastated or anything those two days I didn't get any, but it was strange and I didn't really like it much.

March 21, 2019

I just looked up to *Rainbow*. It's a beautiful song and a good reminder. Forgot to notice it isn't raining anymore. Stuck out in the storm again. It's okay to let go of my umbrella. I had the TV muted last evening and I looked up and it was on the Weather Channel. I had it on the movie channel. The remote was on the end table. I sort of stared at the TV and even said out loud, *"I didn't turn it to the Weather Channel. I guess it's supposed to be on this channel."* Just then, Rainbow!

March 26, 2019

I turned on the music channel first thing and Kimberly Locke's, *Better In Time* was just starting. I cried all the way through it. It says that I didn't think I could live without him but that I deserve to smile again. It also says that there is pain in the healing. I talked to Gregory; felt him so close. Tears rolled down my cheeks as I listened to the words that have so much meaning for me at this stage of the game.

Right after that was Phil Collins, *You'll Be In My Heart*, and that helped. He says to stop my crying, that it's going to be okay. All I have to do is hold his hand and he will protect me. He says that he's going to be here for me so don't cry. He says that our bond can never be broken, that I'm always going to be in his heart. It touched me to my soul. There are no words to describe the peace I feel in my heart when he sends me Rainbows or speaks to me like this in songs. Unbelievable.

March 28, 2019

I dreamed about Gregory! *I was riding on his shoulders! He was running all around with me and we were sort of sneaking up behind friends and people we know to surprise them! He was so playful, a big smile on his face. He looked so handsome and was running around with me on his shoulders like I weighed nothing! He was sort of parading me around like, "Look at her! Look at her!" It was fun, it was playful, it was celebratory. It was so sweet.* Today I celebrate 25 years of sobriety and that's just unreal to me. *"Happy Anniversary to me!"* He was just so excited and playful and was toting me around like I was something special.

March 29, 2019

I turned on the TV and as soon as I switched to the music channel I heard about those Rainbows that will leave me breath-less. The energy in the room changed and I could feel Gregory right here with me. Tears rolled down my cheeks. When it was over I turned the channel to country videos and *Rainbow* was just starting. Tears continued to roll down my cheeks and I was over-whelmed—as always—by the feel of my Gregory in the room and the Rainbows in front of me. I got a couple of beautiful Rainbows yesterday too.

March 30, 2019

I got my Rainbow first thing this morning and I was grateful. Later when I was sitting in the waiting room for a friend at the Cancer Center I looked on the table to a magazine sitting there. I heard, *"There's a Rainbow in there."* I picked it up and scanned the pages of beautiful scenery and knew I was going to see my Rainbow. Nothing. I thumbed through the pages again. Nothing. Hmmm. I set down the magazine and sort of said under my breath, *"Liar."*

Time went by and I knew I was probably going to be there for a while so I picked up the magazine and started reading it from the beginning. I read a couple of good articles and then turned the page. There were several images but my eyes fell immediately to a 90 year old woman in a crazy hat and glasses and wildly colorful jacket. There on her white shirt was a Rainbow! Woohoo! *"There you are!"* I said under my breath with a big smile on my face.

April 1, 2019

I turned on the music and recognized one of my old favorites from Little River Band called, *Cool Change*. The words, it's time for a change, seemed to echo in the room. I could feel Gregory's pres-ence so I knew the words were from him. After that was Pink's, *Just Give Me A Reason*, which says that I can learn how to love again. *"Got it, Honey."* When that was over another old favorite by Pablo Cruise, *Love Will Find A Way*. Encouraging and reassuring words one right after the other!

I had a good day yesterday. I talked to Gregory first thing and had him on my mind throughout the day. *"I'm happy, Honey,"* I said to him several times, *"I love my life again, I really do."* I turned on the TV and got my favorite Skittles commercial and started smiling before I ever got the Rainbow! I looked up and *Rainbow* is just starting. I'm listening to it now. There are beautiful Rainbows transposed over the scenes in this video and it makes my heart swell with happiness. This is an amazing journey I'm on. I feel so loved and protected. I feel at peace. The song ends with the reassuring words that everything is going to be okay. I believe it. Love will find a way.

April 12, 2019

I turned on the music first thing and got *Miracles*, by Jefferson Starship. I smiled because I knew I was going to get my Rainbow. The one that says I can hear Rainbows when he talks to me.

April 20, 2019 (My Birthday)

I had another rough night and woke up with a headache. Seems I can't catch a break. I was nearly in tears by the time I dragged myself out of bed. I sat on the edge of the bed and prayed. I told myself that I didn't expect any Rainbows or signs from Gregory today. I think I didn't want to be disappointed and certainly knew that it's possible he might be a no show on my special day. If he did it on Thanksgiving and Valentine's Day he certainly could do it on my birthday.

I turned on the music and got Elton John's, *Blessed*, and the words seemed to soothe my aching mind and body. He says that I'm going to have the best that life has to offer, that I'll always be blessed. He promises me that. I believed the words and found myself starting to feel better. The next song began and my eyes filled with tears. It was *Beautiful As You*, and I was crying by the time I sat down, knowing I was going to get my Rainbows. It was the most perfect song he could have chosen for me this morning. The tears flowed like a river, soaking my face. I felt Gregory right here with me which is what was making me cry.

April 21, 2019 (Easter Sunday)

Well, I can't remember a birthday that was as special as this one. I celebrated my special day and pampered myself. I got a pedicure and an hour massage. I bought a white candle so I could do a little ceremony with Gregory and take back my birthday. I lit the candle and said a prayer and then stared at it. The energy in the room was filled with a peace that was indescribable. The candle's flame stretched higher and higher and the white glow intensified so powerfully it was almost blinding me! I was overcome with emotion. Tears rolled down my cheeks. *This is incredible.* My day ended with beautiful flowers and an incredible, gourmet dinner with my friend, Libby. I smiled the entire day. *"I did it, Honey, I took back my birthday."*

When I got home I settled in to watch *Change In The Air*. It was a supernatural little movie that I'm still processing. What shocked me more than anything was a part about an hour into it. It was a scene in a yard and in the background was a woman and a man sitting on lawn chairs. It was my dad..... I paused the movie. I rewound it then watched it again until he was out of frame. Then I watched it again. Paused it and stared. Tears rolled down my cheeks. This was my dad sitting there. I was looking at him, watching his mannerisms. The energy in the room shifted and the tears flowed. *"Thanks, Pop, what's a fantastic birthday without seeing you?"* It was unreal. Truly. It made my night! I'm never going to forget April 20, 2019. The year I celebrated again.

We all went to Easter brunch earlier and there were more birthday celebrations for me. I got back home and watched a favorite program. As always, the episode was filled with challenges, with grief, and with joy. At the end when the narrator summed up the life lessons that were highlighted, it made me cry and touched my heart. It seemed to put me in a place of peaceful acceptance about everything. Always bringing me to a place that has more depth and meaning than would be possible without those unavoidable and unpredictable life events.

Being happy is a decision to be made. We can decide to embrace the little things, the precious moments in an ordinary day. Life evolves in its mysterious way and for the most part cannot be predicted. We don't always get what we planned. We trip and fall and get back up again. Our relationships are strained and strengthened and our perspective changes with the darkness and the light. But there is always light. It shines on the path where I've been, it shines on the path I'm on now, and it will shine on my path tomorrow.

April 27, 2019

Woohoo! Rainbows! I've been getting a lot of them these past two weeks, as I often do when I don't feel well. I needed them too! I've had a rough time of it. Wednesday when I was standing in line at the grocery store, back killing me and feeling overwhelmed with all I needed to get done that day, I looked to my right where they have all the candy bars, lighters, and miscellaneous stuff and had to blink my eyes to make sure what I was seeing.

There were these long skinny black boxes hanging on a peg. Three of them, one behind the other. I wasn't sure what they were—they ended up being small umbrellas—but practically jumping out at me in big white letters across the side of each black box was RAINBOW, RAINBOW, RAINBOW! I couldn't believe it! Three Rainbows staring at me. Not colorful Rainbows, just the big, bold word. I needed that! Sometimes life isn't full of color and it certainly wasn't for me that day. Sometimes life seems to be in black and white. But I got my three Rainbows anyway and it made me smile. *"Thanks, Babe, you always know exactly what I need."*

Chapter 38

What If I Never Get Over You?

~~~~~~~

May 5, 2019

(Sunday night 6:02 p.m.)—Holy crap! Holy crap! Holy crap! OMG! OMG! OMG! I'm still crying, I'm shaking, I feel a hot numb all over my body and I can't believe what just happened. As if this book isn't going to be powerful enough! I couldn't even imagine something so profound happening at this stage of the game. I was in the bathroom getting ready for bed and I took a quick glance out the window to the backyard. As I dropped the curtain and it fell closed, I saw Gregory standing in the backyard.....

I hurried and opened the curtain again, a mere second later, but he was gone. I dropped the curtain, opened it, then looked again. A cool numb traveled from my feet to my head and I felt like I would fall over. Tears poured down my cheeks. I closed my eyes. I saw him in that flash. He wasn't solid but more like a ghostly apparition. Tears are rolling down my cheeks and a cool vibration hums within me. OMG.... *"I just saw you standing in our backyard, Babe."* It's taken me some time to recover.

May 6, 2019

Wow, I don't even know what to say. I find myself looking out the back window every time I'm in the bathroom and I replay it in my mind. So powerful. I came downstairs first thing and turned on the music. There was a song called, *Where Are You Now?* It made me smile. *"Well, last night you were in our backyard!"* Unreal.

May 12, 2019

LOL! I love when this happens. I switched the station to the Hallmark channel and it was a close up of a donut on a plate. The woman decorating it poured a bunch of Rainbow sprinkles all over it. I was already smiling because as soon as I saw the Rainbow sprinkles I knew I was going to hear my Rainbow. As she's doing this she says, *"I love sprinkles!"* and I said, *"They're called **Rainbow** sprinkles."* Just then she said, *"Especially the Rainbow kind!"* Makes me so happy.

May 20, 2019

I just got *Rainbow* on the music channel. I somehow knew I was going to hear it this morning so I turned on the TV and had it on low. Then I just looked up and it was starting. I needed it this morning. I haven't been getting very many Rainbows lately.

May 21, 2019

This is so sweet it made me cry. When I came upstairs for the night I turned on the TV and couldn't believe my eyes. It was a commercial and the first thing I noticed was a big inflatable Rainbow in a big backyard filled with children and toys of all kinds. Just then excited children came running around the corner and they all had on bathing suits with big Rainbows on them! One by one, excited, giggly girls ran past the camera with dancing Rainbows on their shirts! I just burst out smiling! Go Rainbows!

May 26, 2019

I no longer get my Rainbows every day. There is sadness in the fact that I seem to be okay with that now. I thought I would always need them. It doesn't feel like loss as much as healing. The story coming to a close as all great stories do. In the kitchen I felt a sense of having come full circle. Of healing all the way to the finish. What an incredible ride. And visions of the new guy play often now and I am excited beyond belief to finally meet him.

I went upstairs and turned on the TV and there was a different commercial with big Rainbow blowup balloons in a festive back-yard party scene. It ends with a family taking a selfie in front of one of the big Rainbows. I felt my Gregory right there with me as a shiver ran up my spine. Seems like every time I think I'm done getting Rainbows he surprises me. I can feel that he's proud of me when I'm in acceptance and excited about my life again. He sends me Rainbows as a thumbs up.

May 27, 2019

Holy cow! I've been bombarded with Rainbows! It just makes me tear up from the love I'm feeling from Gregory so far today. He wins! It's Memorial Day so I'm already thinking about him even more and then he sends me Rainbows so I know he's thinking about me too. It still amazes me. A few minutes ago I turned on the TV and had it muted and was thinking about Gregory and all of a sudden there appeared an upside down Rainbow across the bottom of the screen, sort of transposed over everything. I smiled and a subtle chill ran through me and I felt my heart swell with love. I told Gregory I was so happy that he was sending me Rainbows on Memorial Day, that it means so much.... and just then a Kaboom commercial came on!

The scene is so colorful I was already thinking I was going to get more Rainbows. Then it showed a woman looking at her dirty bathroom and all of a sudden a big furry monster made of blue cleaning rags appeared in the shower, dancing all about as every-thing around him sparkled. Then he danced out of the shower and every time he swung his arms over his head he created colorful Rainbows in the air! *"Now you're showing off, Mister!"* Makes me so happy I can barely stand it!

May 31, 2019

I had a moment in bed late last night when I started thinking about Gregory and I just felt so sad. I cried big tears and talked to him about how much I miss him and our life together. I fell asleep talking to him. Now I've had two Rainbows so far this morning and I know it's his way of letting me know he heard me last night. He's never been able to change the fact that I lost my best friend but he sends me Rainbows to let me know he didn't go so very far away.

June 3, 2019

I got Rainbows all weekend long and connected with Gregory the whole time. I had several crying sessions talking with him and remembering…. *Everything.* The tears have changed. They are more gratitude than grief, mixed with acceptance. They are healing. I miss him so much and I told him so this weekend and then I would get a Rainbow. It was just like old times and I was so happy every time I got one.

June 9, 2019

I got the song *Rainbow* first thing this morning and that's the song that was playing in my mind practically all night! I blew Gregory a kiss, I touched my heart, I told him I miss him. The next song was Nickelback's *Far Away.* He says that he's loved me from the very beginning and that he misses me. He says he's been far away for way too long. Ditto baby.

June 10, 2019

When I turned on the music this morning a Lady Antebellum song I've never heard before was just starting called, *What if I*

Never Get Over You... It says that of course it hurts, my heart is broken. It says that the hardest part is to move on. It says that in time I will be better, but what if time doesn't heal this broken heart? What if I never get over you?

Perhaps that's how it's going to be for a while until I finish the book. Maybe I will continue to vacillate between feeling strong in my new life and ready to move forward and meet someone new, and then quickly running back to Gregory and my memories. In the first few years I remember feeling like I would never get over him. But now? Those moments of holding on seem to be loosening their grip and the thought of letting go no longer terrifies me.

June 13, 2019

I can't believe this. I came down this morning and turned on the music just as Fleetwood Mac's, *As Long As You Follow*, was playing. The Rainbow sort of shouted at me. I was surprised because I forgot about the Rainbow! I love it! And there's that reminder again. There's no need to worry about going it alone now. I'm never alone. He's going to follow me!

June 14, 2019

I came downstairs this morning and turned on the music just as Faith Hill's, *There You'll Be*, was starting. I felt like I was speaking to Greg this time instead of him speaking to me, and it's a sign of my healing. It also reminds me, like always, that he is with me no matter what. It talks about the dreams we've left behind but how blessed we were to have each other. That we were always there for one another and that there's always going to be a place in my heart for him. That for the rest of my life I'll have a piece of him and that no matter where I am there he'll be.

June 15, 2019

I've already had three Rainbows this morning and I can feel Greg right here with me. It's an amazing feeling and I'm so grateful that he doesn't mind that it's been seven years, one month and twenty-seven days since he was walking this earth and I'm still keeping him near. I guess if he really wanted me to move on he'd send the new guy! I could be distracted by that!

June 19, 2019

I write this through tears. I've been so sick and had to push myself to get up and out the door for my appointment with the Kinesiologist. When I got in the car I turned on the radio to an upbeat song called, *Keep Your Head Up*, by Andy Grammer. It says that you only get Rainbows after it rains and no matter what the sun will always shine again. I've been getting a lot of Rainbows since I've been sick and I never take them for granted. I am so grateful that in my darkest hour he sends me Rainbows to light up my life.

June 20, 2019

This blows my mind. I'm propped up in bed in a darkened room mindlessly watching TV and just trying to be distracted from how sick I feel yet another day. I'm worn out and I'm having to fight the urge to beat up on myself for not being able to stay well. Then I found myself thinking about Greg and the Rainbows. Thinking about how they always *spark joy* whenever I get one, whether it's just the word, or actually seeing a beautiful Rainbow.

I could feel him right here with me. My heart was overflowing with gratitude in that moment and I thought about how the Rainbows spark that same kind of joy you get when you see or talk to a treasured loved one. Like talking to the kids or the grandkids on the phone or seeing them. A spark of joy with that connection every time you make it. *"That's what the Rainbows are for me, Honey, like talking to you on the phone and my heart skips a beat every time."*

I had the urge to turn on the TV but I didn't really know why. No connection in music, nothing. I pulled up the program menu and decided to search. I have my normal channels I search through, but for some reason I punched in a number that isn't even a channel I get. It was a cooking show called, Food: Fact or Fiction. And the name of the featured segment? It's called, *Rainbow Connections*. My heart leapt for joy! *"Damn straight, tell ya to your face, Honey!!"*

June 24, 2019

I have been so sick but Gregory has been close the whole time and sending me Rainbows every time I turn around. I smiled, if not laughed, at some of them. Change the channel, Rainbow. Start watching a program, hear Rainbow in the song in the background. I mean, seriously. And I feel him. That's the best part. I've needed that. It's been sweet memories and love so big it's hard to describe. My treasured memories of my time with him feel less like something I've lost and more like something I'm going to have again.

I wasn't planning on writing this morning. It's my day of rest and I earned it after a productive day yesterday. I turned on the TV and it was on Discovery from last night and immediately I heard something like, *there's treasure to be found, over the Rainbow, around the next bend...* All I heard was the Rainbow. I put my hand to my heart. I gave Gregory *the weasel* and I felt him in the room.

I knew I wanted to write that down because I can't tell you how many times it happens and I *don't* write it down. Then I forget about it. I made myself go downstairs and get my laptop even though my whole body feels tired and all I want to do is sit here and sip my tea. But, again, so many of these Rainbow moments get lost and I didn't want this one to. It felt like a, *"Good morning, Baby"* from my love.

I got the laptop plugged in and sitting next to me as I propped back up on my pillows and had another sip of my tea. My mind sort of drifted off, lost in Gregory's essence all around me and the magic of the whole Rainbow thing. *"I mean, really, Dude, you've been sending me Rainbows for over seven years!"* I looked at the TV. It's a commercial for bottled water. On the front is a scene of a big bridge, but the arc of the bridge is a Rainbow! I see this Rainbow in front of me just when I'm communicating with Gregory about how amazing he is to send me Rainbows! Boom, there he goes showing off. I got Rainbows yesterday too and I felt him with me the whole day.

(Moments later)

I was sitting here waiting for this file to save so I could close it down. I searched for the remote to shut off the TV when I heard something about the idea for the first suspension bridge. I looked up and caught my breath. There was a beautiful Double Rainbow across a big gorge that they were contemplating putting this suspension bridge over. I stared at these beautiful Rainbows in front of me and my whole being smiled. *"You're still a showoff..."*

July 7, 2019

As soon as I turned on the music to do Yoga I heard something about all the colors of the Rainbow. It was Taylor Swift's, *Me*, a song I've never heard before. I smiled and settled into my workout. The next song was *Here Without You* and I was so happy to hear it. Last night when I settled in for the night and turned on the Weather Channel I saw a beautiful Double Red Rainbow. It was incredible. For the next 15 minutes it was Rainbow after Rainbow. Beautiful! I gave Greg *the weasel*, smiling ear to ear. *"Go ahead, bombard me with Rainbows at bedtime! I love it!"*

July 20, 2019

Gregory just sent me a Rainbow! The other evening when I was in the kitchen I realized that I hadn't thought of him all day. I couldn't believe it was true, but I searched through the day in my mind and realized I hadn't. I wasn't sure how to feel about that. I also realized I didn't remember when I got my last Rainbow. It felt strangely okay. I couldn't believe it. I didn't think of my husband all day and he didn't send me Rainbows and it doesn't feel like a crisis. It doesn't feel like anything in particular. It just feels normal. I know it's a sign of healing.

(Later)

I ran an errand and as soon as I got in the car the radio was on a Christian station and an upbeat song I'd never heard before was playing. It talked about painting a Rainbow in the sky to remind me that nothing is ever broken, that even when I feel like he's far away, he's going to keep a light on for me. I questioned whether I just heard what I thought I heard. The song is by Phil Joel and is called, *God Is Watching Over You*. It hit me the same way the other Rainbows have hit me today. I can feel Gregory close and that makes me feel safe.

August 2, 2019

I can't remember the last Rainbow I got, but I know that I haven't gotten any for days. I think he wants to show me that I don't need them anymore. I still want them and they bring me so much joy, but he's right, I no longer *need* them. I'm probably okay with that because my life will always be filled with Rainbows. I have a whole book of Rainbows!

A quiet stillness that slightly resembles the familiar numbing sensation of grief, settles over me and I can only believe it is an honoring of where I've been and an acceptance of who and where I am now. It feels like Grace. Like the Rainbows, it doesn't change the fact that Greg died. But, like a healing salve, it pours over my life, smoothing out the sharp, jagged edges.

August 3, 2019

No Rainbows again yesterday. I'm not sure how I feel about that. All I know is I'm not devastated. I know I'll get my Rainbows. I realize that Greg is helping me bring this book to a close. I've been putting it together as it's still being written. Perhaps this is his way of winding things down. I'm ready to hold this magical story in my hands and to read it from start to finish once it's in book form. Once it has a Rainbow and a tornado on the cover. Powerful.

August 5, 2019

As soon as I got in the car and turned on the radio I heard, *"Join us tomorrow and the first Sunday of every month at the Rainbow of Hope Farm..."* Then he must have said Rainbow three or four times as the word seemed to shout at me. A tear filled my eye and I thanked Gregory. I'd written about not getting Rainbows just hours before and then he shows me that when it really counts—when I'm feeling most fragile and alone—he'll send his brightest bit of hope.

When I got home and turned on the TV I couldn't believe it. The most beautiful Rainbow. Not only that, the movie playing was *Love Under The Rainbow*. I sat there staring at Rainbows in the background and reflecting on the walls. Later, when I was upstairs for the night, I got a couple more random Rainbows.

The picture wall is talking to me. I find myself paying more attention to it at random times walking up or down the stairs. But for years now I have mostly walked right by it. Until about a week ago. I found myself staring into Gregory's eyes in one favorite photo. He stares back at me with a light that makes him seem alive again. The whole wall feels outdated. Every picture of me is with Greg and it's a life I find myself struggling to relate to. They seem to swarm around me, coming off the wall like floating memories. I am younger in them, a different woman than who I am today. It was another lifetime.

August 19, 2019

When I turned on my laptop a few minutes ago I couldn't believe what I saw. First, let me say that I got Rainbows all weekend and I could feel my Gregory very close. He's knows I've been struggling, not only with the book, but with my health and not feeling as well as hoped. So I turned on my laptop and there was an amazing sight. Beautiful—*colorful*—trees. I've never seen anything like them.

They're called *Rainbow Eucalyptus Trees*. I read the caption: *"You're not imagining it—these trees are actually sporting* striped bark in Rainbow shades." Seriously? Just below that it says, *"Sometimes nature is just showing off."* That made me smile because of how many times I've accused Gregory of showing off with his Rainbows. Who knew there was a tree named Rainbow?

Yoga was amazing. I could feel an incredible energy all around me. My thoughts throughout my workout were a combination of Gregory and all the love I feel for and from him and our journey, and the new guy and all the excitement and anticipation that the thought of meeting him brings. A new Goo Goo Dolls song began called *Miracle Pill*, and boy, did it speak to me. It speaks of life's up and downs, about doubt and fear and feeling like being left in the darkness. It talks about starting over.

Yep, starting all over. And finally that feels good. At the end of my workout, *Rainbow*, began and I sang every word. I've let go of my umbrella. I know the rain and wind are no longer blowing. I'm no longer stuck out in the storm. The sun came out and brought a Rainbow with it.

August 21, 2019

This morning in the kitchen I felt like just normal life. I realized how amazing it's going to be when the book is finished. I felt a freedom and a joy I haven't felt for some time. I heard a song from the living room. *You're A Hard Habit To Break* (Chicago). Big smile. *"You sure are."* After that I heard, *Hello From The Other Side* (Adele), and a chill ran through me. *"Hi, Baby."*

I made the decision to take some time off from the book to rest and get feeling better, and ever since I've been getting Rainbows like the old days. I want to get the book done but I'm tired. I feel Gregory's presence strong around me. He knows I'm struggling. This *Liver Rescue* has been more brutal than I could have imagined. The next song began as I headed to the living room with my tea. I smiled. *Rainbow*. Of course it was. I sat down and started crying.

Chapter 39

Rainbowland

August 24, 2019

Gregory has been sending me Rainbows all week. I must have gotten three or four yesterday and at least two or more the days before. It's like the old days. I feel him ever near to me and it helps when I'm feeling so poorly. It's reassurance. Three times yesterday when I turned on the TV or came back in the room there was the Lucky Charms commercial. I'm grateful to feel him so close. I could mourn the loss of how it's been the past seven years. It's been an amazing, incredible, unbelievable journey. His spirit kept me alive. He breathed for me. I turned on the music and smiled. Phil Collins, *True Colors*. I gave Gregory *the weasel* on the Rainbow parts.

September 2, 2019

It's Labor Day weekend and that explains the heaviness I've felt around me. But Gregory sent me Rainbows all weekend. I would turn on the TV and there would be a Rainbow. Twice I got beautiful, double Rainbows. I felt him with me as strong as I ever have and I had more than one heartfelt conversation with him. I'm also ready to meet the new guy. Well, almost ready.

September 9, 2019

I have to write about Yoga yesterday morning. I was finishing up and had been thinking about Greg throughout my workout and feeling pretty amazed by my life with him, before and after he died. I was lying on my back for the cooldown when beautiful music began. I reached my hand over my head toward the TV and gave *the weasel*. A chill ran through me. I felt Gregory everywhere. I didn't recognize the song at first but knew to listen closely. He told me I'm the Rainbow in his skies.

It was Joshua Kadison's, *Beautiful In My Eyes*. It made me smile and brought a tear to my eye. Gregory is closer to me in those moments than he ever could be. There's no way to adequately describe it, you have to experience it for yourself. I've experienced it hundreds, if not thousands of times, and I will never get tired of it. It's magical beyond explanation. I got Rainbows all weekend.

September 10, 2019

Ugh. Not feeling very well this morning. It's all a part of the liver cleansing/healing. I've been on the *Liver Rescue* regime for just over ten months. I'm about over it... Grrr. Yesterday, whenever I thought about Greg, I would get a flash of a Rainbow across the TV screen. It was blowing my mind! I sure wish I felt better. I must be getting down to some very old toxins. But I can't tell you how much the Rainbows help.

September 19, 2019

I had a moment with Gregory at the end of Yoga. My sessions are spent with about equal time thinking about him and the new guy. Yesterday was no different. I ended, however, thinking about Gregory. It was the cool down and I was lying on my back. I was surprised when the next song started and I heard about breathtaking Rainbows. I could feel Gregory right there with me and I cried through the whole song. The tears were a mixture of pure amazement that he's still right here and a bit of sadness that I can't touch him.

September 22, 2019

Holy cow! Gregory seems to be outdoing himself! Just before bedtime I turned to the Weather Channel to watch *Weather Gone Viral* OnDemand, and right away started getting Rainbows. I could feel Gregory and a tear filled my eye every time I saw one. Then I started getting tired so I paused it, shut off the TV and went to sleep. Today is my day of rest and when I came back upstairs with my tea I turned on the TV and thought about what I might want to watch. Just then I heard, *"Check your rentals,"* which displays the shows I've watched OnDemand.

I forgot all about what I was watching at bedtime when I clicked on the only show listed. I excitedly hit play. What happened next was amazing even for me. I cried all the way through the last 20 minutes of the show that was all about Rainbows! Not just any Rainbows either. Spectacular, never before seen Rainbows! Front and center was the most amazing shot imaginable. The most perfectly full arced, brightly colored, *gorgeous* Rainbow across the skyline, as a tornado twisted its way toward it! Then, as the cameraman shoots this amazing scene, the tornado moves right to the center of the Rainbow and OMG! it was the most spectacular sight!

I was crying these amazed tears and I had goosebumps everywhere and I could feel Gregory so close I could almost touch him! The whole incredible Rainbow magic that is my life washed over me and I was filled with love and gratitude for Gregory and how he continues to blow my mind with Rainbows. It was the most precious few moments with my love. Indescribable. Unimaginable. Inexplainable. The word Rainbow seems to shout at me and I was smiling through my tears for the whole twenty-minute segment. At one point the meteorologist was just smiling ear to ear when she said, *"I just love Rainbows! Who doesn't love Rainbows?"* You're preaching to the choir!

September 24, 2019

Woohoo! This was amazing! I didn't feel well but needed to go to the store and to Kohl's. Everything was a push. As I was heading past the grocery store to Kohl's, I turned in, telling myself to just get my shopping done. Do the worst thing first. When I was driving out of the parking lot I said to Gregory, *"Look at me! Look at me, Honey!"* Knowing he would be proud of me for taking care of business in spite of how I felt, I said, *"Now bring me a Rainbow!"* I knew I was being kind of bold, but it was in a happy, playful way.

Standing in line for my order at Kohl's, I heard one of my favorite sounds in the whole world. A small child giggling. I turned around and all I saw was this little blonde haired girl bounding down the aisle toward me with a big Rainbow on her shirt! She was so excited to be heading to the toy section right where I stood. All the way to me she was smiling as big as Texas and giggling as she and her big Rainbow skipped toward me. It was magical! *"That's what I'm talking about, Honey! Thank you, Babe."* Then all the way home I couldn't believe it. *"You're amazing, Dude."*

September 26, 2019

Woohoo! Yesterday morning when I was doing Yoga I had Gregory on my mind the whole time. I felt such love. Just as I was finishing up and ready for the cooldown, I felt his energy grow stronger and I just knew I was going to get a song. As the beautiful music began, I didn't recognize it and that always makes me even more excited to hear what he has to say. Lying on my back I reached my hand up toward the TV and gave the weasel, then closed my eyes and listened to the words. It was Billy Ocean's, *The Colour Of Love*.

My heart was overflowing and I couldn't believe I was hearing a song that described the colors of love, and when it asked what is the color of love, I said, *"Rainbows! Rainbows are the color of love!"* I thought to myself, *"This song may not have a Rainbow in it, but it's a Rainbow colored song nonetheless!"* Just then I heard the Rainbow and it slowed my breathing. It says without him here the Rainbow loses it colors. Are you kidding me? Tears filled my eyes and I just couldn't believe it. Another song with Rainbows in it. Magical.

He says that no matter what's going on in the world he will always love me. That's my Gregory. Incredible even for me. Blows my mind that, as I'm putting together the book, I'm still getting amazing Rainbows and feeling him as close as he's ever been. My life feels like the most incredible dream. A dream full of Rainbows!

October 4, 2019

I said, *"Happy Anniversary, Honey,"* to Gregory first yesterday morning but wasn't sure he was going to show up. Then I got Rainbows all last evening! One time when I'd stopped working for the day, I turned on the TV and there was that Lucky Charms commercial just starting! Lol! Then I just kept being surprised by Rainbows. One time it was the biggest smiley face Rainbow across the whole screen sort of vibrating at me! Another time I changed the channel and there was a little Rainbow in the corner of the room. I was smiling all evening and feeling Gregory so close on our wedding anniversary. I thought back to that day and I smiled again.

I didn't expect to get Rainbows yesterday. I definitely haven't been getting them every day and surprisingly I've been getting used to that. I think this is the first anniversary since he died that I didn't cry or even feel sad. My breathing slowed a bit when I thought back to our wedding, knowing that at that time we still had a lot of life yet to live. We had so much fun that day. We hadn't even made it to Michigan yet and had no reason to think we'd be quitting our jobs, moving our family of four across the country and starting over. But we celebrated our first anniversary in Kalkaska and by our second anniversary we were living in this house. Now here I am all these years later, alone.

When I turned on the music this morning a song I've never heard before called, *Prayed For You*, by Matt Stell, was starting. I wasn't thinking about Gregory. I was thinking about the new guy.

It says that before I even met him or knew his name, I prayed for him. Yep. And I wonder how long it's going to be before that prayer is answered?

October 6, 2019

Yesterday I got several Rainbows all afternoon and evening. At least five or six, maybe more. Three of them were big smiley face Rainbows covering the whole TV screen. I was smiling all day. I usually say I could feel Gregory in a strong way, but that's not how it was yesterday afternoon and evening. I could feel him in a subtler way than usual. I can't really explain it but it feels like his energy isn't as strong as it's always been. He's still here and always will be, but I think he's letting me get adjusted to a subtler sense of his energy around me while he tries to distract me with extra Rainbows. It didn't work, but I'm okay with the shift.

October 11, 2019

I turned on the music first thing this morning and it played in the background as I did my morning routine. When I sat down with my tea I had Gregory on my mind and I felt at peace. Then my heart swelled a bit and I thanked him for *30 years*. I put my hand on my heart and I could feel my love there. Just then, *Love Someone*, by Lukas Graham, came on. It says that when you love someone your heart will open and you will make room for them. He says that if you're not afraid of losing that love then you probably haven't really loved. Yep, I know what he's talking about. That's the way I love somebody. With my whole heart and soul. I wouldn't trade what Greg and I had and I'll love like that again. I make no apologies.

October 12, 2019

When I came down this morning and turned on the music, *Come on Get Higher*, by Matt Nathanson, was just starting. The beginning made my heart sink just a little. It talks about all the things I miss. Like the sound of his voice, the feel of his skin, the way one of us breathes out and the other breathes in.

I'm feeling a little melancholy this morning. Not sure if I dreamed about Greg, but I woke up with him on my mind. He's always on my mind and will be as long as I'm working on this Rainbow book. Until it's done, he and his Rainbows are kind of all consuming. I miss him, but mostly I'm just so lonely. I can't imagine how lonely I would be if I didn't have the book, if I didn't have my animals to care for and love on. I look forward to being in a relationship again, to be in that flow of life with someone where when they breathe out you breathe in. Waiting for someone to help me breathe.

(Later)

I had a pretty powerful morning during Yoga. The music was so perfect, every song beautiful and just the right mood for my workout. As one song was ending I felt Gregory's energy wash over me. I was on my back and like before I reached my arm up behind me and gave the weasel to the TV, knowing I was going to hear a song just for me. I can't even explain the feeling in the room but it was full of so much love it made me cry. The beautiful music began and I recognized it as *Beautiful In My Eyes*. A gentle chill ran through me and I knew I was going to get my Rainbow.

As I finished my workout listening to the words, the room was filled with Gregory's spirit full strength and it's such an amazing feeling. And then I heard the part I forgot about and it made me cry. It talks about that long goodbye I keep thinking about. That when we come to that final embrace we'll laugh about how fast time goes. He says we never have to say goodbye because true love lasts forever. He says I'll always be beautiful in his eyes. I cry because the story is so beautiful and I cry because I know that it's coming to a close. Who am I after Gregory and his Rainbows?

October 16, 2019

I've had Gregory on my mind a lot the past few days. I haven't got a Rainbow since Saturday morning. It feels a bit colorless in my world and yet I seem to be able to breathe in it just the same. Still, I miss them. I miss feeling him as close as I do when he's sending me Rainbows. But how else are we going to end this book if he keeps sending the magic? It also has to end with my healing. Physically and with my grief. Fully ready and willing to embrace life without him.

October 17, 2019

Yoga was amazing. I turned on the music channel just as *Home*, by Michael Bublé', was starting. I settled into my warmup as the melody took me right back to when Greg was here and out on storm work. He always said that the closer he got to home the further away it seemed. He said, *"I want to be home."* The next song was also for me, I could feel it. It's called *Nothing's Going To Change My Love For You*, by George Benson, as if in direct response to me writing about not feeling him as close. I was moved by the words. He says I should know by now how much he loves me and that nothing is ever going to change that. It made me so happy.

The song ended and music started that I didn't recognize, but I should have. It was *True Colors*, the Phil Collins version. Tears streamed down my cheeks as I worked out to Rainbows and my love's energy all around me. He tests me. He goes away for a few days just to make sure I can breathe on my own, and when I do, he shows back up to make my day and reassure me that he, and the Rainbows, will never really go away. He just wants to make sure I'm not so dependent on them. Got it.

November 5, 2019

Sunday I got two obvious Rainbows from Gregory and I could feel him when he sent them. Made me smile. Otherwise I haven't been getting them much at all and I'm strangely okay with that.

I guess that's a good sign. He's loosening his grip on me ever so gently, or perhaps it is me who is letting go just enough to move into my future. The one without him in it.

November 7, 2019

Well, I've been getting Rainbows again just as soon as I wrote that I'm not getting them. I think it's his way of letting me know I'm always going to get Rainbows from him, but it's just not going to be every day all the time like it was. I'm good with that. I walked into the living room yesterday and couldn't believe my eyes. Right in the middle of the floor under the coffee table was the most colorful and beautiful Rainbow! The colors were intensified and it even had the most gorgeous blue I've ever seen! I just stared at it. I tried to find the source but couldn't. It was amazing! I could feel Gregory right next to me.

(4:10 p.m.)

I was just finishing up my work for the day and I looked to the stack of printed pages of the first five chapters of, *He Sends Me Rainbows*, and splashed across the page was a beautiful Rainbow! I took a picture. It made me smile. Not only that but Rainbows were reflecting all over the room as a rare flash of sunlight broke through this cloudy, snowy day. Just makes my heart swell with joy!

November 9, 2019

I quit work early for the weekend and came upstairs to relax before dinner. I turned on the TV and right then an upbeat, catchy tune started. The song is called *Sunshine, Lollipops And Rainbows*, by Lesley Gore. It says that because we have each other our life is sunshine, lollipops and Rainbows. Yes, yes it is.

November 12, 2019

I have to write that I got a bunch of Rainbows on Sunday. I could feel Greg so close and I just kept getting them. Ones I've never seen before. It was so great. It was like old times. I've had a couple of conversations with him the past couple of days and shed a few tears yesterday when I told him how much I miss him. A quick flash of us in our heyday and my heart sank. The pang of sadness comes from just missing being in a relationship, as much as it is missing Greg and our life together. It's starting to feel like a long time since he died and I hate that.

November 13, 2019

This is an amazing part of my journey and I can feel the changes as this whole beautiful Rainbow dream comes to a close. I also feel the gentle shift as new love is finding its way to me. This morning, lying in bed, I could actually feel the new guy next to me. I laid there and soaked it all in. What a beautiful place to be. Oh, and I got Rainbows yesterday too and felt my honey close in my heart. I guess that's how it's going to be while I'm finishing our book. Then someone else will show up and scooch his way into the mix and new love and life will take off. That's what I'm counting on.

Chapter 40

Seeing The Future

November 20, 2019

I decided to pick up my little grief and loss book which I haven't read in a long time. I don't know where along the way I stopped needing its daily comfort, but I bet it's been at least a year if not two. I *had* to read that book every morning for the first several years. It saved me. Now, once in a while I'll pick it up and see what the day has to say. That's what happened this morning. I stared at the words that say to take time to plan your future. It seems to be what I can't stop doing. Not necessarily planning it as much as letting it unfold before my eyes. Freaky exciting!

November 21, 2019

Yesterday morning I turned on the music and got ready for Yoga. I was in a peaceful, reflective state. My mind and heart full of Gregory. I settled into my warmup just as a song was ending and a new one began. *Ashes*, by Celine Dion. Beautiful song, all the more powerful because I know that she sings out of hope and grief after deep loss. It's the hope that I was hanging onto as I began my workout and there were no tears. I love that throughout the song it asks if it's possible for beauty to come out of the ashes? But at the end, it says to *allow* beauty to come out of the ashes.

When *Ashes* ended, I recognized the music when the next song began and I smiled. *Rainbow*. Another song to remind me to let the light back in. It's not raining anymore. Besides, I've always had a Rainbow over my head. I love that this song also has a switch in lyrics at the end. Holding onto that umbrella all through the song to letting it go at the end.

November 30, 2019

Well, I needn't have worried about Gregory being a no show on Thanksgiving. I got three Rainbows. I got a couple yesterday too and then first thing this morning I got a beautiful Rainbow that lingered on the screen. The room was filled with peace and I could feel Gregory tucked inside my heart, emanating a calm beauty that can't be described. I smiled and touched my heart. It was clear in that moment that this is how it's going to be now. I'll get my Rainbows when I need them and when I least expect them and I'll feel my Gregory close in my heart and soul.

December 9, 2019

I had a moment earlier and surprised myself by crying. I was listening to Keith Urban's, *When We Were*. I've been feeling quite emotional the past couple of days and have cried at the drop of a hat for no apparent reason. I've had Gregory on my mind and heart in a place that feels just a little too far away for my liking. During that song I started to cry, and in a brief moment my mind traveled back to my life with him. All of it. I accept who I am now but I sure do miss who I was when we were together. The grief felt heavy in that moment and I was surprised by the weight of it.

And then I got a beautiful Rainbow. And then a double Rainbow after that. I could feel such peace in the room and he was as close in that moment as he's ever been. The Rainbows warmed my heart and brought a tear to my eye. *I miss them. I* was in an amazing Rainbow bubble for the longest time. *Years.* And now my life is going along and I mostly don't notice that my world has lost some of its color. But I felt it this morning and my heart felt newly broken. I put on my wedding rings the other day and wore them out to run errands. They've lost their magic. I took them off as soon as I got home.

December 11, 2019

I had Gregory on my mind when I woke up. Halfway through Yoga I started telling him I needed to feel him close. I said, *"Send me a Rainbow!"* Nothing. The rest of the workout was the same and toward the end I said to him, *"What the heck? Not even a crumb?"* I heard him say, *"Let's not go backwards."* *"I know."* I finished my workout and headed to the kitchen to make a smoothie. When I came back upstairs and walked into the bedroom, *Endless Love* was just starting. A tear filled my eye. *"Thanks, Babe, I needed that."*

December 18, 2019

I got three Rainbow winks yesterday and that's what they felt like. They were little Rainbows that could easily have been missed if not for the gentle nudge in their direction. They made me smile.

December 19, 2019

I turned on the music and recognized the song right away. *Just Remember I Love You.* I knew I was going to get my Rainbow, but also not so sure about the words telling me that it keeps raining but the Rainbow's gone. Even so, I was mostly feeling the love from Gregory, his essence everywhere in my living room as this beautiful song played on. After that was, *Wherever You Will Go*, and I haven't heard that song in a while.

I got three Rainbow winks yesterday. I'm calling them winks because they don't have the same punch his Rainbows usually do, but my attention is always drawn to them and my heart smiles. I woke up to *Here Without You* on my mind and realized it's been a long time since I've heard it as well.

December 29, 2019

It's been five days since I've written and seriously I've never felt so sick. According to the *Medical Medium* this is all part of the liver detoxing and healing. Decades worth of toxins. It gives a whole new meaning to nausea. Mostly I feel like I might die. My brain is in the worst fog and I feel like I'm going to pass out every time I stand up. I feel drunk (poisoned) and practically bounce off the walls to the bathroom. It's frightening. I struggled through Thanksgiving, Christmas Eve at Mama's, and Christmas morning at Megan's.

And then the Rainbows. I didn't get any yesterday, but the five days before that I got anywhere from one to three Rainbow winks every day. They were noticeably different, but it took me a couple of days to realize that every Rainbow I was getting was muted in color. Like pastel Rainbows. Soft, quiet colors, but Rainbows, nonetheless. I started smiling every time. It seemed impossible that I was not only getting a few Rainbows every day again, but that they would all be pastel in color. Unassuming, yet drawing me to them every time. As always, they help when I'm feeling down.

January 2, 2020

I've been getting special little Rainbows every day. They are back with color. I've only got one a day the past couple of days, but I can feel Gregory's little hug to me and it warms my heart. I also did Yoga and that felt amazing. I could feel Gregory's presence in the room but kind of on the sidelines. When I was in the cooldown a beautiful song started and I felt gentle goosebumps rush through me. The song is *Someone You Loved*, by Louis Capaldi. I was mesmerized. It talks about needing someone to hold onto now that he's not here to save me. It talks about how much I liked it when he was there to numb the pain for me. It talks about having the rug pulled out from under me and how happy I was being someone he loved.

"Yep, I was spoiled being someone you loved, Honey." And now? Well, I'm not so used to that anymore. Still, it somehow feels okay. I'm at peace. I'm in acceptance. It's been an amazing, beautiful, magical, unbelievable journey and I wouldn't trade where I am right now for anything. When the song ended the upbeat music that followed made me smile and I felt Gregory's playfulness in the room as, *Who Loves You Pretty Baby?* rang out into the room. I smiled from ear to ear and said, *"You do, Baby!"* Woohoo!

January 3, 2020

I turned on the music first thing and it was Goo Goo Dolls', *Better Days*. It couldn't have been more perfect for a new year. It's a song about the chance for better days ahead. It gives me a lot of hope for my future. *Better Days*. It's been a long journey to where I find myself today and it's a pretty great place to be.

January 9, 2020

Gregory has sent me Rainbows every day for the past week. Very subtle now, but I get them and I feel an ever so slight change in the energy around and through me and I smile at him. We're weaning me off. I miss him. I miss our life together. I feel the new guy in a way that both terrifies and excites me. I'm keeping my eye out for him.

January 13, 2020

I took a break from the book in December to get ready for Christmas and have struggled to get back to it. I felt Gregory near and I said to him, *"It's time to get this thing done, Babe,"* and then I started to cry. *"Time to be done."* There it is. I wept and wept.

January 14, 2020

Today is Gregory's birthday. I wished him *Happy Birthday* as soon as I was out of bed. Yesterday gave me a glimpse into the grief I'm going to feel when the book is done. Even though I knew it would be there I didn't expect it to feel quite so powerful. All I can hope for is that when I get to the end of the Rainbow and look back on where I've been, I'll turn back around and see that pot of gold beckoning me to better days.

January 29, 2020

The past two weeks have been excruciating and I've suffered with non-stop pain. Turns out I had pancreatitis and it was brutal. In the midst of it I somehow had the feeling that this was the last of it. It was over. But it was the worst time in my life. There was no comfort to be found. There was only darkness and unrelenting pain. There were no Rainbows. Seriously, the entire two weeks I got no Rainbows. I couldn't feel Gregory. It was the darkest time of my life. Always since he died he shows up big when I'm sick or hurting. That brought its own comfort in the darkness. But even that was gone. There is nothing to hold me there.

January 31, 2020

I talked to Gregory yesterday and told him that I really need a Rainbow. It's been a long time. Within a few minutes I got one! It was a big, colorful, upside down Rainbow transposed across the TV screen. A smiley face Rainbow! *"Thank you, Babe!"* It felt like a spark of joy. Then I got a little Rainbow wink, and then another, and another! In all I got five Rainbow winks in the afternoon. It felt like Greg's way of rewarding me for not only surviving the past two weeks, but also doing it without him. Without his Rainbows. I feel at peace.

February 3, 2020

I've still been sick but I think it's just my liver now. I struggled through Yoga, having to stop several times throughout and just feel sick. Still, I was so aware of my own desire to be healthy. I have given it my all. I pushed through my stretches, tears slowly escaping one, then another. Knowing the worst is over yet disheartened with how terrible I felt in that moment. *"What else are you going to do, L.J.? It's not like you can give up..."*

February 6, 2020

My liver is healed. Everything is. Overnight it seemed, there was no pain and I didn't feel sick. My liver area has hurt for years. I still can't believe it. Comparing myself to myself only three days ago, let alone two weeks ago, and I rejoice. I know the worst is over. The *Medical Medium* says this *Liver Rescue* could take up to three years and with strict discipline it took me fifteen months. Perseverance paid off.

February 8, 2020

I didn't write yesterday but it was a great day. I couldn't believe how good I felt when I did Yoga. I could feel Gregory strong in the room when I was getting ready and it's been awhile since I've felt him like that. The music was soft and beautiful and I just felt a warm glow all around me. I knew he was going to speak to me through songs, something that doesn't happen very often anymore. Right away I heard the upbeat music to Bon Jovi's, *Who Says You Can't Go Home*. I stretched my body and smiled as I felt my Gregory's playful spirit all around and knew I was going to get my Rainbow.

Yesterday I picked up the CD I had made from Uncle Steve's cassette so I could include the words to *The Way* in Dad's chapter of this book. I knew it was going to be hard to hear his voice. When the music started and I heard Steven's sad voice as, *Again Alone*, began, I had a full-blown panic attack. I shut it off and sprung to my feet feeling like I couldn't breathe. I started sobbing. *"I'm not going to be able to do this...."*

I started talking to Steven. *"Help me, Stevarino, help me do this."* I had read the Daily Word just before and it was *Brave.* *"Okay, Steven, help me be brave. Help me just get this done."* It didn't help that the first song is *Again Alone.* It's a heartbreakingly sad song that he wrote after his marriage ended. He was never the same again. The song is so hard to hear. I gathered up my courage, put on my headset and took a deep breath.

I listened to the whole thing, tears rolling down my cheeks one after the other. When it was over, I sat mesmerized by Steven playing his heart out on *Midnight Blues.* Then *The Way* began and I'd forgotten what a beautiful song it is and how much you get to hear his vocal range. It's a comforting song, the way the Blues soothe a wounded heart. It took some time and the song is longer than I remembered, but I got it transcribed and now it's included in Chapter Two.

When I settled in for the evening I turned on soft Seascapes music and a beautiful, soothing song was playing. A peaceful feeling rushed over me and filled the room as the music seemed to soothe my soul. I looked up. It's called, *"The Way"* (Zach Hemsey). I couldn't believe it. I smiled and told Steven, *"I feel you. Thank you."* This morning as I laid in bed I felt peace like I haven't felt in a long time. I thought about the new guy. I can feel him. *"Come find me..."*

February 11, 2020

Riley died last night. They said they believe she had a blood clot go to her heart. I had to make the decision to send her home to be with Greg. She was in so much pain and her back legs were paralyzed. She and Gracie are 15 years old. I was with her when she took her last breath and then was able to spend a few minutes with her. I'm so sad but I know she's with Gregory now and that gives me a little bit of peace. But I'm full of anxiety and the whole house feels dark.

I went to the grocery store, but the closer I got to home the more the anxiety was kicking in. *"You're going to have to help me, Gregory, please help me get peace about Riley. Let me know you've got her, I can't stand this."* I headed upstairs but as soon as I hit the first step I felt like I couldn't breathe. The upstairs—my sanctuary—no longer feels safe. Riley was always up there, usually at the top of the stairs to greet me. It's breaking my heart.

"Please, Honey, help me. Give me peace about everything." I got to my bedroom and turned on the TV for soft music to hopefully calm me down. I was standing right in front of the TV and as soon as the picture came into focus there were a bunch of bright, colorful Rainbows flashing at me! It was a Lucky Charms commercial and I was bombarded by the most brilliantly colored Rainbows I've seen in a long time. I sort of gasped out of surprise.

I realized it's been a long time since I've seen any Rainbows and I was reminded of a time not so long ago when they were a part of my everyday existence. I couldn't believe it. I sat down on the bed. It was as if fireworks were going off all around me. I could feel the celebration of Riley's homecoming and Gregory's joy at having his beloved *Moose* back with him. I was stunned as I sat there and a swirl of emotions rushed over me. I started to cry. And then sob. They were tears of awe and amazement. They were tears of so much gratitude as all my grief over Riley poured out of me and it was okay. I knew she was with Gregory.

Nothing else could have taken this anxiety and grief from me. Gregory's Rainbows! And here's the thing. I wasn't even thinking about Rainbows. Isn't that crazy? It's not like I said, *"Send me a Rainbow, Honey, to let me know Riley's with you."* That blows my mind. It shows that I'm used to not getting Rainbows now. How did that happen and I didn't notice? So his Rainbows a few minutes ago couldn't have been more perfect. Feeling the peace in my heart that I've needed to feel since Monday night, I said, *"You fixed me with your Rainbows, Honey! You're frikken amazing!"*

February 12, 2020

During Yoga earlier I didn't feel well and wasn't sure I was going to be able to keep going. My lungs have been so clogged I struggle to breathe and have little energy. A song began as I laid for a moment hoping to feel better. Ugh. *God help me.* Just then I realized what song was playing and a new determination welled up inside me and I got back into position and gave the workout my all. It's called, *In My Blood*, by Shawn Menendez. It says that I can't give up because it's not in my blood.

That was the determination I could feel within me. It's never been in my blood to give up. The fact that I was unwell for so long did not deter me from having faith in my final goal. To be well. The book can't end without it. It wouldn't make sense. It would have all seemed worthless. The suffering, the pain, the amount of time spent in both.

Chapter 41

Rainbow Paradise

February 14, 2020

I turned on the music channel as soon as I came downstairs. When I sat down with my tea there was a big, *"Happy Valentine's Day!"* sign staring at me from the TV screen. *"Oh, yeah, it's Valentine's Day. Happy Valentine's Day Honey! I wi...."* The sign on the TV seemed to get brighter and I realized, oh, no, I didn't win, Gregory did! He shouted out the first *Happy Valentine's Day!* Woohoo!

During Yoga I was filled with peace and the room seemed to have a glow to it. I've been feeling Gregory stronger since Riley died. A song began that I've never heard before and I couldn't believe my ears. It's called *Adore You*, by Harry Styles. The very first line talks about walking in my paradise of Rainbows. Okay, I think I will! I don't hear the word as often as I used to so it felt a little like revisiting an old friend. The next song is so beautiful. It's called, *God Only Knows*, by For King & Country. Only God knows what I've been through. Well, God and Gregory.

(4:20 p.m.)

I just finished working for the day and when I looked up, there was the most brilliant Rainbow glowing across the coffee table. Unbelievable! Then I reached for my water and there was the most brilliant Rainbow across my hand! Just then the room seemed to get brighter and suddenly I realized there were colorful Rainbows reflecting all over the room! I mean, brilliantly colored ones like I've only seen a couple of times. I just stared at the bold, amazing colors, with my mouth hanging open and gentle chills rushing through me. My heart is overflowing. A smile seems effortlessly spread across my face and I can't believe what I'm seeing! Rainbows dancing all around the room! Who would believe it? *"Happy Valentine's Day, Honey, you amaze the hell out of me!"*

February 18, 2020

Yesterday was a good day. I took a lunchbreak and turned on the TV. Colorful Rainbows bombarded me from the screen. It's the new Lucky Charms commercial that I saw the other day. It really is quite fun! I've been feeling Gregory with me all day and pretty much since Riley died.

February 21, 2020

Before I came downstairs this morning I was a bit teary eyed about how lonely I am. How excited I am to be in love again, and how I can't wait to meet my new guy. *"How long do I have to wait?"* my mind asked no one in particular. I came downstairs and turned on FB to see if my proofreader had messaged me and there it was, it said, *"I don't know who needs to see this, but Isaiah 60:22 says, 'When the time is right, I the Lord, will make it happen.' Sleep in peace tonight. God is in control."* My heart swelled and it made me cry. What a gift. A direct answer to a silent prayer.

February 25, 2020

Yesterday I got no less than four Rainbows. I could feel Gregory and it just made my day every time I got one! I hadn't gotten any for a few days and pretty much didn't expect to. But I had him on my mind a lot.

February 28, 2020

I turned on the music as soon as I came downstairs and heard *Adore You*. It made me smile. And you know what? I think I'm going to take a stroll in that Rainbow paradise you speak about.

(3 p.m.)

After a somewhat disappointing morning of work I went upstairs for a lunchbreak. I turned on the TV and there it was. A couple of children are bringing a snack for their parents. It was on a big silver platter with a rounded cover, like room service. They held up the platter to the camera, took off the lid, and there in the middle of two Ritz cracker concoctions they'd made, was the cutest little Rainbow. They handed the treasure to their parents and began dancing around the room, a big, colorful Rainbow in the background.

I thanked Gregory for sending me Rainbows again. It helps so much. Later, when I went back up for a break and turned on the TV there it was again! Right at the same spot! Serving up a tiny Rainbow on a silver platter! That just amazes me. I'm grateful to know that I was okay when I wasn't getting Rainbows anymore, but it sure is nice when I'm struggling a little bit to have that connection. And who doesn't smile when they see a Rainbow?

March 2, 2020

Two times I went OnDemand and there it was, a big Rainbow! I could feel Gregory with me in the sweetest way. He knows that the book has been a lot of work and that there is still a lot of work ahead of me. He knows I'm ready to write the last page. He's like the loved one standing at the finish line of a marathon, yelling words of encouragement for the last leg of the race. *"You can do it! Keep going! Don't give up! You're almost there! Woohoo!"*

March 4, 2020

"March Forth y'all!" I'm so happy! I feel so good! I woke up with joy in my heart and a big smile on my face clear to my toes.

I'm well! It's over! *Finally, it's over.* I cried about it last night. Humble, grateful tears. As I walked by the buffet the Smiling Buddha caught my eye. I picked him up and held him in my hand. I couldn't help but smile. His hands are raised above his head and the look on his face is pure joy. *"This is me!"*

I had the music on and was in the kitchen heating my tea. My mind went to the new guy and I can feel him closer than I ever have. I allowed my mind to go there. I said, *"I get to do this again,"* and I smiled clear to my toes. Just then I heard beautiful, familiar music. I could feel Gregory's love all around me. The energy in the room changed and I headed to the living room with my heart full of love. It was Commodores', *Three Times A Lady*. The words penetrated my soul and I could feel Gregory speaking straight to my heart.

He's thanking me for the time that we had and how the memories are in our hearts and minds forever now. And then my heart slowed and I felt a touch of sadness rush over me when he said now that we're coming to the end of our Rainbow he wants me to know how much he loves me. A subtle numb washed over me. A swirl of emotions flooded me as I saw in a flash my thirty years with him and then the past nearly eight without him. All the Rainbows, all the magic, all the grief, all the healing. The message I heard loud and clear was something he must say aloud. *That he loves me.* Not like that was ever in question but I can never hear it enough. It was a powerful few moments and his presence and message were strong. The thought came that perhaps this is the end of that long goodbye.

March 6, 2020

Wow, my husband bombarded me with Rainbows yesterday! It's like he's showering me with love and encouragement to keep going. He knows this is hard for me. Everything is coming to a close. Tying up this Rainbow. The good news is what's waiting for me at the end of the Rainbow.

March 10, 2020

Good Lord! My husband has been bombarding me with Rainbows! When I sat down to work I turned on the TV and saw a big bunch of colorful Rainbows! The closer I get to the end of the book, the closer I feel him.

March 13, 2020

I worked on the book most of the day and then took my coffee cup to the kitchen before heading upstairs. I had the TV on mute and when I came back into the living room it was a bombardment of Rainbows! I got a rush of chill bumps and a smile as big as Texas. I stood there sort of in awe. After all this time and all these Rainbows, you'd think it wouldn't hit me the way it does. *"But man, how do you do that, Babe?"*

March 23, 2020

I haven't written for over a week because I've been busy working on the book. I made sure to jot down my Rainbows so I wouldn't forget. I've felt Gregory with me ever since Riley died. I get at least two Rainbows every day and more than that most days. Every time I turned on the TV or walked back into the room there was a Rainbow. I have note after note about the Rainbows I received every day. And songs, it's been like old times.

One time I had the TV muted and was sort of lost in thought. I was staring at the TV but not really looking at it until my thoughts came back to the present and I realized I was staring at the word RAINBOW. Big letters on big sticks, lined up next to each other to spell out the word. A shiver ran through me. A smile did too. Another time I was feeling so much peace and love in the room. I took a deep, cleansing breath. I looked up to see the song playing was called, *Rainbow Bay* (by Sonic Sanctuary). On and on it went for days!

March 30, 2020

I continue to feel so peaceful and so blessed in my life. The weekend was incredible. Gregory is sending me Rainbows like nobody's business and I feel his presence strong around me. I know that he knows how hard this is for me. How the final task of putting together an enormous project like this is like running the last leg of a marathon. You don't think you can do it. I've been particularly moved by the enormous impact of this book. I just cried and cried as I thanked Gregory for the whole beautiful thing. *"I would have died without your Rainbows and songs, Honey, I would have died..."* The grief turned to acceptance and then gratitude and I was overwhelmed once again by the magnitude of everything.

I went to reheat my tea and stopped at the picture wall. I stared at one picture of him for the longest time. I seemed to be drawn into it. He stared back at me. It was as if he was standing right in front of me. I stared at my own young face next to him and was drawn into my own bliss. Snuggled up against Gregory I was as happy as anyone has ever been. He looks happy too.

I turned on the TV to a beautiful scene of a stormy sky from a boat on the water. I thought, *"This would be the perfect sky for a Rainbow."* Just then the scene changed and it was almost identical to the first, only this one had a beautiful Rainbow arcing across the entire width of the sky. Spectacular! There was so much peace in the room I could hardly believe it. I felt complete serenity. I felt Gregory. Then he continued to bombard me with Rainbows the rest of the day! I was laughing at this point and calling him a showoff. Unbelievable!

April 5, 2020

I enjoy my day of rest and watching favorite shows. I was delighted to find that the new season of a favorite program had begun, and I settled in to watch the first episode. The words always seem to touch me to the core. *What determines the beginning of anything new? Does it begin once we take action? Or is it even before then? When we first breathed life into the idea, when we took a giant leap of faith into something completely unknown. And what happens to where we've been when a new life beckons?*

April 7, 2020

I turned on the TV at 5:40 a.m. to check the weather. There it was, a big beautiful Red Rainbow! And then I enjoyed a whole segment on Red Rainbows! I've never felt happier, more excited about my future. I keep getting visions of my new life and I can't even tell you how happy I am! I keep seeing myself with the new guy and he's starting to feel so familiar. More familiar than my memories. Even the years I spent in grief are becoming a memory.

April 8, 2020

I feel a calm I have longed for. Just like with my liver healing, I would get glimpses of that peace, moments when I didn't feel sick, but it didn't last. Now I have felt this peace consistently for some time and my liver has been completely healed since February. The Rainbows continue every day. Sometimes big and brilliant, sometimes little Rainbow winks. They make me smile every time. Who doesn't feel happy when they see a Rainbow?

April 18, 2020

Once again one of my favorite programs has left me contemplating those deeper questions in life and somehow feeling peaceful with the beautiful acceptance of it all. *We don't always get to choose what we have to give up. People and things we love are taken from us. We are not defined by the things we let go of, but by the things we embrace. Family and friends, hope and fear. It is best to accept our humanness, to understand our imperfections and to flourish in the midst of them. None of us walks a path of certainty, but is that not the beauty and adventure of life?*

May 1, 2020

Gregory has been sending me Rainbow winks every single day. At least two or three a day. But on my birthday I got one little Rainbow. I went upstairs for a lunchbreak and turned on the TV just in time to see that familiar silver platter and the children somewhat dramatically lifting off the lid to expose a little Rainbow! It felt super special. Oh, and this is the first time that a dark cloud did not move in around me the month of April. Not even a hint of a shadow. I have been filled with joyful bliss!

May 5, 2020

I had the most amazing day on the book yesterday. I realized that I'm going to be done very soon. I went upstairs for the evening, feeling so peaceful and so happy about everything in my life. I turned on the TV and just stared at the most beautiful double Rainbow on a commercial for a local landscaping company. Time seemed to slow and I stared at those Rainbows for what seemed the longest time. Then my eyes filled with tears and a rush of chills ran through me. *"I don't know how you keep doing this, Babe, but you blow my mind. Thank you."*

I've been feeling so good I can hardly stand myself! This is the me I remember and have missed so much! I got dressed for Yoga and turned on the TV. I wasn't paying attention to the music because I was talking to Gregory and telling him how happy I am. I was bouncing around like a little kid. I was full of enthusiasm. I gave him *the weasel* and told him that I did it! I made it through eight years of grief and illness and now I'm healthier than I've ever been! I'm so happy!

Just then the song ended and I laid down on the floor for the rest of my workout. New music began and I heard once again about taking a stroll in that paradise of Rainbows. A tear filled my eye and I told Gregory, *"That's what I'm doing, Babe, that's what I'm doing!"*

June 30, 2020

I don't get Rainbows every day anymore and it's okay. I get them when I'm least expecting and they always warm my heart and make me smile. The other day I turned on the TV early in the morning and it was still on PBS from the night before. As soon as the picture came on I could see it was a fishing show and a guy was knelt down in his boat after hauling up his net. He pulled the first fish out then said, *"Oh look, hiding under that one is a Rainbow!"* He pulled out the fish, held it up to the camera and said, *"Now that's a nice Rainbow!"* My heart swelled and a tear filled my eye. *"Thank you, Babe, you're so amazing I still can't believe it."* Then I allowed my mind to wander over all the Rainbows and all the magic over the past eight years and I gave Gregory *the weasel* and thanked him for the whole big, beautiful experience.

September 6, 2020

I've been crying those OMG! tears of amazement that were my life for many years. I don't remember the last time I got a Rainbow or the last time I thought about them. I've had Gregory on my mind a lot lately though and didn't really think about why until just a few minutes ago. Tomorrow is Labor Day. I was aware that, like April, I don't have a dark cloud around me for the first time since he died. I feel happy. No sadness, just feeling really good about my life. It surprises me to realize that I don't think about the Rainbows very often.

Today is my day of rest and for some reason earlier I found myself reflecting back to a moment of regret with Greg. It was such a tiny little thing—not validating him or perhaps a tone of voice—and was so long ago that I couldn't believe I was even going there. Just then I looked up to the muted TV and there was a big, colorful Rainbow filling the entire screen and I unmuted it just in time to hear the word. I sat there sort of stunned. It's a Lucky Charms commercial I've never seen before and I was reminded of how often I used to turn on the TV to an animated shower of Rainbows on these commercials.

Then it hit me that he sent me the Rainbows just when I was going to a place that serves no purpose. I started to cry. I could feel him with me. I gave him *the weasel*. I'm so amazed by the whole thing anyway but now he let me know that he's still with me, he still hears my heart and he still knows exactly how to make me smile. He reminded me of all that. That's when the tears really flowed and I cried like I don't remember when. It was a good release. It was being moved by spirit. It was amazing.

September 25, 2020

A lot has happened and I had a major setback with the book. The process of obtaining permission to use all the song lyrics—I quoted nearly 200 of them—was daunting as I began the painstaking process of researching music publishers and contact information so that I could send out letters requesting permission. A decision to purchase a registry of all the music publishers in the U.S. proved to be a waste of money.

A phone call to the contact person on the registry was a further blow. When he asked me what I was contacting them for and I told him, he all but laughed and said I was wasting my time. He said, *"No one is going to respond to your letters. No one cares about your book. Even if they did respond, no one is going to let you use any lyrics without paying for them and you'll be charged a minimum of $1000 a lyric. Just make your book for your children and grandchildren and no one will be the wiser. No one's going to look at it. It's not like you're going to sell them on Amazon or it's going to be a bestseller."*

It got worse when I argued that I wasn't going to shoot myself in the foot because what if I do want to sell it on Amazon or in bookstores? He sort of laughed and then pretty much acted like I was just another wannabe writer with an unrealistic dream in my heart that was never going to happen. He said, *"Just make your little book for your children and grandchildren and call it good. No one even cares! And no one is going to read your letters let alone give you permission to use their song lyrics. You're wasting your time."*

He went on to lecture me about how the whole music industry works, like in movies and how much they have to pay for the music and you could tell he was irritated with me when he said, *"Like I could charge you $100 right now for just talking to me."* At this point the whole thing is sinking in so far I can feel it in every fiber of my being and I said, *"Well, I've wasted enough of your time. I can legally quote song titles and artist names and I can paraphrase all I want so that's what I'm going to do. Have a nice night,"* and I hung up. And then I sobbed and sobbed. A letdown of all the disappointment I felt knowing the book was not going to be what I hoped it would be.

Just then I heard a quiet voice say, *"I don't make dreams smaller, I make them bigger."* I took a deep breath and after a day of rest I hit the ground running with a new determination to use my creative writing skills, in hopes of somehow doing justice to the powerful messages I'd received through songs without compromising the magic. Within a few days it was done and I was back on track. When all was said and done I felt I owed 'Doug' a great big *"Thank You!"* for taking me off the path that was going nowhere and putting me on the one that will get me where I need to be. *I'm responsible for the action, God's responsible for the outcome.* It will be what it will be.

The next day I got in the car and had the music on but wasn't paying attention. My mind was full of Gregory and the journey we've been on the past 38 years. The whole thing felt surreal. I was thinking about finally finishing the book and what that means for me now. All the work it took to get to this place and how grateful I am for every labored step. In that moment everything felt so perfect, so peaceful. Reflecting back, I told Gregory, *"We did it, Babe."*

I felt the car fill up with his peaceful energy and a tear filled my eye. There was silence as one song ended and the next one began. Somehow I knew that, unlike all the songs he's ever sent me, this one was going to be from my heart to his. Tears filled my eyes as the beautiful music began. In that moment I felt I had come full circle and everything made sense. It's called, *When I See You Again*, by Wiz Khalifa. *It's been a long time without you, Babe. An incredible journey from the start. We'll talk about it when I see you again.*

September 30, 2020

I dreamed about Gregory! I was in the living room and he came in from the hallway. A song came on and I started singing and dancing seductively. I said, "Mere, Honey, I need to practice!" I was so playful and having so much fun. He took me in his arms and was dancing around with me. My hair was pulled up in a loose bun and I had on a low cut gown and looked very sexy. We were so playful as he twirled me around, dipped me down and then pulled me to him. We stared into each other's eyes with a knowing that this would be our last dance for a while. I woke up.

To Be Continued ...